Development Issues
for the 1970s

Development Issues for the 1970s

Richard J. Ward

Foreword by William S. Gaud

DUNELLEN

NEW YORK • LONDON

© 1973 by the Dunellen Publishing Company, Inc.
386 Park Avenue South
New York, New York 10016

and

Kennikat Press, Inc.
Port Washington, New York

International Standard Book Number 0-8424-0060-5.

Library of Congress Catalogue Card Number 72-86223.

Printed in the United States of America.

Martin Robinson & Company Ltd. * London

To

Cecilia Butler Ward

Contents

List of Tables and Figures

Tables

Figures

Foreword

This book deals with many of the critical development issues which surfaced in the 1960s and have become the priority concerns of the 1970s. They are issues which absorbed much of my time and attention in my eight years with the Agency for International Development, where our concentration on the future prospects of the developing countries identified the urgent importance to the development process of such matters as population growth, nutrition, unemployment, income distribution, debt service burdens, and trade.

These issues must be faced up to and dealt with if the Third World is to achieve its long-term goals. It is essential to define them and take them to the conference table, the classroom, and the public, in the hope that aroused interest and free discussion will suggest ideas and innovations leading to their solution.

Mr. Ward is an experienced development economist who has been involved in both governmental and private approaches to development in many parts of the world. His book identifies, explores, and illumines many of the more urgent problems which now confront us.

Though our knowledge is still far from complete, we have learned much about the development process in the last decade. We have learned, for example, that while economic growth is essential to development, economic growth alone is not enough. Development is a complicated blend of economic, social, and political growth and progress. Today we realize, more than ever before, that development is concerned primarily with the quality of the life of the individual and not merely with the economic well-being of the state in which he lives.

From this it follows that the true state of a nation's development cannot be measured simply in macroeconomic terms. Country X may have a relatively high per capita GNP, a good growth rate, rapidly growing exports, and a manageable debt burden. However, if millions of its citizens are outside the money economy, if 40 per cent of them are living on a subsistence level, if the number of its unemployed and functional illiterates is increasing — above all, if it has a high and still unchecked rate of population growth — it should look to its development priorities.

To realize this is one thing. To translate it into action is quite another thing. Mr. Robert McNamara, president of the World Bank, deserves the thanks of us all for his continuing effort to increase the world's awareness that this is what development is all about, and to channel the activities of the World Bank Group and other development agencies in directions that will enable the developing world to deal with its pressing human problems.

It is a waste of energy to search for a quick and easy way out. There is none. The ingredients of success are patience, perseverance, ingenuity, and a generous but carefully thought out use of resources — plus one thing more: time. The world moves fast today, but not so fast that we can expect the citizens of the developing countries to do in a decade, or even in two decades, what it took us generations to accomplish.

As in the 1960s, the public sector will, in the 1970s, continue to play the leading role in development. It alone can establish the policy and infrastructural framework on which to build modern societies. However, many of the developing countries now have, or are rapidly acquiring, the infrastructure that is needed for industrial development. These countries want to develop — and they must develop — as rapidly as possible. If they are to do so, they should not leave to the public sector the job of building up their industries. Their budgets and their governments are already overburdened with other essential tasks. They need not only more resources, but more managerial talent, improved technology, and additional opportunities for training their growing labor forces. In my view, a country that is bent on development cannot afford to ignore private initiative, private enterprise and private investment.

Most of the developing countries recognize this. True, many of them impose restrictions on private investment, both foreign and domestic. To the extent that such restrictions are designed to insure that private investments fit the priorities of their development plans, one cannot quarrel with them. In today's world every private investment should meet two tests: it should contribute to the development objectives of the host country, and it should also serve the interests of the investor. If host countries and investors will see to it that all private investment meets these two tests, a long step will have been taken towards dispelling the suspicion and distrust with which private investment is viewed in some quarters.

We in the United States can do much to help the developing nations achieve their goals, but let us keep one or two things in mind as we proceed. First — and here we are on common ground with the rest of the developed world — we must remember that the problems for which we are seeking solutions are not our problems but the problems of the developing nations. Only they can decide how they want to solve them and in what priority. If asked, we can consult, advise or help. We should not, however, take over, and we should not try to make their decisions for them. Patience and forbearance — these are vital qualities in any relationship, and surely so in this one.

Second — and here we have less company — we can take little pride in the support we are currently giving the developing nations. The richest nation in the world was 15 months late in ratifying its contribution to the International Development Association. It ranks among the bottom few of the developed nations in the percentage of its GNP that it contributes to development. In a period when the debt service burden of the developing world was steadily rising, the United States did not soften its loan terms; it hardened them. Despite eloquent protestations of support for international development agencies, the United States took years in deciding to support the efforts of the Asian Development Bank to give loans on soft terms to the least developed nations of Asia, has yet to support the efforts of the African Development Bank to do the same thing in Africa, and is now engaged in a drive to reduce its contributions to the development agencies of the United Nations. What is most remarkable is that, despite this far from brilliant record, many of our fellow citizens feel that the United States is not only doing right by the developing world but is doing more than its share.

There was a time when the United States did lead the way in giving support to other nations, but a generation has passed since the days of the Marshall Plan — a generation which has transformed Western Europe, Japan and Canada. We are by no means the only nation giving substantial support to the Third World. Many others are also doing so, and not a few of them seem more aware of and responsive to the needs of the developing countries than we.

Mr. Ward's book will give its readers a clearer picture than most of us now have of the process and the problems of development. I hope and believe it will contribute to a better understanding of this important and complex subject.

WILLIAM S. GAUD
Executive Vice President
International Finance Corporation
Formerly, Administrator of the
U.S. Agency for International
Development

Introduction

The UN "Decade of Development" ended with the 1960's, but the development task remains as crucial for the current decade. Despite the doldrums into which aid-giving appears to have fallen in the United States, considerable gains have been made in the less developed world over the past decade or two. Yet, many critical problems remain to be faced in this new decade. The gap in living standards between rich and poor countries continues to widen in absolute terms. Both income and social inequalities are far — indeed very far — from being resolved. Political awareness of these inequalities is, in fact, spreading rapidly, adding pressure to the need for action. Recent evaluations of the development process — its aims, achievements, and shortcomings — conclude with forceful pleas for continued effort to avert broad-scaled social and political upheaval by dedication to the task of developing the poor regions of the world.*

This book assesses some of the key issues and problems which emerged from the Decade of Development and which will continue to absorb the attention of students of development in the present decade. Each of the chapters derives from subject matter of con-

*Lester Pearson Report, *Partners in Development* (Praeger; New York, 1969); United Nations, *A Study of the Capacity of the United Nations Development System,* Vols. I-II (Geneva, 1969).

cern to U.S. policy making or to specific problems of less-developed countries. Much of the data used to describe and explore the various problems is unavailable elsewhere. These chapters, while reviewing progress made, raise new questions and pose positive alternatives which warrant inquiry.

Part 1 focuses on the dynamic race between food and population. Is the world facing mass famine, as some modern treatises claim? The last decade produced the "green revolution" in agricultural productivity. It also revealed complexities in the population-control programs which will need to be resolved in this decade. The first problem area discussed in Chapter 1 is world agriculture and its transformation from a subsistence-oriented sector to a generator of surpluses. Can this trend continue? An optimistic view concerning the cooperative ability of earth and man to increase food output is developed with a statistical review of possible food and population projections in India and Pakistan to the year 2000. The chapter also proposes a whole "new think," to use De Bono's phrase, on the overall approach to the agricultural sector more suited to the rapidly unfolding future than the tradition-bound past. Provided the current momentum of progress can be sustained in agriculture, there is also the possibility, examined in the second chapter, that the agricultural sector in other Asian countries can increase its absorption of labor, despite much theory and tradition to the contrary. This could in turn check the migration of people to the already overburdened urban centers in India and in other less-developed countries.

With all of the encouraging prospects for agriculture, brought about by dramatic increases in the use of fertilizers, pesticides, new miracle seeds, irrigation, and other inputs, there is still the question of seeking a broader approach to population control than methods now being promoted convey. This is especially warranted where results from current family-planning efforts have not been too significant to date. The alternatives outlined in Chapter 4 are suggestive of areas in which investigation might be undertaken.

The final problem area covered in Part 1 recognizes the hypothesis developed by Robert Solow, Moses Abramovitz, Solomon Fabricant, John Kendrick, and others concerning the causal impetus behind productivity trends in the United States. The hypothesis is that the major contribution to economic progress is not in material inputs but in a "residual" human factor which embodies knowledge, training, improved organization, and dynamic and innovative change. The first part of this chapter describes Hans Singer's efforts to identify and quantify these intangible elements in the residual factor in order to deal with them and apply them more rationally and effectively. The task of quantification has not been easy. The second part of this chapter responds to Singer's effort and reflects some of the experience of others in dealing with the human coefficient in the development equation.

Part 2 examines a number of current important development problems and prospects for their resolution. Social or income inequality is of growing concern in the underdeveloped countries. It may have been instrumental in toppling President Ayub Khan of Pakistan in 1968. Research in this area is sparse, but Chapter 6 reviews the case of India and Pakistan to suggest a need to prevent development from becoming a boon only to the privileged few.

From long years of aid received on varying terms, some developing countries are faced with sharply rising debt-service payments and declining net aid. The United States had a high debt service just before the turn of the century, but it declined in importance thereafter; it also had serious periodic defaults on such indebtedness. Unless appropriate measures are taken, India and Pakistan will have international-debt burdens that will eat up half of the foreign exchange received from foreign aid. Chapter 7 raises some of the less-known questions which warn of critical balance-of-payments pressures in this decade unless firm corrective measures are adopted.

The next chapter provides perspective in demonstrating that the performance of the less-developed countries has largely measured up to the expectations set for the Decade of Development in 1960, despite severe droughts in Asia and setbacks in some countries caused by local conflicts and inroads made by population expansion. In fact, by historic measure, the performance has been impressive compared to the developed world. Can the pace be maintained in this decade? Can hope be strengthened in more demonstrable evidence of growth besides that evidenced in the economic indicators?

For more than a decade, the United States and other donor countries have required aid recipients to use the aid provided to purchase goods only from the donor country. This has not only often reduced the net value of the aid but also diverted trade from normal trade channels. On the other hand, it has been difficult, especially in the United States, to generate political support for aid-giving without consideration of the effect on the U.S. balance of payments. Even with growing multilateralism of aid, this pressure will likely be a recurring problem. Chapter 9, therefore, reflects on this problem, which will remain with us in the decade to come.

Chapter 10 questions Gunnar Myrdal's prognosis for the future of foreign assistance on a number of points. He tells us that aid is ineffective; indigenous motivation and investment are the prime movers. He is critical of other Western aid approaches. Whether he is right or wrong is a question the years just ahead must resolve.

The six chapters in Part 3 deal with various planning strategies and potentials. The first seeks to prescribe a balance between "big push" overheating of an underdeveloped economy and a momentum of progress adequate to achieve satisfactory and balanced improvement in development and living standards. The desire of the underdeveloped countries to plunge ahead and to catch up with the modernized world and its people is understandable and has to a degree been successful in the past. Now, we must deal with the realities and rigidities of these economies and the sensitive interrelationships inherent in economic phenomena.

Based on the author's experience in Afghanistan, Chapter 12 demonstrates what kind of planning strategy those who provide foreign assistance on a concessional basis will increasingly demand in future planning proposals of less-developed countries seeking aid. All too often these plans have been a long, uncoordinated string of projects, with all too little assessment of why mobilization of indigenous resources is not more effective. Often the planning strategies, when they do contain economic analyses, are "rigged" to make a case for the need for foreign exchange, when in fact an objective assessment including optimum commitment of indigenous resources to development is more likely to attract hardheaded donors. This is particularly true at the present time, when funds are scarce everywhere in the advanced countries, particularly in the United States. This is but one form which self-help may take in a better relationship between less-developed countries and their donors.

Chapter 13 uses a particular case to demonstrate how planning had helped to identify, among sector investment alternatives, the highest yield programs.

In the long run, foreign concessional (noncommercial) or low aid should decline in favor of normal trade or foreign-investment generation of foreign exchange. The past decade grappled with this problem vigorously. The coming decade should uncover new approaches to this long range problem. Chapter 14 reviews the status of this issue and sets the stage for postulating new ways of approaching it in the 1970's.

The strategy of development undergoes constant change. At one phase the emphasis is on industrial project building, at another on agriculture, or at another on trade-policy questions. In mobilizing forces for new initiatives, what often appear to be exaggerated claims are made for the impact anticipated from pursuing any particular line of effort. Only in this way can whole programs and widely scattered, busy administrative machinery be mobilized behind the plan of the moment. Western governments, and particularly the United States aid program, have been organized in the past behind a strategy to liberalize trade; to decontrol licensing, pricing, and other administrative hindrances to free-market behavior; and to dismantle state monopolistic enterprise in the less-developed countries. Drawing on some recent studies, Chapter 15 questions the comparative returns from pursuing these objectives over what an alternative emphasis or strategy might bring, particularly in the area of manpower development geared to promoting technological change. The current decade will see greater attention given to these new approaches to the growth process.

The final essay appropriately explores future directions of research and suggests that research in the currently vital area of agricultural growth must not overlook the long-term development effort. That is the question for this decade. For example, the industrial sectors of the less-developed economies, even in large countries, are surprisingly and distressingly small. Agricultural growth is essential, but in the long run what should be the relative roles of various major sectors in the growth process, particularly as to their capacity to provide employment and rising living standards to the people of the "late coming" economies?

Satisfactory solutions to all of the problems explored in these chapters will not likely be found in this decade, but a strong case could be made that by the end of the decade, the economists' methodologies, models, strategies, or systems, irrespective of the schools of thought to which they belong, will need to be in place and in process of implementation if progress and peace are to have significant meaning for the human race.

Prologue:
The Impact of
Monetary Reform

One of the most dramatic and economically important events of the early 1970's was the announcement of the Nixon economic program, on 15 August 1971. In addition to its series of policy steps to stimulate U.S. domestic investment, consumption, and hence employment, measures were proposed which significantly affected the world trading community. In suspending the U.S. dollar from its historic international convertibility into gold, in imposing a temporary 10 percent surcharge on most imports into the United States, and in providing export incentives and investment credits in favor of purchase of domestic machinery, the enormous U.S. market suddenly became less accessible to other countries. For those nations for which international trade represents a substantial proportion of their national income, the effect of the Nixon-policy package bordered for a time on the traumatic. Some countries were forced by the demand for their currencies to revalue, others contemplated retaliatory measures to counteract the effect, some devalued, and still others toyed with compensatory adjustments more directly related to their trade vis-à-vis other nations.

This chapter reviews briefly some of the implications of the Nixon economic program for the less-developed world, for those countries which at the time were said to be "innocent victims and helpless bystanders" in the atmosphere of monetary uncertainty created by floating currencies. Months after the Nixon announcement, firm trends or expectations could not be predicted, as each nation sought optimum adjustments suited to its own trade and overall balance-of-payments needs. The overriding concern was that delay could only heighten the danger of further retaliations in restrictionism and trade discrimination. No one doubted that the world of trade and international monetary and investment exchange which had functioned since the Bretton Woods Agreement of 1944 had come to an end and that the impending monetary reform would establish the framework for international trade for many years to come.

Recent Import and Export Trends[1]

A review of recent trade patterns will help set the stage for the international monetary and trade reorganization set in train by President Nixon. The value of exports of primary producing countries had risen by 11 percent in 1970, compared to 13 percent in 1969. However, these rates were considerably above the annual average rate for the 1960–1970 period of 7.5 percent. The slowdown in 1970 was due to the economic recession in the industrial countries, which receive most of the primary goods exported from the less-developed countries. The outstanding export gainers among these were in the Far East, with Taiwan, Hong Kong, and Korea leading the way. This success was registered heavily in manufactured goods and was attributable to the price competitiveness of these exports. Of the Southeast Asian countries, Indonesia and the Philippines experienced higher growth patterns in 1970 because of a 20 percent rise in petroleum exports (Indonesia) and higher world prices for copper and sugar (Philippines). The exports of Thailand, Malaysia, and Burma were unfavorably affected by the decline in rubber and rice prices. The rate of export growth in the Middle East slightly exceeded the global average, while Africa's exports increased at less than the global average in 1970.

The exports of the less-developed countries in the western hemisphere increased less in 1970 than they had the year before, while the average increase for South American countries as a group did not change significantly in 1970 over the previous year. The exports of Mexico and several Caribbean countries had declined.

The value of imports of primary producing countries increased sharply at the outset of the 1970's, at 11 percent in 1969 and 13 percent in 1970. This increase was substantially a result of the sharp rise in import prices, which were up 5 percent in 1970, compared to 3 percent in 1969. Putting the import and export performance together, however, the overall position of the less-developed countries, in terms of their balance of payments, had improved both in 1969 and 1970, caused significantly by the growth in exports of oil, minerals, and manufactures. Needless to say, there were wide variations in these trends in the performance of individual countries, but the increased export of nonprimary goods has given the developing world hope of eventual balance-of-payments stability. The export–import data and the overall trade balances are shown in the accompanying tables.

Meanwhile, throughout the 1960's the monetary-exchange relationships between the dollar and key European currencies and the Japanese yen had been gradually leaving their Bretton Woods moorings. From the dollar gap of the early post-World War II period, a combination of circumstances had produced a serious dollar glut abroad. The United States had spent hundreds of billions of dollars abroad in foreign aid, in military outlays for wars and overseas bases and personnel, in tourism spending by U.S. citizens traveling abroad, and in business investment, especially in Europe. As a result of these capital outflows of U.S. dollars, foreign governments alone held $30 billion in dollar balances in October 1971, while the long period of convertibility into gold in the face of the dollar glut had drained the U.S. gold down to $10 billion, as compared to $18 billion in 1960 and about $25 billion in 1950.

To these trends must be added the gradual loss of export markets by U.S. industries, in part because of overvalued currencies abroad but also because of more technologically efficient competition from abroad, particularly from German and Japanese enterprise. Also harmful to U.S. trading advantages were persistent restrictions abroad against America's goods, while U.S. trade barriers were being reduced over time through the cooperative efforts promoted in the General Agreement on Tariff and Trade (GATT) and Kennedy Round negotiations. The final outcome of these collective assaults on the U.S. trading position was to produce deficits in the overall U.S. balance of payments every year since 1951, with the exception of 1957 and 1968, and even, finally in 1971, the first U.S. deficit in trade in this century.

There was no doubt that the international monetary system was overdue for a major overhaul in relative currency and trade relationships when President Nixon launched his new trade and currency policies in August 1971.

Table 1. Primary Producing Countries: Changes in Value of Total Exports, 1960–1970[1]

	1970 (Billion U.S. dollars)	Compound Percentage Annual Rates			Percentage Changes from Previous Year		
		1960–70	1960–65	1965–70	1968	1969	1970
MORE DEVELOPED AREAS							
Europe	**9.79**	**10.4**	**9.1**	**11.7**	**6.4**	**17.1**	**17.4**
Finland	2.31	8.8	7.6	10.1	6.7	21.4	16.1
Ireland	1.04	9.2	7.5	11.0	1.8	11.7	16.2
Portugal	0.95	11.2	11.9	10.4	8.7	11.9	10.9
Spain	2.39	12.7	5.9	19.9	14.9	19.4	26.0
Greece	0.64	12.2	10.1	14.4	−5.5	18.2	16.1
Turkey	0.60	6.5	7.6	5.4	−5.2	8.3	12.5
Yugoslavia	1.68	11.5	14.0	9.0	1.0	16.7	13.8
Southern Hemisphere	**8.17**	**7.2**	**6.3**	**8.1**	**4.2**	**14.0**	**7.1**
Australia	4.77	9.3	8.7	9.9	1.4	19.7	13.0
New Zealand	1.23	3.8	3.6	4.0	1.6	19.9	1.2
South Africa	2.18	5.7	3.8	7.6	10.3	2.0	−1.1
Total, more developed areas	**17.96**	**8.8**	**7.6**	**10.0**	**4.6**	**15.5**	**12.4**
LESS DEVELOPED AREAS							
Asia	**14.50**	**6.5**	**3.8**	**9.2**	**10.8**	**14.6**	**11.8**
Far East	4.78	18.4	14.8	22.0	20.6	28.3	24.1
Hong Kong	2.51	13.8	10.7	17.1	14.2	24.9	15.4
China, Republic of	1.43	24.2	22.4	26.0	25.1	30.9	36.0
Korea, Republic of	0.84	38.2	39.6	36.7	42.2	36.7	34.2
Southeast	6.60	3.6	0.8	6.5	8.0	14.5	6.8
Philippines	1.07	6.6	6.5	6.8	3.3	0.7	24.9
Thailand	0.70	5.4	8.8	2.3	−3.4	7.6	−1.6
Malaysia	1.68	3.6	0.8	6.5	10.7	22.6	1.8
Singapore	1.55	3.2	−2.6	9.6	11.5	21.9	0.3
Indonesia	1.18	3.9	−3.0	7.6	13.2	14.0	18.7
South	3.13	3.0	4.0	1.9	7.1	1.4	5.4
India	1.96	3.9	4.9	3.0	8.7	4.6	6.8
Pakistan	0.72	6.3	6.1	6.5	11.6	−5.4	6.2
Middle East	**10.91**	**8.5**	**8.0**	**9.0**	**9.4**	**9.1**	**7.5**
Oil exporters	8.71	9.0	8.6	9.4	9.2	7.2	8.5
Iran	2.37	10.9	9.1	12.7	−2.6	11.7	13.1
Kuwait	1.58	5.1	5.3	4.9	5.9	6.1	7.1
Saudi Arabia	2.15	10.1	11.1	9.0	8.9	5.3	5.2
Other Middle East	2.21	6.5	5.9	6.9	10.3	16.7	7.6
Israel	0.78	13.7	14.7	12.7	15.3	13.9	7.1
United Arab Republic	0.76	3.0	1.3	4.7	9.9	19.8	2.3
Africa	**11.95**	**9.7**	**8.3**	**11.2**	**16.1**	**16.4**	**11.4**
North Africa	4.33	13.5	12.2	14.7	29.0	15.4	8.2
Libyan Arab Republic	2.37	72.0	135.0	24.3	58.5	16.1	9.1
Algeria	1.00	6.0	2.7	9.5	4.8	23.1	7.4
Morocco	0.49	3.3	4.0	2.7	6.1	7.8	1.4
Other Africa	7.62	8.1	6.8	9.4	9.6	17.0	13.3
Zambia	0.99	. . .	. . .	13.2	15.8	40.8	−7.7
Kenya	0.29	6.1	5.3	6.1	4.9	8.8	7.0
Congo, Democratic Republic of	0.75	4.5	−5.6	17.3	15.9	26.3	16.0
Nigeria	1.24	10.1	9.6	10.6	−13.6	51.7	39.4
Ghana	0.46	4.6	−0.2	9.6	16.1	18.1	17.6
Ivory Coast	0.47	11.6	12.0	11.1	30.8	8.5	1.7
Western Hemisphere	**15.87**	**5.7**	**5.2**	**6.1**	**5.0**	**10.1**	**9.4**
Central America, Mexico, and Caribbean	5.05	5.9	5.9	5.9	7.5	7.9	5.2
Mexico	1.40	6.2	7.9	4.5	10.4	14.0	−2.2
Trinidad and Tobago	0.48	5.3	7.0	3.6	7.3	0.2	1.9
South America	10.82	5.6	4.9	6.2	3.7	11.2	11.4
Argentina	1.76	5.0	6.7	3.4	−6.6	17.8	9.4
Brazil	2.74	8.0	4.7	11.4	13.7	22.9	18.5
Chile	1.18	9.2	7.0	11.4	3.0	23.9	1.3
Peru	1.04	9.3	9.1	9.4	8.0	−0.1	20.8
Colombia	0.75	4.8	2.9	6.8	9.4	11.6	19.7
Venezuela	2.64	0.8	0.4	1.2	0.3	−0.6	4.6
Other Areas	**0.49**	**8.3**	**4.2**	**12.7**	**16.7**	**17.1**	**19.5**
Total, less developed areas	**53.73**	**7.2**	**5.9**	**8.6**	**9.8**	**12.5**	**10.2**
Total, primary producing countries	**71.69**	**7.6**	**6.3**	**8.9**	**8.7**	**13.2**	**10.7**

Sources: *International Financial Statistics* and Fund staff estimates.

[1]Based on customs data, not adjusted to balance of payments concepts. Regional figures are comprehensive, including data for countries not listed separately.

Table 2. Primary Producing Countries: Changes in Value of Total Imports, 1960–1970[1]

	1970 (Billion U.S. dollars)	Compound Percentage Annual Rates			Percentage Changes from Previous Year		
		1960–70	1960–65	1965–70	1968	1969	1970
MORE DEVELOPED AREAS							
Europe	16.60	12.4	13.9	11.0	4.6	17.2	21.2
Finland	2.64	9.5	9.1	9.9	−8.1	26.8	30.2
Ireland	1.62	9.9	10.5	9.3	10.4	18.8	14.6
Greece	1.96	10.8	10.1	11.5	17.5	14.4	22.7
Portugal	1.56	11.0	11.1	11.0	11.2	10.0	20.1
Spain	4.72	20.6	33.0	9.4	1.1	20.1	12.3
Turkey	0.92	7.0	4.3	9.8	11.6	−2.1	22.0
Yugoslavia	2.87	13.3	9.3	17.4	5.2	18.8	34.5
Southern Hemisphere	10.26	7.0	7.5	6.5	4.5	8.3	16.0
Australia	5.10	6.5	6.8	6.2	12.0	4.1	11.8
New Zealand	1.24	4.7	5.7	3.6	−6.3	12.1	23.9
South Africa	3.92	8.7	9.5	7.8	−1.9	13.5	19.5
Total, more developed areas	26.86	10.0	10.9	9.1	4.4	13.5	19.2
LESS DEVELOPED AREAS							
Asia	19.52	7.0	5.0	9.1	6.8	10.6	10.5
Far East	6.41	14.4	9.2	19.9	22.1	24.2	16.7
Hong Kong	2.91	11.0	8.9	13.1	13.1	19.4	18.2
China, Republic of	1.52	17.8	13.4	22.3	12.1	34.3	25.6
Korea, Republic of	1.98	19.1	6.1	33.8	46.9	24.7	8.7
Southeast	9.26	6.9	4.1	9.7	7.2	12.3	10.7
Philippines	1.21	6.3	6.2	6.3	9.2	−2.0	−3.5
Thailand	1.25	10.7	10.2	11.2	8.5	8.0	0.9
Malaysia	1.39	4.3	3.8	4.8	6.7	1.6	17.9
Singapore	2.46	6.3	−1.3	14.6	15.4	22.7	20.9
Indonesia	1.29	5.0	4.4	5.5	3.6	19.1	17.1
South	3.85	0.5	4.0	−2.6	−6.4	−7.3	1.1
India	2.13	−0.8	4.1	−4.6	−9.5	−12.3	−3.2
Pakistan	1.15	5.8	9.8	2.0	−6.9	−1.1	13.5
Middle East	8.26	7.8	8.2	7.5	12.2	11.2	7.1
Oil exporters	4.39	9.6	9.3	9.9	12.4	8.2	6.4
Iran	1.78	12.0	8.5	15.6	20.4	14.7	14.1
Kuwait	0.63	10.0	9.3	10.6	3.0	5.7	−3.3
Saudi Arabia	0.77	12.6	16.6	8.8	25.1	2.2	0.4
Other Middle East	3.88	6.1	7.2	5.0	11.8	14.7	7.9
Israel	1.44	11.1	10.6	11.6	43.9	18.3	9.0
United Arab Republic	0.87	2.7	6.9	−1.4	15.9	13.3	15.5
Africa	9.80	5.3	3.9	6.4	8.6	8.8	10.4
North Africa	2.80	2.4	−2.8	8.1	17.0	11.3	1.2
Libyan Arab Republic	0.55	12.6	13.6	11.6	35.5	4.8	−18.0
Algeria	1.02	−1.8	−8.0	8.6	27.6	23.8	0.8
Morocco	0.67	4.9	1.8	8.2	6.6	2.0	19.0
Other Africa	7.00	6.8	7.3	5.8	5.4	7.7	14.6
Zambia	0.49	...	...	8.2	6.2	−4.1	—
Kenya	0.42	6.8	4.9	8.2	6.0	1.4	15.8
Congo, Democratic Republic of	0.51	8.0	6.4	9.7	21.1	32.3	23.8
Nigeria	1.05	5.7	5.0	6.5	−13.6	27.7	52.4
Ghana	0.41	1.3	4.3	−1.5	−3.8	12.8	19.3
Ivory Coast	0.39	11.5	12.6	10.5	18.9	7.3	15.1
Western Hemisphere	17.22	6.0	4.9	8.8	9.7	8.6	12.0
Central America, Mexico, and Caribbean	7.72	7.1	6.0	8.2	7.9	6.2	12.6
Mexico	2.46	7.6	5.6	9.5	12.3	6.0	18.4
Trinidad and Tobago	0.54	6.3	10.2	2.6	2.4	12.6	12.5
South America	9.50	5.1	4.1	9.3	11.4	10.7	11.6
Argentina	1.68	3.0	−0.8	7.0	6.7	34.8	6.6
Brazil	2.76	6.6	−4.6	20.3	27.9	5.2	22.9
Chile	0.94	6.0	2.8	9.3	2.2	16.1	9.2
Peru	0.63	5.4	14.8	−2.9	−25.8	−2.0	4.5
Colombia	0.84	4.9	−2.4	13.1	29.5	6.7	22.0
Venezuela	1.94	4.7	4.1	5.1	16.3	2.9	6.6
Other Areas	0.62	6.5	8.7	4.4	14.0	−4.6	—
Total, less developed areas	55.42	6.4	4,7	8.2	8.9	9.5	10.3
Total, primary producing countries	82.28	7.5	6.5	8.5	7.5	10.7	13.1

Sources: *International Financial Statistics* and Fund staff estimates.

[1]Based on customs data, not adjusted to balance of payments concepts. Regional figures are comprehensive, including data for countries not listed separately.

Table 3. Primary Producing Countries: Trade Balances, 1967–1970[1]

(In millions of U.S. dollars)

	1967	1968	1969	1970
MORE DEVELOPED AREAS				
Europe	**−4,499**	**−4,560**	**−5,349**	**−6,806**
Finland	−205	39	−39	−330
Ireland	−395	−401	−524	−587
Greece	−691	−925	−1,041	−1,314
Portugal	−358	−416	−443	−610
Spain	−2,076	−1,908	−2,300	−2,323
Turkey	−167	−274	−217	−316
Yugoslavia	−455	−533	−660	−1,193
Southern Hemisphere	**−1,388**	**−1,474**	**−1,214**	**−2,490**
Australia	−435	−854	−341	−330
New Zealand	40	115	208	−18
South Africa	−993	−735	−1,081	−1,747
Total, more developed areas	**−5,887**	**−6,034**	**−6,563**	**−8,901**
LESS DEVELOPED AREAS				
Asia	**−4,745**	**−4,659**	**−4,695**	**−5,022**
Far East	−1,134	−1,423	−1,645	−1,636
Hong Kong	−293	−314	−279	−391
China, Republic of	−165	−101	−163	−96
Korea, Republic of	−676	−1,008	−1,203	−1,149
Southeast	−1,952	−2,055	−2,209	−2,664
Philippines	−351	−432	−400	−143
Thailand	−379	−492	−534	−556
Malaysia	131	188	473	291
Singapore	−300	−390	−491	−910
Indonesia	−122	−52	−105	−107
South	−1,659	−1,181	−841	−722
India	−1,159	−756	−367	−173
Pakistan	−456	−305	−333	−428
Middle East	**−2,318**	**2,367**	**2,437**	**2,662**
Oil exporters	3,467	3,677	3,904	4,320
Iran	804	523	543	599
Kuwait	720	780	830	956
Saudi Arabia	1,212	1,227	1,281	1,384
Other Middle East	−1,149	−1,310	−1,467	−1,658
Israel	−220	−475	−590	−657
United Arab Republic	−226	−44	−10	−110
Africa	**429**	**1,061**	**1,857**	**2,155**
North Africa	562	980	1,232	1,527
Libyan Arab Republic	702	1,222	1,492	1,812
Algeria	85	−56	−75	−14
Morocco	−93	−101	−77	−177
Other Africa	−133	81	625	628
Zambia	175	249	581	498
Kenya	−96	−106	−89	−127
Congo, Democratic Republic of	180	200	234	239
Nigeria	54	48	200	189
Ghana	−34	24	44	46
Ivory Coast	61	111	124	81
Western Hemisphere	**−339**	**−971**	**−860**	**−1,348**
Central America, Mexico, and Caribbean	−1,849	−2,008	−2,055	−2,669
Mexico	−610	−706	−648	−1,063
Trinidad and Tobago	23	45	−8	−59
South America	1,510	1,037	1,195	1,321
Argentina	368	199	36	83
Brazil	−13	−251	46	−17
Chile	188	194	298	234
Peru	−27	251	262	415
Colombia	13	−85	−63	−91
Venezuela	1,011	771	706	701
Other Areas	**−270**	**−300**	**−210**	**−130**
Total, less developed areas	**−2,607**	**−2,502**	**−1,471**	**−1,683**
Total, primary producing countries	**−8,494**	**−8,536**	**−8,034**	**−10,584**

Sources: *International Financial Statistics* and Fund staff estimates.

[1]The data in this table are on a customs basis, not adjusted to balance of payments concepts. Regional figures are comprehensive, including data for countries not listed separately.

Table 4. Selected Less-Developed Countries:

Balance-of-Payments Summaries, 1968–1970

(In millions of U.S. dollars)

		Current Balance [1]	Central Government Capital and Aid	Private Long-Term Capital [2]	Short-Term Capital and Net Errors and Omissions	Overall Balance [3]		Ratio of Year-End Reserves to Imports
Cases of improvement in both current balance and overall- balance[4] from 1969 to 1970
Argentina	1968	−17	−75	−20	145	33		65
	1969	−220	−18	58	−42	−222		34
	1970	−134	−52	97	164	134	(75)	40
Ceylon	1968	−64	43	−2	−10	−33		14
	1969	−142	128	−2	4	−12		9
	1970	−79	83	—	−1	16	(3)	11
Ghana	1968	−56	25	14	19	2		37
	1969	−50	45	10	−25	−20		25
	1970	−28	22	21	−25	2	(−10)	17
Peru	1968	−23	48	25	−68	−18		18
	1969	−5	77	29	−70	31		28
	1970	125	95	−78	28	184	(170)	48
Philippines	1968	−304	49	102	79	−74		13
	1969	−283	128	90	25	−40		10
	1970	−34	114	125	−107	116	(98)	21
Cases of improvement in overall balance[4] from 1970 to 1970 despite deterioration or lack of improvement in current account
Brazil	1968	−520	14	205	371	70		12
	1969	−353	−32	557	227	399		29
	1970	−502	142	377	453	529	(470)	43
Indonesia	1968	−251	213	38	−15	−15		...
	1969	−361	236	43	34	−48		...
	1970	−401	305	56	17	12	(−23)	...
Mexico	1968	−738	120	441	248	71		34
	1969	−729	90	614	30	5		32
	1970	−1,035	232	454	386	82	(37)	30
Nigeria	1968	−274	43	163	71	3		23
	1969	−176	29	139	21	13		20
	1970	−179	56	187	5	86	(69)	21
Cases of deterioration or lack of substantial improvement in overall balance[4] from 1969 to 1970 despite current account improvement
Iran	1968	−366	407	71	−125	−13		20
	1969	−540	515	102	−58	19		18
	1970	−376	425	111	−283	−102	(−123)	12
Uganda	1968	−8	17	−3	8	14		26
	1969	−9	21	−3	−6	3		27
	1970	10	22	...[5]	−33[5]	4	(−1)	31
Cases of deterioration or lack of improvement in both current balance and overall balance[4] from 1969 to 1970
Colombia	1968	−188	113	88	56	69		27
	1969	−210	118	158	−12	54		32
	1970	−284	106	124	69	36	(15)	25
Congo, Democratic Republic of	1968	−38	82	7	19	70		38
	1969	−1	55	—	−15	39		42
	1970	−61	54	−17	−4	−13	(−28)	32
India	1968	−680	970	−17	−170	103		27
	1969	−287	736	−37	−36	376		45
	1970	−444	684	−23	−33	310	(184)	47

13

Table 4. (*concluded*). **Selected Less-Developed Countries:**

Balance-of-Payments Summaries, 1968–1970

(*In millions of U.S. dollars*)

		Current Balance [1]	Central Government Capital and Aid	Private Long-Term Capital [2]	Short-Term Capital and Net Errors and Omissions	Overall Balance [3]		Ratio of Year-End Reserves to Imports
Cases of deterioration or lack of improvement in both current balance and overall balance [4] from 1969 to 1970 (*concl.*)								
Malaysia	1968	10	16	82	−49	59		44
	1969	216	56	57	−162	167		58
	1970	65	21	67	−124	50	(29)	53
Pakistan	1968	−442	453	55	−11	57		25
	1969	−413	323	146	9	65		32
	1970	−698	321	199	40	−106	(−138)	17
Thailand	1968	−205	96	82	39	12		89
	1969	−275	66	105	68	−36		79
	1970	−319	45	105	100	−69	(−69)	73
United Arab Republic	1968	−245	270	−17	−34	−26		20
	1969	−296	246	−15	63	−2		15
	1970	−458	432	−10	3	−8	(−33)	12
Zambia	1968	−26	49	56	−60	19		39
	1969	321	18	...[5]	−170 [5]	169		75
	1970	155	−34	...[5]	16 [5]	145	(137)	105

The Nixon Policy Impact

With the floating of the U.S. dollar, trends and relative disequilibria in trade that had accumulated over time would condition the degree of currency adjustment to be expected or the degree to which compensating factors or policies would be initiated by various countries to offset the effective dollar devaluation that resulted vis-à-vis revaluing currencies. So long as currencies of the less-developed countries retained a fixed relationship to the U.S. dollar, the floating procedure itself need not have affected trade of the developing countries with the United States, while exports of less-developed countries to Germany and Japan would be facilitated by the revaluations of these currencies. However, the 10 percent surcharge placed on most manufactured goods by the Nixon policies affected unfavorably imports from less-developed countries into the U.S. market.

Prior to the August policy announcement, an UNCTAD Expert Group set up to review international monetary issues affecting developing countries had been meeting with members of the International Monetary Fund to consider the appropriate use by less-developed countries of Special Drawing Rights (SDRs). The group proposed that a link be created between SDRs and development assistance through a contribution of this international currency unit to the International Development Association (IDA) or by a contribution from member countries of their national currencies to IDA in some proportion to the SDRs allocated to each country, in relation to their respective quotas in the Fund. However, measures to increase the official flow of development capital to the less-developed countries could conceivably be offset by a reduction in the private flow of investment capital if discouraged by tariff barriers prohibiting the manufactures of developing countries from entering the U.S. market. U.S. private investment in developing countries is often predicated on the capacity of the enterprise created to export to the United States. On the other hand, revaluations of the German mark and Japanese yen could induce more foreign investment in developing countries from those two countries, relative to U.S. private investment flows, if these countries imported more from the developing countries as a result of the relative decrease in such import prices.

Thus, the Nixon policies produced a dynamic dialogue and adjustment period in relative currency valuations and raised issues for the less-developed world as to how developing nations would fare in the new international monetary and trading system, especially with respect to export of their manufactures. Before the Nixon program was introduced, efforts were already underway to utilize international monetary currencies to further the cause of development. It is likely that during this decade the development gap between the developed and less-developed world will widen increasingly, leading to demands for a more systematic multilateral method of transferring still more resources from the more-developed to the less-developed world. The SDRs could provide the medium for translating this need into an equitable-share plan, based on country quotas in the International Monetary Fund, for tapping the world's pooled reserves. In his address to the board of governors during the international meetings in Washington, on 27 September 1971, Robert McNamara, president of the World Bank, urged that "whatever steps be taken to improve the operations of the international monetary system must be such as to permit a continuing increase in capital flows to meet the targets to which developed countries have subscribed: an increase in public development assistance from $8 billion per year in 1970 to $12.5 billion per year in 1975."[2] Mr. McNamara also stressed the dependence of the less-developed countries for their continued growth on "a rapid expansion of trade with advanced countries."

Obviously, changes in the international monetary mechanism can seriously affect both the flow of assistance capital to the developing world and the ability of that world to export to the developed world, without which the long-term prospect for their ultimate economic self-reliance would be a lost cause.

In sum, the developing countries came to the International World Bank and Fund meetings in Washington, in 1971, with a list of grievances they were eager to see remedied by an international monetary system designed to reverse the chronic widening of the development gap between the developed and the less-developed worlds. Currency-valuation shifts significantly reorient trade patterns among the countries involved, but there is common agreement in the less-developed countries and in development-assistance institutions that the final currency and trade relationships would leave the less-developed countries no worse off, if not better off, in their trade advantages with the developed world, and provide a systematic multilateral capital-flow mechanism that will give strong impetus to reversing the widening development gap between the less-developed and the more-affluent worlds.

The sentiments expressed by the developing-country finance ministers and central-bank governors at the international meetings in Washington can be summarized in the following requests, made by the less-developed country ministers before the World Bank and Fund group members:[3]

1. Remove existing trade and payments restrictions, including new or existing tariffs or surcharges on imports into developed countries.

2. Reestablish fixed exchange parities with relatively narrow fluctuation bands but wider than the one percent band prevailing since Bretton Woods in 1944.

3. Replace the long-practiced system of unpredictable bilateral or multilateral assistance flows with a universally agreed plan of capital flows based on use of SDRs, tied to established country reserve quotas in the International Monetary Fund and made available on concessional terms.

4. The resultant assistance which accrues to the developing countries should be made on more-concessional (lower interest and time repayment) terms than in the past.

5. Development loans should be less tied to international bidding requirements, and provide more local cost financing.

6. Recognition in the foreign assistance process that growth is not simply a matter of annual increments in GNP but also gives rise to serious social strains. These include unemployment, especially among younger laborers, from 15 to 24 and including those with college degrees; educational reorientation toward developmental needs rather than toward civil service occupations; health, nutrition, and family planning; urban social upheaval. More assistance must flow into these areas of development stress.

7. Finally, more long-term commitments of assistance for developing countries, rather than ad hoc or annual aid allocations based on repetitive "cliff hanger" negotiations.

These do not exhaust the various requests for reform which were voiced by various finance ministers and central-bank governors at the fall 1971 Washington meetings. Ostensibly, the most important new issues were related to the revaluations of developed-country currencies and the threat of reciprocal trade restrictions induced by the surcharge imposed by the United States on imports. The gravity of the issues were such that the ministers and governors characterized the meetings, in the words of J. M. MWanakatwe, minister of finance and governor of the Band and Fund for Zambia, as "a watershed in the monetary history of the world."

Prospects for, and Nature of, Reform

It is not possible to predict the final outcome of the Bank and Fund negotiations initiated in the fall of 1971. Two months after the Nixon policy announcement, the German mark had revalued by about 10 percent, the Japanese yen less. Some countries had devalued. The 10 percent surcharge placed on foreign imports by the United States omitted primary goods but not the manufactures of less-developed countries. The United States had hoped for revaluations of 15 percent for the yen, 12 percent for the mark, and 10 percent for the French franc.

The U. S. surcharge was particularly distressing to developing countries, which had been striving to diversify exports. The so-called Caucus for the Developing World, comprised of 77 developing countries, met in Bangkok in early October 1971 and voiced strong attacks on the U.S. trade surcharge. The Indian delegation complained that the Third World had done least to upset the U.S. balance of payments yet would suffer most from the protective measures implicit in the Nixon program and that while India might weather the shock, many developing countries would be severely disrupted. India estimated that 21 percent of its exports to the United States would be affected, valued at about $55 million, mainly leather, footwear, engineering products, chemicals, carpets, ferromanganese goods, and other products. Because of their high elasticity of substitution, India could not raise prices of these goods to U.S. customers and so would suffer losses in the U.S. market. Moreover, India's minister of foreign trade pointed out that while one-third of India's imports come from the United States, India's exports to the United States were paying for only about 35 percent of these imports. Thus, India's trade balance with the United States would worsen as a result of the Nixon policies. The Indian case typifies the criticism of the developed countries whose opportunities in the U.S. market for their increasingly important manufactured exports were dampened by the new U.S. trade policy.

Concerted opposition to the U.S. surcharge was by no means confined to the developing countries. Consequently, the combined efforts of both developed and less-developed countries to bargain the surcharge out of existence were considered to have a good chance of success — in time. How much time, it was felt, depended upon the willingness of other countries to reduce trade restrictions again U.S. exports, and the degree to which certain countries assumed a greater share of the overseas military burdens hitherto borne by the United States. European countries were being urged to support their own military forces to relieve the United States of some of its NATO expenses, and other countries around the world were being pressured to pick up some of the costs of maintaining military systems (bases, support or training forces) on their own territory. Simultaneously, Pierre Paul Schweitzer, managing director of the International Monetary Fund, was urging the United States to accept a modest devaluation of the U.S. dollar with respect to gold, implying a continued role for the metal in a revised fixed, but more flexible, parity system.

It seems fair to predict that an improved international monetary mechanism will indeed result from these pressures and continued negotiations. The general lines of agreement which seemed likely to emerge from a settlement of the momentous monetary revisions initiated in the fall of 1971 were the following:

1. Currency readjustments producing revaluation of undervalued developed-country currencies, particularly the mark, the yen, and the franc.

2. Replacement of the U.S. dollar and gold as the primary international monetary reserve with a mutually acceptable and more flexible asset (such as gold plus SDRs).

3. An adjustment on the more-fixed exchange-rate fluctuation around parity, characteristic of the past, to a 2 or 3 percent spread.

4. A more dynamic exchange-rate system for adjusting to market forces regularly rather than with formally announced adjustments of considerable and disturbing magnitude.

5. A reduction in allowable speculative activity by large money blocks (such as Eurodollars).

6. A means to provide assistance funds, based on country quotas in the Fund, through multilateral agencies on a more systematic, concessional longer-term basis, and a continued orientation away from bilateral assistance to the developing countries.

These do not reflect all the concerns expressed by developed and less-developed countries over the world monetary scene in the fall of 1971, but they represent revisions that seem most likely to be implemented. Unless the new arrangements allow exceptions based on some of the requests for redress expressed by the less-developed countries, the U.S. market, at least, will remain somewhat less accessible to the manufactures of less-developed countries than prior to the Nixon program announcement of August 1971. For the cause of export development, this would further postpone target dates for balance-of-payments stability. To this extent, the total package ultimately negotiated or bargained for in the aftermath of the Nixon program will be more important to the developing nations in the 1970's and beyond than the benefits or burdens devolving upon them from any particular measure.

Notes

1. Trade data taken from International Monetary Fund, Annual Report (Washington, D.C., 1971).

2. From printed text of statement of Robert McNamara, 27 September 1971, Washington, D.C.

3. Derived from statements made at the Bank and Fund Boards of Governors 1971 Annual Meeting, Washington, D.C., 27–28 September, by ministers of finance and/or central-bank governors of Philippines, India, Ceylon, Zambia, Indonesia, Burma, Trinidad and Tobago, Malawi, Barbados, Tanzania, Malaysia, Algeria, and Korea.

Part 1
Food and Human Welfare

1 Food Versus People: Must We Choose?

Every so often the prophets of doom and gloom predict the end of the world through starvation. Today the prophets are abroad in platoons: Some recent books and articles have been insisting that mass famines will take place by 1975. William and Paul Paddock, for example, in their book, *Famine–1975!*, envisage disaster: "The locomotive roaring straight at us is the population explosion. The unmovable landslide across the tracks is the stagnant production of food in the undeveloped nations, the nations where the population increases are greatest. The collision is inevitable. The famines are inevitable."[1]

In his article, "The Fight Against Famine Is Already Lost," Paul Ehrlich of Stanford University claims that even with the help of technology no source on land or in the sea will be adequate to feed the growing numbers in the world. In his words, "The battle to feed humanity is over. . . . Sometime between 1970 and 1985, the world will undergo vast famines. Hundreds of millions of people are going to starve to death."[2] The food crisis in his view calls for, among other things, punitive taxes on all products used for the nursery.

Many of the recent dire predictions about the capacity of the world to produce food stem from the high population growth rates prevailing in many parts of the underdeveloped world and from the serious droughts that devastated southern Asia in 1965 and 1966. India's food-grain output had reached 89 million tons, an all-time record, in 1964, only to drop to something over 70 million tons in 1965 and 1966. A 20 percent drop from the record high was a serious blow to the projections that were being made on the basis of the years of building up agricultural technology. Only timely and substantial assistance from world-food-surplus countries averted starvation in some Indian states.

But even while these predictions were being made, the picture in agriculture was in fact undergoing a massive transformation. The question now in the minds of many is whether we are witnessing in southern Asia and elsewhere a dramatic comeback of agriculture attributable to good climatic conditions or whether we are dealing with a reversal of long-term trends in the population–food relationship. There is ample evidence to indicate that the latter answer is the true one. A technological revolution in agriculture has actually been under way for a number of years, a fact that had been hidden by the droughts in southern Asia. It now threatens to cause not worldwide famine but food surpluses.

The signs in agriculture are unmistakable. Targets can be misleading, padded as they often are with wishful thinking. But a review of some of the manifestations of the upsurge in world agriculture is reassuring. While the population explosion leaves no room for complacency, the scare literature has given scant attention to the fact that both India and Pakistan established targets of achieving self-sufficiency in food by 1971. Already, Pakistan is exporting well over 100,000 tons of rice to Near Eastern buyers — hardly a practice to be indulged in by a starving nation. Some countries in southern Asia and the Near East are already self-sufficient in food; Thailand and Turkey are among them. Iran in recent years has exported over 100,000 tons of wheat to southern Asian countries, and Turkey expects soon to have food for export. A number of other smaller countries, such as Afghanistan, Ceylon, and Nepal, have set targets for food self-sufficiency in grains in a number of years.

A recent study of Latin American agriculture by a U.S. Department of Agriculture economist states that "in most Latin American countries the total food supply available is adequate to meet minimum needs of the population."[3] Another study suggested that in the future Latin America will be called upon to export food to other parts of the world.[4] Even though Latin America's population is rapidly approaching 300 million, the picture with regard to food is a hopeful one because of the continent's vast potential. Already beef exports from Brazil are increasing, and farmers, spurred on by better prices, are shifting from dependence on the coffee crop to food-grain production. Experts agree that in Brazil, where fertilizer, miracle-seed varieties, and pesticides are only now slowly finding their way onto the farms, the potential has hardly been tapped. The real problem there is not related to the capacity to produce food but to a lack of purchasing power due to large-scale unemployment and food-marketing and distribution problems. This second study concludes, "The world will continue to have excess production capacity by 1980."[5]

A central fact in the whole situation is that India's drought problems constitute half the world's food-deficit problem. If this can be solved, we will have cut the problem down to manageable size (even a 10 percent increase in India's annual rice and wheat output would eliminate its current food-grain gap). The problem then becomes one of food balance, of providing a nutritionally improved diet for the average Indian.

Another potential source of food the world famine alarmists overlook, despite its proximity, is the United States. Only a few years ago the country was suffering from enormous surpluses. Newspaper headlines were reporting the farm dilemma: "Record Oversupply of Wheat Plagues Farmer and Congress"; "Wheat Surplus Is Big Headache." Cartoons abounded on the U.S. dilemma. In the midst of the southern Asian droughts of 1965 and 1966, the farmers in the United States resisted the government's attempt to increase planted acreage by over 30 percent, because they feared a sharp drop in prices. Under pressure, they increased acreage planted by 20 percent, which still left millions of acres idle in the soil bank. In recent years, the United States has produced record wheat crops, which refilled the storage bins just when countries in many parts of the world found their own supplies increasing relative to needs. A *New York Times* headline of 28 April 1968, affirms the facts: "Farmers Dismayed by the Prospect of Bumper Grain Crops."

The U.S. farmer's capacity to produce food is thus not in question; the effect of surpluses on the price of his output is. In fact, if all the soil-bank lands were used to produce wheat, the United States could make at least another 30 million tons of wheat available to the world in one year. Although the price question is vital in its effect on incentive to produce, it is not realistic to talk of worldwide famine when our efficient capacity to produce is not being realized. We shall continue to have marketing and resource-allocation problems but not capacity problems.

The story is similarly hopeful in other big producing countries — Argentina, Australia, Canada, France, and the Soviet Union. A report by D. Gale Johnson to the Senate Committee on Foreign

Relations, 4 April 1968, concluded that carry-over stocks of wheat in the early 1970's will be at the high levels of the early 1960's. Even the prospects in mainland China are improving, with imports, which amounted to 27 million tons from 1961 to 1965 — all from the free world — now declining. From his review of even this gigantic feeding job — over 700 million mouths — Johnson concludes that it is "not unreasonable to plan for the cessation of such imports over the next few years," thus releasing more suppliers to the rest of the world markets.

To what extent are the targets to achieve self-sufficiency in food padded with wishful thinking? Agricultural production in India and Pakistan in 1968 was up over 20 percent compared to 1967's production. It is true that good weather played a part in this dramatic comeback in southern Asia's food output, but enlightened policies and especially the rapid spread of technology — the vastly improved seeds, the enormous increase in fertilizer use, the application of pesticides and better cultivation practices, and the tapping of new water sources — all helped to revise our thinking about food output.

The new miracle inputs have helped to bring about this agricultural revolution in southern Asia. In the 1950's, agriculture in India and Pakistan was stagnant. The Indian planners adopted the Russian planning philosophy of emphasizing heavy industry. Western aid donors were told that Indian planning was sophisticated and needed little advice. As the lag in agriculture became increasingly apparent, the Indian government's attitude changed and Western donors began to take more interest in Indian planning, orientation in their development programs gave agriculture top was that in both India and Pakistan a change in attitude and orietation in their development programs gave agriculture top priority. Traditional practices that depressed and discouraged farm-production incentives through compulsory sales to the government and forced levies were abandoned; instead support prices for food-grains were established. These changes, together with selective subsidies, helped farmers to get agricultural inputs of fertilizer, better seeds, and pesticides. The consumer-oriented policy of keeping the prices of farm goods down (which, at the same time, discouraged farmers from producing) underwent a dramatic reversal. Higher food prices are now permitted and are creating increased investment in the high-yield inputs. New profit possibilities have spurred farmers to invest and adopt more modern farming practices.

The results have been dramatic. In five years West Pakistani farmers invested $50 million in tube wells, which gave them a dependable source of water for their crops. In East Pakistan the number of pumps farmers have bought tripled between 1964/65 and 1967/68, and acreage covered by these pumps increased from 130,000 acres to nearly 400,000. The East Pakistanis set a target of 14,000 pumps to be in use by the 1968/69 season covering 840,000 acres. Only a few years ago Pakistan's use of fertilizer was negligible. In 1960 it was 30,000 tons; by 1967 it was 185,000 tons; in 1969 it reached 400,000 tons. A heartening aspect of this rise in consumption of this vital input is that most of the farmers pay cash for their purchases.

The story is similar in India. Before 1960, fertilizer use was rare. In 1964 it had reached 600,000 tons; by 1967, 1.3 million tons; and in 1969 it reached over 2 million tons. The U.S. aid program will finance $200 million worth of fertilizer imports from the United States, but India will put up $100 million of its own scarce foreign exchange for fertilizer imports, plus $20 million for better seeds and for pesticides, and will allocate $45 million for a new fertilizer plant. In Turkey, too, there was little use of fertilizer prior to 1960; consumption then rose to 80,000 tons in 1964 and to about 320,000 tons in 1967. Estimates for the 1970's show still further increases.

Underdeveloped countries are also making amazing progress in increasing their own capacity to produce fertilizer and in adapting their own seed strains for their particular environments. A 160,000-ton fertilizer facility, the Coromandel Plant, started production in India in December 1968. American firms have taken an active role in this development. International Minerals and Chemicals of Chicago and Chevron Chemicals of California have 47 percent ownership in the Coromandel enterprise; private Indian partners retain 53 percent. Already the owners of this plant are planning to expand capacity to over 200,000 tons. Standard Oil of Indiana (AMOCO) in another venture owns 49 percent of Madras Fertilizer Limited of India. The U.S. Agency for International Development has been helping these enterprises by providing risk guarantees to the American investors.

Other fertilizer plants are being organized on a cooperative basis. One such plant with a foreign exchange cost of over $50 million has the support of the central farmers cooperative of Indiana and two Mississippi cooperatives, Coastal Chemicals and Mississippi Chemicals. The American participants seek to raise the foreign exchange through U.S. financial institutions, while the Agency for International Development will help with risk guarantees.

Three other fertilizer plants are under construction in Pakistan, with the help of foreign private interests from other Western countries. An Esso-Pakistan fertilizer enterprise is already under construction in Pakistan, and three others are in the advanced stages of preparation. Thus, these less-developed countries are committed to programs of action toward consolidating the agricultural transformation underway in their regions.

There has also been a revolution in the use of new high-yield varieties of wheat, rice, and other food-grains. The new seeds produce two to four times as much as the old varieties. They are now planted on about 13 million acres in India, nearly 4 million acres in Pakistan, and close to 400,000 acres in Turkey. These countries are importing enormous quantities of the new seeds, and we have only begun to see the results. The word will spread among farmers in these countries until they are all achieving impressive increases in food output. The miracle seeds in wheat and rice have spurred research in corn, millet, and sorghums, and the results are equally encouraging. Some of the nation's best experts warn of the impending problems of buffer-stock building, storage, transportation, and better distribution, new markets, and the need to diversify as price indicators point the way for farmers.

As the United States gradually withdraws PL 480 food assistance or makes it more expensive by requiring dollar repayment on harder terms, farm prices in many food deficit countries will begin to rise. Governments in these countries will no longer suppress food prices. The new enlightened attitudes that give farmers adequate price incentives to invest in the new seeds, in fertilizers, in pesticides and other improved contributions to agriculture, will help these countries show dramatic progress toward the ambitious targets they have established for themselves. The targets may not be achieved in the time spans they have set, but with at least normal climatic conditions the massive increase in agricultural innovations will very likely put the prophets of doom to rout.

The situation in the Near East and southern Asia can be duplicated in other parts of the world. Many experts in this field are therefore concluding that, in the foreseeable future, excessive food supplies will be the rule rather than the exception. We will still be grappling with the problems of adequate nutritional balance, with distribution bottlenecks, marketing complexities, storage, shipping, and price incentives versus political pressures. But the problems associated with shortage will become problems of surplus if the present upsurge in agriculture continues. Added to these hopeful signs is the potential in the oceans, in food concentrate substitutes, and in innovative technocracies related to utilization of the sun's energy — too vast to confine to any numerical approximation.

A further slackening of pressure on food supplies is resulting from the sharply increased family-planning programs in many parts of the world. For example, India, Pakistan, and Turkey are undertaking major family planning programs and allocating greater portions of their budgets to such programs. Increasing awareness is shown for attacking this difficult and delicate problem from many different angles.

In the summer 1968 issue of *Horizon,* Roger Revelle, head of the Harvard Population Center, lists as the major influences on eventual stabilization of population growth in the less-developed lands compulsory education for eight or more years: jobs for women; more readily available consumer goods to divert income (thus postponing marriages for some); a strong social security system, which would lessen concern about having many male children to insure survival of a few; and industrial growth so as to absorb more workers from rural areas where there are fewer reasons for postponing marriages.

India is increasing the age at which marriage will be allowed. Many other ways in which the population factor can be affected have not been adequately tested. When they are, the pressure on food supplies will be lessened further.

Recent events have clearly demonstrated that the farmers of the underdeveloped countries of the world have the capacity to increase their output very considerably. The farmers of the developed countries could also double their output if they needed to. The U.S. soil bank could be fully reactivated, and measures could be taken to increase the productivity of small farms enormously. The potential agricultural output of the United States, Europe, and Latin America combined is far greater than present output levels suggest.

Every generation has its share of pessimists for the human race. They always seem to underestimate man's ability to innovate and contrive new techniques to postpone the Malthusian hypothesis another hundred years. In the case of food production, it will not be man's ability to apply ingenuity or the earth's capacity to respond to it that will threaten famine, but the will to use the technological means at our disposal and to plan the storage and distribution systems needed to handle the yields. That will be the critical problem through the decade of the 1970's.

Notes

1. P. 2.
2. See his *The Population Bomb* (New York: Ballantine, 1968), Prologue.
3. Martin Kriesberg, "Food Needs and Market Demand in Latin America — A Fresh Appraisal," Unprocessed paper prepared for 10th World Conference of the Society for International Development, Washington, D.C., 7 March 1968.
4. Montague Yudelman, *Agricultural Development in Latin America: Current Status and Prospects,* Inter-American Development Bank document, (October, 1966).
5. Kriesberg, p. 1.

2 The Factual Base and the Future

The Food-People Race

Forecasters who predict famine and mass worldwide starvation by 1975 or 1980 often use India's two worst drought years as the basis of their predictions. This chapter uses Indian and Pakistani data to speculate on the scope of this problem.

Table 2.1 projects Indian and Pakistani population and food-grain production under various plausible assumptions and demonstrates the unlikelihood of mass starvation in either country. What the data suggest is that the real issue in the food-population question in the long run is not likely to be food so much as the quality of capital investment (the return to capital) and the quality of life associated with high productivity. Montague Yudelman of the University of Michigan concluded from his research that the problem in Latin America will not be food availability in terms of survival, but other pressures and bottlenecks which doubling the number of people there could generate.[1] The burden of future analysis, therefore, should be on the quality of economic progress, on the kinds of pressures that a doubling of population may exert on the commitment of capital in these countries.

The table shows that even under the worst assumptions of an increased population growth rate and 3 percent annual food-grain production growth (as compared to the 2.8 percent annual growth

Table 2.1: Population-Food: Past, Projected, Per Capita Food, India, Pakistan

(1957, 1967 Actual; 1968 Estimate; 1975, 1985, 2000 Projections)

	1957	1967	1968	1975	1985	2000
I. Population (millions)						
India						
1. 2.4% per annum	405.7	510.6	522.8	617.1	782.3	1119.0 A
2. 2.4% 57–65; 2.8%	405.7	514.4	528.8	641.4	845.5	1285.0 B
3. Graduated increase[1]	405.7	517.3	531.8	650.2	889.1	1431.0 C
4. Graduated decrease[2]	405.7	510.6	522.8	614.2	738.7	979.2 D
Pakistan						
1. 2.6% per annum	93.4	120.0	123.1	147.2	190.0	279.3
2. 2.6% 57–65; 2.8%	93.4	120.4	123.8	150.4	198.1	299.1
3. Graduated increase[3]	93.4	121.4	125.0	154.8	211.9	339.0
4. Graduated decrease[4]	93.4	120.0	123.1	146.5	184.9	251.7
II. Food-grains						
India						
Total production (000 M.T.)	72,3375	75,049	97,000	117,015	157,258	245,322
	72,3376	75,049	97,000	124,000	183,547	286,150
Human consumption[7]	68,400	76,900	86,800			221,322
						258,150
Annual per capita (lbs.)	326*	307	339	372x	455x	403 A
		305	335	333x	324x	351 B
		303	333			315 C
						461 D
						470.6
						490.6
						367.9
						537.7

32

Pakistan	1950	1955	1960	1965**	1966**	1967**
Total Production [8] (000 M.T.)	13,800	16,400	19,000	23,355	32,944	55,350
	13,800[9]	16,400	19,000	24,041	35,587	64,056
	13,800[10]	16,400	19,000	24,975	40,680	85,428
Human consumption[8]	13,700	16,800	18,000 (Est)			
Annual per capita (lbs.)	274†	279	298	347x	397x	623[14]
		278	296	306x	279x	301
		277	294			
		279	298			

III. GNP (Data Book)	1950	1955	1960	1965**	1966**	1967**
India[11]	22,830	27,790	34,470	38,112	38,645	42,200
Pakistan[12]	5,883	6,370	7,634	9,566	10,140	10,769

3% p.a. food 1969—at 4 pop. growth assumptions
4% p.a. food 1969—at 4 pop. growth assumptions

*Average of 1956, 1957, 1958.

†Average of 1957, 1958, 1959.

x Best assumptions (highest food, lowest population); worst assumptions (lowest food, highest population).

**Growth rates of 1965, 1966, 1967 at 1966 prices applied to 1964 base.

Notes to Table 2.1

(While projected figures are included, it is assumed that there will in fact be fluctuations within the long-term average growth per year projected.)

1. At 2.4% p.a. 1957–1961, increased .2% for each 5-year period, 1961–1980, maintained at 3.2% p.a., 1980–2000.

2. At 2.4% p.a. 1957–1970; 2.3%, 1970–1975; 2.2%, 1975–80; 2.1%, 1980–1985; 2.0%, 1985–1990; 1.9%, 1990–1995; 1.8%, 1995–2000. (Assumes progress on family planning. India aims to reduce the rate to 1.5%.)

3. At 2.6% p.a. 1957–1961, increased .2% for each 5 year period 1961–1971, 3.2% p.a. 1971–2000.

4. 2.6% p.a. 1957–1970; 2.5%, 1970–1975; 2.4%, 1975–1980; 2.3%, 1980–1985; 2.2%, 1985–1990; 2.1%, 1990–1995; 2.0%, 1995–2000.

5. 1957–1968 at 2.8% p.a. 1968 excellent year, so no increase shown for 1969. 1969–2000 at 3.0% p.a.

6. 1969–2000 at 4.0% p.a.

7. From USAID/Delhi, "Review of Indian Agriculture," June 1966, ch. 14: gross availability minus 10% for seed, feed, wastage. Figures have been rounded.

8. Past series from USAID/Pakistan, *Statistical Fact Book,* 1968, Table 6.8 and U.S. Department of Agriculture data for estimates of 1967 and 1968. Growth from 1957 is 3.2% p.a. based on average of 1957–1959 and average of 1965–1968. 1967 was an excellent year, and 1969 is not expected to exceed it, so no increase shown for 1969. Projected growth from 1969 at 3.5% p.a. Consumption is roughly equivalent to production (because seed, feed, and wastage roughly equal imports, and exports are small).

9. From 1969 on growth assumed 4% p.a.

10. Growth from 1969–1970 assumed 3% due to high levels achieved in 1967 and 1968 by unusually favorable weather conditions. From 1970 on assumed Mission target of 5% p.a.

11. AID, Statistics and Reports Division, Data Book. Relative changes would not alter the correlation significantly so we have not converted to the (1966) devalued rupee rate. 1950–1964 is at 1962 prices. The figures for 1965, 1966, and 1967 were obtained by applying the constant growth rate of those years (at 1966 prices) to the 1964 base figure, the last in the historical series provided by the AID Data Book. The historic food-grain series is from USDA statistics. (Data in $ million equivalent)

12. Same technique but food-grain data is from USAID/Pakistan, *Statistical Fact Book,* 1968, Table 6.8.

13. Production reduced by 10 percent to cover seed, feed, wastage.

14. Assumes consumption equal to production projections minus seed, feed, and wastage (10% of production).

trend since 1950), India's per capita consumption of food-grain will be 315 pounds per year by the year 2000, compared to about 305 pounds in the 1966/67 drought year and 335 pounds per capita in the 1967/68, a good year. If the population growth is maintained at 2.4 percent a year while food-grain availability grows at 3 percent a year, per capita consumption could increase by 20 percent by 2000. If food-grain availability increases by 4 percent a year on the average while the population growth rate gradually declines to 1.8 percent a year (targets the current green revolution and family-planning efforts might achieve) the food-grain availability per capita could increase by nearly 40 percent. The most pessimistic estimate of a population in India of 1.4 billion by 2000 turns out to be worse than Coale and Hoover's worst estimate under their "sustained fertility" assumption (1.1 billion),[2] while the most optimistic assumption of 980 million in 2000 in the table is considerably worse than the Coale and Hoover's most optimistic assumption (fertility reduced by 50 percent between 1956–1981) of about 570 million. Therefore, the ranges of per capita food consumption indicated (omitting income elasticity of food-grain as a consideration) would seem a reasonable basis, at least, for making judgments and qualifications. Modest success with the agricultural and family-planning efforts in these two countries will produce rising per capita availabilities of food-grain. A compound interest on food-grain growth can exhibit the same explosive characteristic as population.

How much food-grain per capita is equivalent to self-sufficiency? If we assume the record crop of 1967/68 was shy of self-sufficiency by 10 million tons (a high estimate), 366 pounds per capita per year would represent self-sufficiency. This could be reached by 1974 only under the best of circumstances — a drop of population growth of 2.3 percent per annum, a rise in food-grain output by 4 percent per annum after 1969. If food-grain output grows to 4 percent per annum while the population rate gradually increases to 3.2 percent per annum, self-sufficiency will not be achieved until 2000. The achievement of self-sufficiency by 1975 will require average growth in food-grain output of 4 percent per year (India's Fourth Plan suggests that it is "reasonable to expect" 5 percent) and a restrained population growth of no more than 2.4 percent a year. To the extent that Indians substitute other foods for food grains, the self-sufficiency level on food-grain alone can be reduced. A balanced diet will require more meat, fish, eggs, fruit, and vegetables, all of which are sorely lacking in the Indian diet.

Table 2.1 shows the correlation between GNP and food-grain consumption. Past data (1950–1967) indicates a close correlation — as GNP rises, consumption of food-grain rises, but not as rapidly as GNP. This could reflect (1) a switch to other foods as GNP rises, (2) more employment (those who were eating anyway, but who then find work and add to value added), or (3) increased productivity in many sectors. We could expect the line to turn up toward the GNP axis as self-sufficiency is approached, possibly indicating a further switch to other foods, or downward toward the food-grain axis if income elasticity of food-grain consumption rises.

These data argue against the likelihood of mass starvation in India, given reasonable expectations about population and agricultural progress,[3] but the doubling of the Indian population as a minimum condition raises other serious investment questions which should be the focus of attention. The alternative cost of capital committed to schools, housing, roads, and social services of various kinds would be the loss of irrigation complexes; factories; and technological advances in chemical, manufacturing, metallurgical, and many other fields which provide the strongest underpinnings for economic development. Based on current capital-per-worker ratios and social investment per capita, an order-of-magnitude estimate can be made of the size of the investment required to service a doubling of the Indian population, to what extent the GNP growth can reasonably support it, and how much foreign capital would be required.

This suggests that over the longer pull we are really dealing with a quality-of-life issue rather than starvation or the capability of densely populated countries simply to carry on. This conclusion, in turn, gets us back to the most basic of development questions: how much can more food increase productivity? Can a more rapid growth in income per capita influence population growth more dynamically than current family-planning programs? If the number of people doubles in India by 2000 and all are better fed than today, will such a society be more satisfied or more stable than one in which population increases half as much and is considerably better off on a per capita basis but still as far below Western standards, relatively, as they are today?

Little attention has been given to two other aspects of population growth. One is the degree to which unemployment can be reduced in the most densely populated countries; the other is the impact of a reduced population growth on demand. Both of these are, in turn, related to productivity trends. Increased productivity on the farms could actually increase the capacity of the agricultural sector to absorb labor, particularly in large-food-deficit countries.[4] In view of the critical pressures building up in the urban centers of the less-developed world, measures for slowing down the out-migration from agriculture should no longer be considered anti-progressive. On the demand side, rising productivity can satisfy Say's law as well as a rising population can but may conflict with efforts to check unemployment.[5] These issues, too, rather than the availability of goods, will more likely constitute the more vital problems of this decade and beyond.

An Approach For This Decade

The current food surpluses at home and abroad and the note of optimism in the figures presented above allow little room for complacency if the Malthusian population–food specter is to be held at bay. When suddenly it seemed apparent that India's fickle monsoons had plunged one-sixth of the earth's population to within the shadow of massive famine in 1965, communications were slow in creating an awareness of the situation beyond the countries where the threat occurred. At the same time, in the face of the great needs of India and Pakistan, the U.S. supply of food seemed by no means to be unlimited; the image of mountains of surplus grains suddenly proved to be something of a mirage, as hungry mouths around the globe consumed our stockpiles. At the 1965–1967 rates of utilization and production of feed grains, another decade at most could have seen our storage granaries emptied.

These trends have been reversed. Yet, we will need at least by the end of this decade to have devised a dynamic strategy for an ongoing growth pattern in agricul.ure, free of the periodic threat of collapse in output of vital grains. We need an "agro-dynamics" for this new decade, which will bring a macro-organized approach to the world's food problem to replace the chaos of the past.

It is indeed strange that with all of the experience in producing a dramatic revolution in the agriculture of the United States in the last twenty-five years, we seem not to have sold our techniques and our formula for high productivity to other parts of the world, not even to rural sectors of the developed Western countries. Even with the current green revolution in Asia resulting from miracle seeds and fertilizers, optimal farm capacity, or agrocapacity, is far from being achieved even in much of rural America or Europe. Within a radius of a few miles of Paris, Berlin, Vienna, Rome, or Nashville, Tennessee, for that matter, one finds primitive plumbing and water use and animal-drawn plows. Even in the densely populated Northeast, beginning only thirty miles north of New York City, depressed rural expanses cover much of the area between cities. Multimillions of acres in our southern and western states are submarginally utilized. If optimally organized, the agriculture of Ireland alone could feed all of Europe. Inspection of the outcountry reveals that much of Ireland's farm sector is as it was fifty or even seventy years ago — almost feudal in its unexploited potential.

In the Western world, farm surpluses and insufficient idle farm acreage have been among the greatest problems. Owning a small or even a medium-sized farm is regarded close to a form of exhibitionism or, at least in choice of career, a sign of personal or family withdrawal or defeat. This, despite the paradox that one-half of the world's population is undernourished, while three to four million still die annually from starvation.

Admittedly, population does outrun world food supply occasionally in some regions of the world, not because we do not know how to affect farm productivity dramatically, but because we have failed to organize or cooperate to introduce high-yield formulas to more regions and countries around the world and to reach the depressed areas with surpluses.

Man's efforts have been too widely scattered to have mobilized any one area of the world to utilize fully its arable areas. The UN Food and Agricultural Organization, the Agency for International Development, the World Bank, the Ford and Rockefeller foundations, many private firms, and other organizations have all done excellent work, with an immeasurable flow of technical advice; pilot projects; research; irrigation and other water systems; land development; crop, animal, and seed improvement; fertilizer use; plant protection; and farm credit.

Yet, with it all, we could still face periodic famine in the underdeveloped world. The efforts have been genuine and useful and many of them individually dynamic and uplifting to many regions and millions of people, but they have not been enough. They have been too uncoordinated and piecemeal, too oriented to the local scene. As a result, the green revolution has not entirely dispelled the Malthusian gloom on the horizon. Good Asian monsoons and dramatic increases in farm inputs have brightened the prospects, but still we need an entirely new, unified, but more broadly based, approach to maintain growth, conceptually encompassing all arable areas of the world. We could call it Operation Agro-Dynamics (OAD).

First, the scattering of numerous independent efforts, should be replaced by the coordination of all programs by a country committee of Operation Agro-Dynamics. The committee would consist of a few international and indigenous agricultural and land-use experts in each country who would develop a total land- and water-use plan for the country. A comprehensive countrywide survey of all the arable potential would be laid out.

Second, the country committee would develop a large-scale

operation in the "Optimum Agro-Area" (OAA), in which there would be a maximum possible application of known techniques to food production. This would include farm units as large as necessary to produce optimum yields, using fertilizers, insecticides, the best seed and crop strains, and mechanical equipment — all the devices that have made some sections of Western agriculture dramatically successful. This might ingeniously combine U.S. extensive farming methods with those of Denmark or the Netherlands and possibly certain Far Eastern intensive modes of farming. Labor for the area would be paid well and drawn from the most skillful farmers available. Price and profit incentives would have to be adequate. All facets of the project would be combined to produce a dynamic example of what modern techniques can do for a large area. Small-scale pilot farm projects have been tried for many years, each proving conclusively the benefits to be gained from a variety of improved farm methods. To meet the possible widening of any food-population gap, however, the effort must be expanded manyfold, and OAA envisages the adaptation of vast sections of the countries where OAD is instituted.

As history has proven, whenever agriculture is successful, the total effort becomes labor saving on the growing end and employment creating on the supply and distribution ends. This feature will require OAD to coordinate its thrust with all other sectors of the economy, since labor will be released to seek work in agrobusinesses in the rural sector, in public works, or in services, such as distribution, marketing, retailing, and servicing equipment.

Once the OAA is functioning, the process of converting the population and of implementing the program widely begins. The first step would be to convert the OAA gradually into a cooperative operation, ultimately owned and managed by those involved in it directly or indirectly. This may involve a share system of ownership, based on pre-OAA land portions owned or estimated pre-OAA farm income.

Any program which proposes to produce sharp increases in agricultural productivity will inevitably involve the release of laborers who must be absorbed elsewhere in the economy. In every country in which agriculture has advanced into even a semblance of modernity, the number of farm laborers as a percent of the total labor force has declined dramatically. In the developed economies the labor force in farming ranges from 10 to 30 percent of the total labor force. In the less-developed countries agricultural labor reaches from 50 to 70 percent of the total. In the Western world, the industrial revolution presupposed an agricultural revolution to release workers for the rapid proliferation of production units in the industrial sector and rapid demand for complementary or supplementary productive activities in the services sector. It is naive to expect that the rural sector in the less-developed countries can absorb the effects of mechanization and continued population growth.[6] Thus, their surplus of labor presents a different problem than the developed countries faced in their earlier stages of growth. Any big push for new takeoffs in agricultural productivity in the less-developed countries must, therefore, be matched or coordinated with programs to absorb the labor released as a result of the application of optimal techniques.

Some labor will be absorbed in harvesting, storing, processing, packaging, and the wholesale and retail distribution of farm output. Producing new inputs for the OAA will absorb others. These efforts will not be enough. The development of the industrial and service sectors will have to continue apace to help absorb the effects of any effectively successful and dynamic agro-operation.

In this respect, the country committee of OAD will have to meet with central country planners who are primarily concerned with the other sectors. Again, it is a matter of man's ability to organize his total environment for optimum production capacity to satisfy his basic and other felt or aspirant needs. The total effort should include estimates of rates of opportunity or job creation so that the reduction of labor use in agriculture can be coordinated with planned job generation in other sectors of the economy.

I have referred before to the backwardness which still prevails in much of the rural areas of even the developed world. OAD should by no means preclude development of optimal farm-output conditions in these areas, which are equally important to solving any prospect of a world food crisis or mass unemployment. In fact, if some LDCs are incapable of absorbing OAD released labor, a possible alternative would be for OAD to generate the required surpluses in the advanced economies, transporting them to the deficient areas, while they in turn focus on more labor-intensive programs.

To illustrate, if optimization of food production in India eventually releases labor as a result of the spread of OAA farming techniques, India may have to focus on becoming a gargantuan industrial complex, using its exports to buy food from developed, surplus-possessing countries. In the advanced countries, this could have the multiple effects of increasing world food supplies, absorbing more people in the rural sector (thus reducing pressures on the urban centers), promoting exports to the less-developed countries in exchange for more of their imports, broadening the market base for farm goods, and leading to improved terms of trade for the farm sector.

This latter approach would involve a survey of the rural sectors of all the advanced countries to produce an optimal-farm-productivity plan for each country. The central board of the OAD, possibly established at the United Nations, would pursue the task of organizing country committees and Country Research Teams (CRT) to carry on the broad surveys and country consultations required.

OAD would also bring into play more dramatically and with accelerated research if necessary, the processes of desalination, nuclear plantology, ocean farming, and other frontier areas of potential food expansion. All of these activities have been going on for decades, but the efforts have been small-scale relative to the need; uncoordinated and unintegrated with total country or regional food-resource planning. OAD in every instance will not neglect these areas of contribution to the total country plans. Nor should it neglect to seek more effective cooperation in distributing, through normal trade channels, the surpluses of one area to cover the shortages of another. U.S. government surpluses, we now feel, have encouraged dependence on our food supplies and nurtured casual national attitudes toward agricultural and land reform. The future will require more stringent conditions on the use of such surpluses. But unless efforts are coordinated — on the macroeconomic and national as well as international levels — and unless widespread application of the optimal concept is adopted, both in the developed and underdeveloped countries, the gains of the green revolution in a few areas will not be sufficient to provide the sustained advance in living standards needed to create the modernization process which leads to a decline in population growth.[7]

Man's responsibility and rational intellect must organize the resources at his disposal. Malnutrition is a scourge which could bring economic and political chaos decades from now that no amount of alternative aid efforts could rectify. If this situation is allowed to come to pass, the innocent will reap the ravages, not of nature, but of responsible man's irresponsibility.

Appendix on U.S. Wheat Supplies

The world food situation has been profoundly influenced by U.S. productivity in wheat. U.S. consumption seems to have leveled off over the period shown in Table 2.2. U.S. farmers are reputedly dismayed over bumper grain crops because of depressed price im-

Table 2.2: Recent U.S. Wheat Trends
(In Millions)

	1964/65		1965/66		1966/67		1967/68 (Preliminary)	
	Bushels	Metric Tons	Bushels	Metric Tons	Bushels	Metric Tons	Bushels	Metric Tons
Supply								
1963–64 carryover	901.4	24.5	817.3	22.4	535.2	14.6	425.0	11.6
Production	1283.4	34.9	1315.6	35.8	1311.7	35.7	1524.0*	41.5
Imports	1.1	.03	.9	neg	1.7	.04	1.0	.02
Total available	2185.9	59.4	2133.8	58.1	1848.6	50.3	1950.0	53.1
Demand								
Domestic use	643.6	17.5	731.2	19.9	681.2	18.5	655.0	17.8
Food	509.2	13.9	515.1	14.0	502.2	13.7	510.0	13.9
Seed	65.6	1.8	61.9	1.7	78.3	2.1	70.0	1.9
Feed	68.7	1.9	154.1	4.2	100.6	2.7	75.0	2.0
Industry	.1	neg	.1	—	.1	—	—	—
Exports	725.0	19.7	867.4	23.6	742.4	20.2	750.0	20.4
Stock carryover	817.3	22.4	535.2	14.6	425.0	11.6	545.0	14.8

Source: Data provided by USDA.

*Highest production since 1940.

plications. When there is 8 or 9 million acres of land in the U.S. soil bank, it can, if activated, produce an additional estimated 30 million tons of wheat. According to the U.S. Department of Agriculture, 4 or 5 million acres were expected to come out of soil bank in 1968, and the rest in 1969, because the Soil Bank Act was expected to run out in 1970. Some, if not most, of the lands could go into crops other than wheat. The pressures for U.S. export of wheat may, in any case, increase rather than diminish. This further reduces the pressure on world food supplies and increases pressure for diversification of land use.

It remains to be seen in the 1970's what policy stance either U.S. farmers or officials are likely to assume when the success of the new agricultural inputs in the less-developed countries threatens the markets for U.S. cereals exports. It is surely not early and may even be late for promoting numerous means to avoid uneconomic solutions to this impending event.

Notes

1. Montague Yudelman, *Agricultural Development in Latin America: Current Status and Prospects,* Inter-American Development Bank document (October 1966).

2. Ansley L. Coale and Edgar M. Hoover, *Population Growth and Economic Development in Low-Income Countries,* (Princeton, N.J.: Princeton University Press), p. 332.

3. A conclusion also reached by Coale: "Even in that circumstance [doubling of population], there appears to be every technical possibility of somewhat higher per capita incomes at the end of a generation than today" ("The Economic Effects of Fertility Control in Underdeveloped Areas," in *Human Fertility and Population Problems* [Cambridge, Mass.: Schenkman Publishing Co., 1963], p. 148).

4. This is covered more fully in the next chapter.

5. One recent effort to deal with this issue through the effect on demand of lower population growth rates is Goran Ohlin, *Population Control and Economic Development,* Development OECD (Paris, 1967). I am also indebted to Professor T. Curtin of the University of York for discussions on this subject.

6. There is, however, disagreement on this point; cf. Bruce Johnston and John Cowie, "The Seed-Fertilizer Revolution and Labor Force Absorption Problems," Food Research Institute, Stanford University, unpublished MS (January 1969). See also the next chapter.

7. See chap. 4.

3 Absorbing More Labor in Agriculture

Some of the arguments and insights put forward by recent articles in support of reducing the out-migration of labor to nonfarm sectors in the less-developed countries have long been neglected in development planning in the last decade in favor of more prestigious industrial development.[1] In view of the pressure migrant redundant farm labor can impose on urban areas, I have indicated below how further positive emphasis and substantiation might be developed to support the argument that "programs aimed at facilitating the outflow of labor from the farm sector probably deserve only low priority in the initial investment plans of underdeveloped countries."[2] This is particularly of interest in view of the prevailing differences of opinion as to whether there is, in fact, surplus labor in the agricultural sectors of some less-developed countries where it is widely believed to exist. While Enke claimed of India that during 1961–1966 existing underemployment would worsen "despite an estimated migration of almost one-and-a-half million job seekers from country to town, the increase in rural under-employment possibly being nine million,"[3] Paglin questioned the existence of any underemployment at all in India's farm sector,[4] and Schultz believed that Indian farmers, given the structure of their environment, were quite efficient.[5]

It is entirely possible, I would contend, that the traditional expectation of a declining share of agriculture income and labor force in country totals as development proceeds can only be achieved in the less-developed economies as yields are substantially advanced over their current low levels. Meanwhile, these sectors could, as in Japan,[6] absorb far more laborers, provided the developing countries clear the way for the myriad inputs needed. Given the critical levels of unemployment in this decade in less-developed countries, new approaches of this kind require urgent attention.

Potential Labor Absorption

Tables 3.1-3 show the potential labor-absorption capacity, income originating, and per capita income potential which could conceivably result from an optimization of acreage yields in the farm sectors of a number of countries now experiencing yields far below those in, say, Japan or Taiwan. I have omitted livestock, forestry, and fisheries, but the thrust would generally be the same.

If we assumed (unrealistically) that 1970 is a target year for maximizing yields, and the work force in agriculture increased at the rate of the total population increase from 1950 to 1960 (slightly less than its current rate, assuming effective family planning), a combination of increased land use and increased yields which would support 175 workers per 100 hectares would enable this sector to absorb more than its own labor force growth to 1970 and considerably more by 1980.

For example, India's labor force in agriculture in 1960 was reported to be 134 million. Using all arable lands available in India and assuming no gain in labor intensiveness per 100 hectares, the number of workers agriculture could absorb would be 168 million, as against labor-force growth to 163 million by 1970. (The latter figure, however, assumes the growth rate of the total population applied to the agricultural sector, when, in fact, the rate of the rural sector may be higher, depending upon the success of family planning.) If growth in yields, on the other hand, enabled India to support 175 workers per 100 hectares instead of 83 (1960), thereby achieving 70 percent of Japan's demonstrable labor-absorption capacity, the increase in workers which could be absorbed would be about 352 million, or about 189 million more than a 1970 conservative forecast of the agricultural work force, or 218 million more than the 1960 labor force, an increase of 260 percent. If the maximum target year is moved up (more realistically) twenty years instead of ten, India's agricultural work force, increasing 2 percent

*Thanks are due to Mordecai Ezekiel for helpful discussions on this subject.

Table 3.1: Employment-Absorption Potentials from Rising Agricultural Productivity[a]

(Selected countries)

	Agricultural[b] workers per 100 hectares of arable land, 1960	No. of arable[c] hectares now in use, 1960 (000)	Total agri-[d] cultural workers, 1960 (000)	Maximum[e] arable land, (000) hectares	Workers with[f] max. land & 1960 worker per 100 hectares (000)	Workers with[g] max. land & max. workers per 100 hectares (000)	Increased[h] workers without gain in workers per hectare (000)	Increased[i] workers with 175 workers per 100 hectares (000)	Annual population growth rate (1950-60) (percent)	Agriculture[j] work force By 1970 (000)	By 1980 (000)
Greece	52.6	3,700	1,946	4,625	2,433	4,625	487	2,679	1.0	2,156	2,641
UAR (1961)	166.7	2,500	4,167	3,750	6,251	6,563	2,084	2,396	2.4	5,292	6,709
India	83.3	161,000	133,630	201,200	167,600	352,100	33,970	218,470	2.0	163,029	200,440
Iran	22.2	16,860	3,743	49,438[k]	10,975	49,438	7,232	45,695	2.2	4,660	5,802
Israel (1961)	33.3	400	133	500	167	500	34	367	5.2[l]	170	219
Jordan	14.7	966	142	1,256	185	220	43	78	2.6	183	237
Pakistan	83.3	25,535	21,270	26,535	22,104	46,436	834	25,166	2.2	26,588	32,969
Turkey[m]	38.5	25,290	9,737	29,084	11,197	29,084	1,460	19,347	2.9	12,853	17,429
Japan[n]	250.0	6,000	15,000	7,200	18,000	21,600[o]	3,000	6,600	1.2	16,950	19,050

a Excludes livestock, forestry, and fishing.

b U.S. Department of Agriculture, *Agriculture in 26 Developing Nations, 1948 to 1963*, Report No. 27 (November 1965), Table 49. Japan is included for comparison with a high yield country.

c Agency for International Development, Statistics and Reports Division (Washington, D.C.); also USDA, *op. cit.*, Tables 14, 67.

d Column 2 × column 3 divided by 100.

e USDA, *op. cit.*, Tables 14, 67. The Pakistan figure assumes an increase of 1 million hectares or 4 percent over farmed area in 1960, based on a recent report from the AID Mission, Pakistan. The USDA gives the range for the United Arab Republic as 25-74 percent potential expansion; I have used 50 percent here.

f Column 4 × 175, where 175 is above the UAR (166.7) but below Taiwan (199) or Japan (250).

g Column 5 × 175 for Pakistan, India, and the UAR; column 5 × 100 for Greece, Iran, Israel, Jordan, and Turkey. Expanded workers per hectare assumes increased yield per hectare.

h Column 5 – column 3.

i Column 6 – column 3.

j Assumes growth in the agriculture work force at the same rate as population growth. Also, the 1950-60 rates are used in the projections.

k U.S. Agency for International Development, Statistics and Reports Division.

l Much of this is attributable to immigration. I assume 2.5 percent growth, inclusive of future immigration.

m In 1960 about 15 percent of the irrigable land was irrigated. By 1965, 25 percent was irrigated. Also, from 1950 to 1960 the economically active in the population actually declined 9 percent. Gains in agriculture may slow the trend, but probably will not reverse it.

n Actually, from 1950 to 1960, the economically active in agriculture in Japan declined 17 percent, and this trend is more likely to continue than to reverse. Also, with its high farm productivity, Japan still is a sizeable net importer of agricultural products, excepting rice. See the USDA study, Tables 51, 77.

o Assumes a 20 percent increase in workers per 100 hectares of arable land.

Table 3.2: Potential Income Gain from Agriculture with Maximum Land Use and Comparable Yield Estimate

(Selected countries)

	No. of arable[a] hectares now in use, 1960 (000)	Yield per[b] hectare, 1960 (dollars)	Total yield[c] ($ million)	Max. no. of[d] arable hectares (000)	Maximum[e] $ yield per hectare	Maximum[f] total yield ($ million)	Maximum[g] gain from agriculture ($ million)
Greece	3,700	205	759	4,625	300	1,388	629
UAR	2,500	643	1,608	3,750	700	2,625	1,017
India	161,000	91[h]	14,651	201,200	300	60,360	45,709
Iran	16,860	n.a.	—	49,438	250	12,360	21,412[i]
Israel	400	557	223	500	600	300	77
Jordan	966	63	61	1,256	200	251	190
Pakistan	25,535	133	3,396	26,535	300	7,961	4,565
Turkey	25,290	127	3,212	29,084	250	7,271	4,059
Japan	6,000	961	5,766	7,200	1,000	7,200	1,434

a See Table 1.
b USDA study, Table 6. By way of comparison, the Taiwan yield per hectare is $477.
c Checks substantially with Table 67, USDA study.
d Table 3.1.
e Assumptions, based on comparisons with other countries and estimates of potential by country.
f Column 5 x column 6.
g Column 7 — column 4.
h Studies by Farm Management Research Centers in India show that gross output per acre averages higher on small farms than on large (rupees per acre): smallest—219; second smallest—188; second largest—170; largest—159. This is due to larger labor inputs on small farms (USDA report, No. 27, page 41).
i Assuming Iran's yield per hectare equal to Turkey's in 1960.

Table 3.3: Potential Per Capita Income Gain from Maximum Agricultural Yield

| | Total 1964 population (000) | Projected total population | | Per capita[a] income, 1964 (1962 prices) | Maximum[b] yield from agriculture ($ million) | Gain in[c] total agricultural income ($ million) | Per capita income gain[d] | | 1980 percent gain per capita over 1964 |
		1970 (000)	1980 (000)				1970 (dollars)	1980 (dollars)	
Greece	8,580	9,130	10,082	556	1,388	472	52	44	11
UAR	29,800 (1965)	34,389	42,614	139	2,625	763	22	18	12
India	475,000	536,750	655,500	83	60,360	34,282	64	52	63
Iran	23,400 (1965)	26,720	32,292	221	12,360	16,059	60	51	23
Israel	2,480 (1965)	2,882	3,569	1,116	300	58	20	16	1
Jordan	1,850	2,161	2,794	223	251	143	66	51	23
Pakistan	110,900	126,650	157,478	82	7,961	3,424	27	22	27
Turkey	30,800	36,652	48,972	222	7,271	3,044	83	62	28
Japan	96,900	104,070	117,249	671	7,200	1,075	10	9	1

a   U.S. Agency for International Development, Statistics and Reports Division (Washington, D.C.). UAR data is for 1963.
b   Derived from Table 3.2.
c   A 25 percent cost factor for all inputs has been deducted from the gross gain.
d   Assumes maximum land use and maximum yields by 1970 and 1980.

per year, would reach about 200 million in 1980, as compared to 163 million in 1970. The potential maximum projected of 352 million would still be able to absorb the difference, plus 152 million. The expansion of workers used per 100 hectares, it bears remembering, would be based on rising productivity, with all the inputs this implies, commensurate with these projections.

Although one-fourth of the 3.5 percent annual growth of Pakistan's agriculture during the second plan (1959/60–1964/65) was reported to be due to extension of area, further gains in expanding land use in Pakistan appear to be very limited. The potential gain in worker absorption per 100 hectares through rising yields, however, is also assumed to increase from 83 to 175, the same as in India. Here again, this sector could more than absorb the growth of its own labor force, if yields were optimized. In all the countries shown but the United Arab Republic and Jordan, the optimization of yields as formulated here would readily absorb the growth in the labor force. Part of the labor-absorption capability, as it has been in the past, can come from improved and increased irrigation which requires two to four times more labor (depending upon the crop) than nonirrigated lands, but fertilizer, seed improvement, agricultural education, and other inputs are involved as well.

For the more arid countries of Greece, Iran, Jordan, Israel, and Turkey, where the irrigation potential is less, the capacity to absorb workers was taken as 100 workers per 100 hectares rather than 175. In view of their current levels of one-third of this, this target may be ambitious, but even with a considerable degree of error there is ample room for absorbing an agricultural work force projected at the rate of total population growth.

Potential Income Gains

The potential gain in income from rising productivity in the agricultural sector is equally relevant. Again taking the maximum number of arable hectares available and making some arbitrary assumptions about potential yields per hectare in dollars, as compared to recent yields, and assuming the results are essentially in real terms without projecting future money values and farm price indices, India and Jordan could increase their income from agriculture more than three times, Pakistan and Turkey could more than double theirs, and Greece and the UAR could increase their income substantially (Table 3.2). Before World War I, Japan increased yields dramatically per hectare and without drastic reforms, while maintaining growth simultaneously in its industrialization drive.

The chances of India or Pakistan reaching such returns are remote, but the potential for tripling yields in these countries should not be considered utopian.

Cost Considerations

There are, of course, serious cost considerations to be taken into account in bringing acreage up to the yields required to support the number of workers dealt with in these somewhat mechanical projections. There are complexities to this which defy ready benefit-cost formulas, but some orders of magnitude and the feasibility of attaining these goals must now be addressed.[7] Cost estimates of the inputs of fertilizer, seed, pesticides, water, and other inputs of the more obvious physical type can be developed. Net-yield estimates from irrigation complexes around the world lead us to assume that if the water is available and if appropriate water-use practices, fertilizer, cropping patterns, and other inputs are employed, land can produce better living standards. Basic soil conditions vary, but in India's case "the natural fertility of land is as high as in Japan."[8]

The inputs which are difficult if not impossible to quantify and add to the equation, but which may in many instances be crucial to a positive benefit-cost outcome, have to do with vital environmental factors. There is, in sum, a high correlation between the level of economic development and value of output per agricultural worker. The environmental factors involved may be briefly noted but cannot be neglected in judging whether India or any of the less-developed countries can realistically strive for such ambitious targets. The Department of Agriculture's study, for example, noted that seven of the top ten countries in yields per unit of land had higher literacy rates.[9] Higher education brings many low-cost elements into play, with high correlations between yields and ability to perceive independently, to understand an extension agent's directions, or to read about and act upon advantages to be derived from better cropping patterns, water use, and plowing practices; willingness to use even small savings for high-yield capital inputs; ability to seek and utilize market potentials for surplus outputs; and many other possibilities related to a higher level of education, but not necessarily a direct cost factor for the farmer. There are, in addition, other factors which private entities or governments can do, or should provide, which contribute significantly to a higher farm yield. These have to do with the availability of private or government-sponsored information or extension services, research and information on plant breeding, improved seeds, more incentive-oriented tenancy conditions, better distribution and marketing facilities, more incentive-inducing pricing practices. All of these factors affect both the cost of inputs and expected yields from physical outputs. Providing these environmental or infrastructural inputs in India, Pakistan, or elsewhere requires a broad-gauged program, a portion of which, at least in the early stages of implementation, must be launched and, where necessary, financed from general revenues rather than from specific charges against the farmer. At the same time, taxes on rising rents as pressure is applied to land could assist in providing the general revenues.

With these important qualifications in mind, some specific order-of-magnitude costing can be done, geared to the projection of land use and yields made in Tables 3.1–3. The results will reduce net per capita gains by approximately 25 percent, still leaving the labor-absorption and per capita-income targets worth pursuing, as the per capita-income data of Table 3.3 indicate.

It will simplify the approach if we confine our probing of specific costs to India, drawing upon criteria developed from various applied cases in India or elsewhere. Fertilizer costs are an important consideration in achieving the maximum yields projected in the tables. What might be the cost of the fertilizer input to this result in the case of India? The method can be applied to the other countries. In 1962–63 India was applying only 3.4 kilograms of fertilizer per hectare, while Japan applied 20 kilograms. In both rice and wheat Japanese physical output yields were over three times those of India.[10] Let us assume that as one of the necessary inputs, India must sharply increase fertilizer use per hectare to achieve the yields we have. posited. However, rather than apply the Japanese level, we will assume for India a higher proportion of wheat output (which uses less fertilizer than rice). Instead of 270 kilograms per hectare, I have assumed 200 kilograms per hectare. At the same time, the Indian fertilizer price has been far above either the Pakistani or Japanese price per kilogram. Therefore, I have used the Pakistani price of 12.6 cents per kilogram rather than the Indian price of 34.5 cents per kilogram — a price which, while an average of the nitrogenous and phosphate fertilizers, reflects the differential in each separate category as between Indian and Pakistani prices.[11] The results on cost of fertilizer per hectare to achieve the yield target for India in Table 3.2 are shown in Table 3.4.

The cost of fertilizer per hectare, using a Pakistani price of 12.6 cents per kilogram of fertilizer, results in cost per hectare to cover increase in hectares, projected at three-fourths the Japanese rate of

Table 3.4: Cost Per Hectare of Fertilizer, Indian Case

	(1) Comparison of fertilizer use per hectare 1962–63 (Kg)	(2)a No. of hectares to maximize assumed yields (000)	(3)b Total annual fertilizer need, with present use level (M.T.)	(4)c Total annual fertilizer need, with 75% Japan level (M.T.)	(5)d Total cost per year of fertilizer to India at Indian price ($ million)	(6) Cost of fertilizer to India per year at Pakistan price ($ million)	(7) Cost per hectare using Indian price (dollars)	(8) Cost per hectare using Pakistan price (dollars)
India (Japan)	3.4 270.1	201,200	684,000	40,240,000	13,883	5,070	67	25

a From Table 3.2.
b Column 1 x column 2 converted to metric tons.
c This is 75 percent of the Japanese level per hectare of 270 kg.
d India's 1962–63 price was 34.5 cents per kg, Pakistan's 12.6 cents, and Japan's 21 cents (USDA study, p. 55).

use (200 kilograms or 440 pounds per hectare), of $25 per hectare out of the projected yield per hectare in Table 3.2 of $300. In 1960–61 the Japanese were paying about $56 per hectare for fertilizer to reach the level of 200 kilograms per hectare would 20 to 1 on this input, while India was paying only $11.70 per hectare on a yield of $91, a ratio of 9 to 1. Using the Indian price of pertilizer to reach the level of 200 kilograms per hectare would produce a ratio of yield to fertilizer cost of 4 to 1, while using the Pakistani price would produce a yield to fertilizer cost of 12 to 1. The Indian per hectare yield of $91 left little available for inputs, but a yield of over three times that level should allow more to be invested in fertilizer, as well as in other inputs. Thus the assumed level of yield could readily absorb an added fertilizer cost commensurate with that yield.

Fertilizer is but one capital cost behind the assumed maximum yields shown in Table 3.2. Cost of improved water sources, seeds, implements, and the hidden or indirect costs of all the other infrastructural factors mentioned earlier must be taken into account, though explicit cost data on all of these factors is difficult to estimate. A gross order-of-magnitude estimate of this total capital investment required can be derived from projection of 1960 gross capital formation data per hectare of arable land. In 1960 gross capital formation for Indian agriculture was estimated to be $13 per hectare.[12] In Pakistan it was $6 per hectare, in the UAR $47, in Taiwan $55, and in Japan $129. If we assume that India must achieve Taiwan's or Japan's ratio of capital formation per hectare to a yield of about 1 to 8 or 9, this would call for an expenditure of $40 out of the $300 yield per hectare assumed in Table 3.2. This could represent the cost of fertilizer, seeds, and other inputs (*ex* capital) needed to achieve the $300 per hectare yield in India.

There is much uncertainty in these estimates and some chicken-and-egg sequential dilemmas, but one is led to conclude that if the price incentives are evident on the yields-versus-use of inputs, the decisions can and will be made by farmers to use them. U.S. Department of Agriculture data clearly indicate that the cycle of frustration in Indian agriculture has been due partly and probably significantly to faulty price relationships. India's ratio of fertilizer prices to prices of crops produced, for example, has in recent years been a strong disincentive to use this input. India would need to obtain a rice yield of 5.23 kilograms to pay for 1 kilogram of fertilizer, while in Pakistan the ratio was 1.15 and in Japan 1.35; on wheat, India's was 3.67, while Pakistan's was 1.50 and Japan's 1.80.[13]

Cost of credit has also been higher in India. A 1963 FAO study indicated that about 30 percent of all India farm loans were contracted at interest rates over 50 percent, and about 50 percent of the loans were at rates above 25 percent. This is no doubt another important price deterrent which adds to the cost of investing in inputs of various kinds.

With more appropriate prices of inputs to Indian agriculture, as our illustrative case, the cost of achieving a $300 per hectare yield need not, by ratios prevailing in higher yield countries, exceed $75.[14] Specific ratios may be determined for other countries where data is available.

Translating these potential aggregate income gains, minus costs of approximately 20 percent, into per capita gains (Table 3.3) reduces the impact relatively, particularly for Turkey, Jordan, Israel, and the UAR, in view of their higher population growth rates. The impact is nevertheless quite significant. The chances were all but nil that the targets for maximizing or optimizing yields could be reached by 1970. Whether it be 1970 or 1980, the gain in per capita income derived from agriculture is not widely altered in absolute terms, but the potential gain over current levels by 1980 differ significantly from one country to the next. The gains in the countries dealt with range from 63 percent in India to 11 percent in Greece. The gain in Turkey would be 28 percent, in Pakistan 27 percent. Where per capita incomes are already high (Israel, Japan), the gains are relatively small.

If we can concede some validity to the approach implicit in the data presented here, then we should be in a position to do some rethinking on Owen's statement (common in the literature) that, at least in the earlier stages of development, "the so-called 'drift to the city' of farm population goes hand in hand with general economic development." Historically, this has been true, but we need to consider the possibility now that far greater yields in agriculture, which are clearly possible, could support larger rural enclaves more effectively than has been the case in the past.

Notes

1. Wyn Owen, "The Double Developmental Squeeze on Agriculture," *American Economic Review,* LVI (March 1966), 43–70.

2. Ibid., p. 64.

3. Stephen Enke, *Economics for Development* (Englewood Cliffs, N.J., 1963), p. 568.

4. Morton Paglin, "Surplus Agricultural Labor and Development: Facts and Theories," *American Economic Review,* LV (September 1965), 830.

5. T. W. Schultz, *Economic Crises in World Agriculture* (Ann Arbor, Mich., 1965).

6. Kazushi Ohkawa and Henry Rosovsky, "The Role of Agriculture in Modern Japanese Economic Development," *Economic Development and Cultural Change* (October 1960). Appropriate account has to be taken of the high labor absorption of rice culture as compared to wheat and other crop complexes.

7. The complexity of the problems related to costing investment alternatives are recounted in UN, ECAFE, "Criteria for Allocating Investment Resources among Various Fields of Development in Underdeveloped Countries," *Economic Bulletin for Asia and the Far East* (June 1961), reprinted along with other selections on this subject in Section V, "Allocation of Investment Resources," in Gerald Meir's *Leading Issues in Development Economics* (New York: Oxford University Press, 1964).

8. USDA study, noted in footnote (a), Table 3.1.

9. Ibid., p. 14. I have dealt with some of these in R. Ward, "Focus in Jordan Agriculture," *Land Economics* (May 1966).

10. USDA study, Table 34, p. 46.

11. Ibid., Table 40, p. 55.

12. Ibid., Table 58, p. 80.

13. Ibid., Table 42, p. 57.

14. A 25 percent ratio of costs to income is not uncommon in field reports: for example, Government of Jordan, Department of Statistics, *National Accounts,* 1959–1965, p. 42. Where prices of inputs are high, this proportion will be higher. This figure would include all capital carrying charges plus the cost of maintenance inputs. The tendency of rising rents to absorb some of the gains could be offset by taxing these rents and using the general revenue obtained to provide the environmental and infrastructural inputs needed (improved research, extension service, farm-to-market roads, marketing and distributional information and services, municipal water systems, agricultural training institutions, etc.). I am indebted to Lester Chandler of Princeton for discussions on this notion.

4 Alternative Means to Control Population Growth

Introduction

Population growth in many underdeveloped countries is undoubtedly a serious problem. Pressure for action is at a high pitch. To date, policies to combat population growth seem to have focused on promoting massive use of contraceptive devices: the intrauterine device or "loop," the oral pill, condoms, sterilization and other direct methods, not excluding abortion. The United States has vigorously urged family planning programs on less-developed countries and has helped finance purchase and shipment of considerable quantities of some of these devices, for example, to India, at the request of the Indian government. The U.S. government is also considering helping populous Asian countries build plants in their countries to manufacture these devices. Companies with distributive outlets in India (i.e., Lever Brothers, Lipton Tea) are considered to be good agents for marketing the devices in the rural villages. The World Bank, particularly under Robert McNamara, has given population control high priority. The results of these efforts thus far have admittedly been disappointing. Rejection or indifference to these methods is widespread, partly due to unforeseen side effects not well understood by recipients. Time may change this, but even by 2000, present predictions see but a modest impact on population growth from contraceptive methods now being applied.

Thus far, demographers seem at a loss for alternative approaches to population control that could produce effects within a reasonable time span. Even Catholic demographers from whom we might have expected proposals for practical operational programs in consonance with traditional Catholic teaching have had amazingly little influence on this process, now in full swing, at least in the Asian countries.

Some relief from the pressure of feeding people is evident in the agricultural transformation underway around the world, spurred by vastly greater use of fertilizers, pesticides and new miracle seed varieties.[1] Projections of the potential growth in food-grains in India, even with only moderate success in the agricultural revolution, as compared with the worst expectations about population growth, show (in Chapter 1) that by the year 2000 the Indians will be eating considerably better than they are now. Even if India's population continues to increase at about 2.6 percent a year, while food increases at its historic rate of about 3 percent a year the per capita consumption of food-grains alone will increase. However, there is a good chance that food-grain production will, in fact, increase more rapidly. Both Pakistan and India are projecting 5 percent per year growth rates in food production. Pakistan projects full food self-sufficiency soon and is already exporting surpluses, reflecting the anticipated results of the current exponential rise in the new agricultural inputs. These dramatic increases in agricultural productivity could also help the serious unemployment problem in Asia and check the flow of labor to already overburdened cities.[2] Confirming the green revolution is now the key task.

Thus, population-control specialists often point with alarm at the exponential growth curve for population, but fail to include on the same page the likely exponential growth in food-grain production. In fact, exponential growth patterns are discernable not only in population and food, but in knowledge, electronic-cybernetic change, various technological applications, and in numerous other sectors of our dynamically changing world. Emphasis on promoting exponential growth in technology that will utilize the world's untapped capacity is an avenue of attack on the population question which has always appealed to optimistic social scientists, and rightly so. The favorable trends in food output should provide planners more time to work on other longer-range programs for influencing population growth as alternatives to contraception.

Of course, man's needs go far beyond food and it is urgent that social scientists have something more dynamically practical and applicable to say in this new decade to today's planners on population, both in the underdeveloped and developed worlds.

This paper maintains that there are alternative practical approaches to influencing population growth which may find more acceptance than current methods. Furthermore, more penetrating research by social scientists on the positive growth factors in the development process, such as more domestic and foreign investment, more technology to help export industries of less-developed countries, more technical and policy advice from advanced countries, more commitment to education, and more attention to urban problems, should turn up other factors that can help check population growth.

New methods of arresting the growth of population are not easy to find, but there are a number of areas in which some fruitful work could be done, and it is to these that this essay is directed. These areas require intensive research far beyond the treatment afforded here, but a beginning may be made by calling them to the attention again of demographers, who have failed to stress their potential impact. Each of these means of reducing population growth is an alternative to the use of contraceptives. Quantitative estimates of material benefits and costs are omitted. It is probable that promoting widespread use of contraceptive devices would be far less costly than meeting the costs of more education and some of the social costs associated with alternative population checks. However, the benefits of the alternatives may in the long run produce far greater returns. For example, returns to education have been calculated by T. Schultz, Harbison, and others and found to be high.[3] Similar calculations must be a necessary part of further examination of the following areas of potential influence on the population equation.

Alternative Population Checks[4]

Compulsory Education for Children

Less-developed countries could extend the age to which young people must remain in school and could be more effective in improving the content of education and in imposing compulsory-education regulations.[5] This would serve the dual purpose of reducing fertility by offering secondary education as an alternative to child marriages and, by increasing the literacy rate, open alternatives for employment or careers conducive to postponing marriage. While education costs will rise significantly, less-developed countries have demonstrated their ability to manage the cost of increased educational facilities. In Egypt, for example, between 1953 and 1964, 4,000 new schools were built and 58,000 additional teachers were trained. About 52 percent of the children between the ages of 6 and 12 attended primary school in 1963 in contrast to 42 percent in 1958. At the same time, industrial, commercial, and agricultural vocational school attendance increased sharply. Increases in attendance in schools and training centers are already common in other less-developed countries. What is needed now is an attempt in these countries to determine how much this effort can be expended in the overall development strategy and what impact it might have in the short and long run on population growth. This could have the secondary benefit of forcing less-developed countries to take care not to divert scarce resources to nondevelopmental and often destructive purposes. We need much more scientific data in this area, but it is an area where expanded activity should be welcomed by the less-developed countries.

Influence of the Delay in Age of Marriage

In 1965, S. N. Agarwala, the Indian economist, estimated that an increase in average age of marriage of Indian women from the existing 15.6 years to 19 or 20 years would result in an annual crude birthrate 30 years later of 33.9 births per thousand population instead of 47.8, a decline of 29 percent. He found a rise in age at marriage of Indian females from a mean of 12.3 years in 1924 to 16.7 years in the 1955–1959 period (Table 4.1).

Table 4.1: Mean Age at Marriage and at Cohabitation by
Year of Cohabitation
(11 Punjab Villages)

Item	1924	1925-34	1935-44	1945-49	1950-54	1955-59
Mean Age at Marriage	12.3	13.4	13.9	15.0	15.6	16.7
Mean Age at Cohabitation	15.8	15.7	15.7	16.1	16.5	17.5
Number of Wives	276	381	556	371	338	310

The average age of marriage increased by 2.7 years between 1924 and 1945 while the mean age at cohabitation remained almost constant.[6] After 1945 both the age of marriage and age at cohabitation increased with the greatest increase between 1955 and 1959. As a consequence wives now starting cohabitation are expected to bear on the average of 1.3 children less than did wives aged 45 or more in 1959. The people of these Punjab villages have achieved delayed cohabitation sufficient to affect the expected number of children born. Thus, a trend to later cohabitation of women has a strong potential toward lower birthrate and warrants an effort to develop methods promoting later cohabitation through postponed marriages or longer waiting periods before cohabitation.

Delayed marriage can be promoted by programs that increase the opportunities for higher education, that promote urbanization, and provide more opportunities for women in the labor force. Such programs would require government support and possibly an administrative system to ensure compliance. There would be social and family consequences which would also require careful attention, but providing rational solutions to these should be less difficult than dealing with the effects of extreme poverty.

Increased Knowledge of the Decrease in the Mortality Rate

The Indian practices of child marriages, employment of children, and beginning of procreation at puberty are promoted by the permeating influence of death. To offset the fear that too few offspring will survive, marriage partners seek to produce many children. To counter this, a program could spread the knowledge that a lower mortality rate has been achieved so that less purposeful effort to generate large families could prevail.

In Taiwan, for example, fertility has been falling slowly without benefit of a large, organized family-planning program. Ronald Freedman points out that because of Taiwan's low mortality rate, from two to four children is considered ideal. Most of the people know about the decline in infant mortality and are aware that this means most of their children will survive to become adults. Those who tend to limit family size have other characteristics in common: they are better educated, are in touch with mass media, own modern objects of consumption, live in nuclear or parent-centered rather than joint families, are the least favorable toward traditional family practices, have little farm experience, and are migrants from large cities or who work in an impersonal setting as employees of nonrelatives. These factors influence the fertility rate indirectly but have a more significant influence than direct contraceptive methods in a rapidly changing culture. The mass of Indians, on the other hand, prefer at least four surviving children to balance their feelings of relative insecurity about being provided for in their old age.

The following can also contribute to a declining birthrate:

1. The reduction in level of infant and childhood mortality will

increase the economic cost of supporting a family under conditions of constant fertility and hence may serve as a stimulus to fertility reduction in various ways not necessarily associated with direct contraceptive methods.

2. Reductions in mortality at young ages are also usually accompanied by reductions in mortality at older ages. Therefore, a general reduction in mortality at all ages would not statistically have to increase the number of children per productive adult. More important, studies have shown that a decline in mortality is often followed by a decline in the birthrate.

3. On a biological level, a high rate of infant mortality will lead to an increased fertility in any society where a substantial proportion of mothers breast-feed their children. If a child survives and is breast-fed by his mother, during the period of the mother's lactation, her fecundity is greatly reduced and her chance of conceiving a second child therefore declines. Mothers in this case would have to be adequately fed.

4. One anthropologist (Dr. Laila Sh. El Hamamsy, Social Research Center, American University, Cairo, Egypt) argues that a high death rate among infants and children causes parents to refrain from investing large amounts of emotional energy in any one of their children. The pain of bereavement following the death of a child is related to the amount of energy invested in the child. However, the more emotional energy one puts into any one child, the less emotional energy is left over for other children. Therefore, these studies suggest that the investment of large amounts of energy in any one child should lead one to desire fewer children. A higher survival rate among children should, therefore, lead to a reduction in family size.

It is apparent from these observations that the overall population would not necessarily increase if great strides are made to decrease the mortality rate.[7] However, the long-run psychological effect on the parent of realizing that deaths will not decimate the family could more than compensate for the tendency of the population to rise and could result in further decreases in the birthrate. Some effort could be made to educate the populace about the decline in mortality among infants who have had the basic inoculations and precautions. The concern for having enough children will be replaced by a more relaxed attitude which, even without birth-control methods, could lead to a declining birthrate. Such attitudes could reduce the frequency of sex experience or increase the acceptability of following an improved rhythm technique.

Rural-urban migration will indirectly curtail the birthrate. A study done by Dr. Ulia Olin of the UN, "Feedback Mechanisms in Human Population," shows the effects of crowding on the central nervous system of both animals and humans. Crowding produces stress and stress leads to enlarged adrenal glands reducing fertility. Social competition is more intense in urban than in rural areas, leading to a greater incidence of low-key nervous tension. Over a long period of time such tension decreases the biological proclivity to reproduction. Where suitable urban conglomerations can be developed or promoted, migrations to such centers would appear to help reduce the birthrate, while exposing families to improved social and cultural opportunites.

In underdeveloped countries, on the other hand, urbanization has been progressing more rapidly than the ability of governments to provide adequate social services or jobs. Therefore, remigration toward the outer perimeters of urban centers is probably more desirable. There is already evidence that this process is taking place. In Bombay, census tabulations showed that the net migration into Bombay decreased from about 950,000 during 1941–1951 to less than 600,000 during 1951–1961, despite increasing rural density and rural unemployment. To meet the growing rural density close to Bombay, the state government of Maharashtra made a concerted effort to decentralize industrial establishments so as to absorb the rural population and those who left the city. New industrial areas were also established at convenient distances from the metropolitan area.

Rural-urban migration is an integral part of industrialization and economic development, but it also may become a major instrument of social change. About 30 percent of males and 20 percent of females left Bombay within three or four years after entering the city. A concomitant advantage was that the rural population was exposed to urban ways of life. Studies have proven that the migrants from rural areas are the most literate group in the rural environment. When they leave their respective areas, the most productive manpower is lost to the rural sector.

Moreover, the longer the exposure to city life, the greater the resemblance to city-born persons and the greater the dissimilarity with populations in states of origin. A study of migrant Indian women aged 15-19 proved conclusively that the proportion of single women increases significantly with an increase in the length of residence in the city and that migrants who decide to leave the city do take their newly learned norms with them. Rural migrants who take advantage of educational opportunities also demonstrate a lower birthrate through postponement of marriage and career-directed motivations. The strategy of establishing incentives for a permanent rural-urban migration to new satellite towns or industrial sites near an urban area should, on this basis, reduce the birthrate. The investment and other costs of providing the social infrastructure would be high but must be balanced against the savings resulting from a reduced growth rate of population and against other benefits which well-ordered suburban complexes can produce. The new town-satellite city would have the atypical stresses and tensions of a larger urban area, but it would be better organized economically and socially. The situation would be conducive to developing a highly productive labor force and a well-educated population with newly acquired urban values. The environment would promote later marriages or offer activities or jobs for wives, both of which would reduce fertility. The new town could serve as an educational medium between the urban area and the villages. Such a concept of the urban conglomerate — modern and progressive — is badly needed for the crowded less-developed countries.[8]

Child-Labor Laws

By passing and enforcing child-labor laws, the economic utility of offspring (as income producers and security in old age) is diminished, leaving simply the noneconomic utility for parents to take into account. By having to support children fully, parents undergo increased direct costs of food, recreation, and space in crowded urban circumstances. They appreciate more fully the costs of raising children. This will help to convince parents of the need to consider appropriate alternatives. A modern, urban middle-class way of life opens up virtually unlimited nondomestic avenues of recreation and cultural interest. This gives parents opportunities for alternative social outlets for their energies and could help them accept morally acceptable birth-control methods, even if considerable planning and effort is required.

It would be the responsibility of the governments of less-developed countries, as in other countries, to impose child-labor laws, though it is difficult to administer them in underdeveloped rural areas. "Disguised employment" has been successful there. The government would have to provide provincial officials to carry out the laws. Punitive taxes against the family in case a child works before the proper age could help keep village children in school and dependent on the family, thus rendering them less free to marry at an early age.

The Net Economic Cost of Children

An institutional change that accompanies economic development and is detrimental to a high-fertility level may be an increase in the net economic cost of children relative to that of other consumer commodities which parents might buy in place of supporting children. The net economic cost of children is equal to the gross expenditures involved in child-bearing minus the productive return (as distinct from their nonmaterial value) which the children themselves bring into the family. As the economic well-being of a society rises, child labor becomes less frequent and, hence, other factors remaining equal, the net economic cost of children rises. An increase in the net economic cost of children relative to other commodities which parents might buy in their stead is a cause of fertility decline. Families in traditional cultures tend to see many advantages in numerous children but seldom weigh the direct and indirect costs. A program to promote more awareness of the benefits and costs of children, both to the family and to children themselves, could be helpful.

People in a rapidly developing country may be slow to develop a taste for newer consumer goods available to them as their incomes rise. Rather than spend their money on new consumer articles to which they were not accustomed, they might wish to expand their consumption of more familiar articles. This expansion might include the consumption caused by additional children. This could be offset by making goods readily available to families. In this sense, a liberal import policy could help to stimulate disincentives to have more children by making a broad spectrum of goods available to family consuming units. Families would have less inclination to marry young or strive deliberately for larger families to the extent that cultural goods can be promoted. These purchases need not lead to crass or petty materialism but to a commitment of energies and time to cultural exposure.[9]

Effects of Greater Mobility

A high degree of social as well as geographic mobility may be associated with a fading of traditional and hereditary customs and status requirements and may lead to an increasing use of conspicuous consumption, in the modern economy sense, as a means of demonstrating high status. An increase in conspicuous consumption, in turn, would necessitate a diversion of funds from other types of consumption — including the consumption expenditures of raising a large family. There are numerous studies going back to the Victorian period that demonstrate the association the middle class of Western societies makes between fewer children and a higher living standard. An increased rate of vertical social mobility is inimical to high fertility. Social as well as geographic mobility results from increased education and urbanization. We need to explore further how either mass education or selective education can affect social and geographical mobility, can most effectively reach those who would postpone marriage to prepare for a career, and can reach those who would, if better educated or trained, have less desire to strive deliberately for large families and therefore be more amenable in their sex relations to abstinence or the rhythm method.

Increased Number of Women in the Labor Force

Employment of women outside the home leads to smaller families. Such employment will often entail alternative preoccupations to rearing children: companionship, recreation, mental stimulation, creative activity, or financial remuneration. Giving up employment will frequently be experienced as a cost — one of the costs of having children. Employment is a means of introducing into women's lives the subjective awareness of opportunity costs involved in childbearing — an awareness that traditional feminine roles and activities are well-designed to circumvent. In a recent study two French demographers, Collver and Langlois, found a high negative association of fertility with women's participation in work. The regression equation shows that the number of children per 1,000 women declined by seven for each one percent increase in the work-participation rate. From the population viewpoint, the most desirable industries to be introduced into an underdeveloped country would be those using large numbers of female workers: modern factories, stores, offices, etc. A policy of this type could involve some direct governmental outlays but more significantly the abolition of legal restrictions and informal barriers. Women employed in "cottage industries" would enhance economic development, but the traditional forms of social and family relationships would still be maintained. Little or no progress would be made toward transforming the entire socioeconomic structure into that of a rapidly growing modern economy unless women could be lured away from their traditional environments into interests away from the home. Once in the labor force, the horizon for feminine activity broadens. Other useful social activities could occupy women outside of the home. To assist this process, urban social, religious, athletic, or similar activity clubs might send representatives to the traditional areas to help diversify wives' interest. Where these organizations do not exist, foreign aid could finance participant trainees to study their structure in other countries. Successful generation of outside interests could also enhance incentives for further general or vocational education. In the process socioeconomic barriers might well be broken down and the ultimate result could produce a decline in the birthrate through diffusion of rural or traditional customs which promote high birthrates. Some of the effects of working wives on family welfare may be undesirable, but the disadvantages are probably less than those produced by alternatives which perpetuate extreme poverty.

Increased Reliance on Social-Security Programs

If the older people in the underdeveloped countries could rely more heavily on the security of pensions rather than on sustenance from their kin, there would be less desire for large families. There is a strong tendency to strive for large families spread over a wide span so that there is a guarantee of at least one son living as the couple survives through an extended old age. With no organized security system among rural populations, the only security against destitution in old age is the support from one or more of their surviving offspring. Less-developed countries do have pension systems, particularly for government employees, but they are not prevalent among the mass of the poor, where subsistence incomes would make them difficult to implement. However, industrial workers could be covered by contributory pension systems and some thought could be given to including other categories of workers. Combined with experimental government-organized social-security programs and guarantees of protection in old age, these could have some influence on the present disposition to create very large families as a hedge against destitution in old age.

Conclusion

Broad areas have been delineated within which population-control efforts might take place in the years ahead. There are undoubtedly others that need to be explored.[10] Specific recommendations for policy steps indigenous governments might take will require probing these areas in given environments. At present, control efforts seem to be massive but too narrowly committed only to contraceptive techniques. Investment in additional areas affecting population-growth trends will be required to bring more effective results within a shorter time span. It is also conceivable that the net yield on investment in more broadly based programs to influence population trends might exceed rates of return on investment in capital projects or other development programs.

There is still time for social scientists to revive emphasis on the positive aspects of economic development.[11] If all the energies channeled into defining and deploring the population crisis and forecasting *Famine — 1975!*[12] were devoted to seeking ways to increase the investment in development in the underdeveloped countries, the impact on population growth might be highly significant. In addition to seeking new ways to influence population growth directly, social scientists could be pressuring for the following: (1) a greater flow of aid from the developed to the under-developed world; (2) improved or preferential trade policies of the developed economies to permit the poorer countries to sell their most advantageous economic wares in advanced country markets; (3) increased commitment of the developed countries themselves to development, seeking reductions in allocations to burdensome military establishments or to other nondevelopmental projects;[13] (4) firm fiscal and monetary policies and liberalized trade policies in underdeveloped countries to check inflation (which kills export sales), diversion of resources and overvalued currencies, while improving the international competitiveness of their goods and services; (5) a vastly increased effort in education to reduce widespread illiteracy (in India it is nearly 75 percent), upgrade levels of training to broaden workers' options and promote broader professionalism in the art of technological research and innovation so that these countries can take the leap into technically advanced levels whicu, as in the case of Japan, make them highly competitive i world markets.

Given the numerous alternative approaches to ameliorating the world's population problems, it is unfortunate that social scientists have not been more innovative. There is every opportunity to stress the positive approach which, by increasing per capita-income growth, can affect population pressures more than narrowly conceived population control programs. "The key to a more stable population," as Barbara Ward has put it, "lies beyond any particular kind or strategy of birth control, it lies in the general increase in economic and social confidence and elbow-room."[14] A world of rising living standards, by generating the first of these, may well lay the foundation for providing the last. The problem of integrating these approaches into population planning will be a critical one in the 1970's.

Notes

1. Trends in current agriculture are summarized in chap. 1.

2. Some attempts at estimating this potential is undertaken in chap. 2.

3. T. W. Schultz, *The Economic Value of Education* (New York: Columbia University Press, 1963); F. Harbison and Meyers, *Education, Manpower and Economic Growth,* (New York: McGraw Hill, 1964).

4. Indebtedness to the authors is too heavy to have footnoted in every instance the particular ideas accepted from them.

5. Gunnar Myrdal gives great stress to the lag in both juvenile and adult education in less-developed countries in *Asian Drama,* 3 vols. (New York: Pantheon, 1968), chap. 9.

6. In India, child marriages are by custom contracted some time prior to actual cohabitation of the partners.

7. This is the basic argument made by Roger Revelle, head of the Harvard Population Center in "Too Many Born? Too Many Die," *Horizon* (summer, 1968). Paul Schultz of the RAND Corporation has also been researching in this field, financed by AID and the Ford Foundation.

8. It is also surprising but obvious to those who travel to such cities as New Delhi, Lahore, Kathmandu, Ankara, Dacca, etc., that air pollution is often far worse than one would experience in New York or Los Angeles.

9. It is not frivolous to suggest that plans underway to bring rural electrification to India may have a measurable effect on frequency of sex experience and, therefore, on the birthrate.

10. Research under the direction of Dr. Stephen Enke at General Electric's Center for Advanced Studies (TEMPO) identifies "implicit pronatalist programs," whereby governments unnecessarily encourage population growth (allowing child labor, early marriages, inadequate social security, inflation which increases dependence on children, uncertain inheritance laws, compulsory military service which takes sons from the farms).

11. And even of population growth. Both Ohlin and Clark have dealt with the dampening effect a declining population would have on the demand function; cf. Goran Ohlin, *Population Control and Economic Development* (Paris: OECD, 1967; Colin Clark, *Population Growth and Land Use* (New York: Macmillan, St. Martin's Press, 1967) and in other works.

12. Authored by William and Paul Paddock.

13. Global expenditures for military purposes in 1967 were $182 billion, $50 billion more than 1964. By contrast, the DAC countries net disbursements of public and private aid amounted to only $11.4 billion (*Survey of International Development* bulletin, 15 February 1969, p. 4). What would even half the military outlay do for mass education, youth and adult, and consequently to population growth?

14. *The Lopsided World,* (New York: Norton, 1968) p. 80.

5   Renewed Emphasis on Human Investment

Measuring the Impact of Social Factors*

If we ask ourselves whether social or human factors are preconditions for economic development or economic development is the
precondition for social and human development, the obvious answer
is "both." This is another case of the chicken-or-the-egg question.
In a feedback process, it all depends where you start, and this is a
matter of choice. However, for what it is worth, the results of the
UN Research Institute for Social Development for a specific group
of underdeveloped countries for the specific period of time, 1950–
1960, suggests that the need for economic growth as a precondition
for social development was at that point the stronger force of the
two, although the other need was much more clearly established
than could have been assumed a priori — the need for human investment as a precondition of economic development.

Human resources have only recently been recognized in their
true importance. Experience and research have shown that only
a comparatively minor part of economic progress can be attributed
to the input of the material or physical factors of production —

*The first part of the chapter is by Hans Singer of the UN. It first appeared
as "The Notion of Human Investment," *Review of Social Economy,* 24
(March 1966), 1 ff. The second part of the chapter is an assessment.

more capital, more labor, more land, more natural resources. Most of it is due to what economists have begun to call the intangible factor or residual factor. This is really the human factor — better quality of labor, better education, better training, more knowledge, better housing, better nutrition, better organization, etc. This realization has opened up new approaches — through education, training, community development, use of idle manpower and eradication of disease — to using the vast latent human resources of the developing countries.

At a recent meeting organized by the UN Children's Fund in Italy, attention was drawn to the widespread malnutrition among children of one to four years of age in the poorer countries. The terrible fact is that such malnutrition is irreversible, in the sense that these children, however much their situation may improve afterwards, can never repair the damage that has been done. For instance, they will not be able to take proper advantage of educational facilities even where these can be provided and will never become effective producers.

The second big problem raised at this conference was the problem of employment for the young people now emerging from the spreading primary school systems of the poorer countries. They are dissatisfied with the primitive and traditional village and tribal customs and tend to drift to the towns where, however, there are few employment opportunities for them. It can be seen how at this point the field of human resources and the field of technology interconnect. We need employment and training for young people in the developing countries, and we need technology which provides this employment and training.

At the present time, there is almost perfect unanimity among economists, sociologists, and other scholars on the importance and influence of the development of human resources in the economic and social development of developing countries. As pointed out in a report of the secretary-general of the United Nations, "Emphasis on the mobilization of human resources as a precondition for achieving the aims of the development decade, and as a necessary area for intensified international action, does not perhaps need much general argumentation at this time. Educated and trained people are always the chief, and in a longer run the only, agents of development. The unutilized talents of their people constitute the chief present waste and the chief future hope of the developing countries."

The views of the economists have performed a sort of cycle in the last twenty years or so. About twenty years ago when the attention of economists had not yet been attracted to the then very peripheral problems of underdeveloped countries, they tended to believe that these were matters of interest mainly to sociologists, anthropologists, psychologists, or other lesser breeds of this kind. Then economic development became the big growth sector in the economic science. In the flush of enthusiasm, economists tended to think in terms of economic growth models. Those were the great days of the Harrod-Domar formula, of average and incremental capital-output ratios, of rates of saving and investment, of closing and widening gaps in gross national product (GNP). Then came the days of disillusionment. Doubts began to creep in as to whether the matter was that simple. What was the meaning of GNP gaps when the GNP concept was applied to countries with subsistence economies, with tribal or other communal forms of organization, with different economic motivations? What was the meaning of capital formations or saving in such conditions?

A very appropriate point was brought up by Dudley Seers and Richard Jolly in their paper, *The Treatment of Education in National Accounting,* which was prepared for the General Conference of the International Association for Research in Income and Wealth, in Lom, Norway, 1965, which states as follows:

> The second example shows the dangers for policy in defining investment and thus saving too narrowly. In giving aid to developing countries, there is an understandable wish to put money where it pays, i.e., in countries within sight of reaching self-sustaining growth. How near a country is to this target is judged (by one major donor country at least) partly by the current savings ratio. Savings in this case is defined under present conventions and thus ignores expenditures on human capital formation. It should be obvious that any aid policy based on this sort of definition may be far removed from the findings of recent research into the importance of education as a major cause of economic growth.

The doubts were reinforced when quantitative research arrived at the conclusion that capital investment failed to account for much or most of economic growth, that there was a large unexplained "residue." It was found that when you deal with unhealthy, undernourished, illiterate people, some extra food or the eradication of malaria or some instruction or training can be more important in raising their productivity than physical capital; what then becomes of the conventional line of division between consumption and investment? The incremental capital-output ratios of the Harrod-Domar formula turned out to be so unstable as to be useless as instruments of economic planning according to a purely economic model, even though it took economists many years to draw this obvious conclusion.

Even worse, the social worm was right inside the core of the economic apple: the rate of investment turned out to be determined by investment opportunities, but the perception of such opportunities was a matter of the quality of people and involved pre-investment work; moreover, the utilization of such investment opportunities as were perceived was found to be a matter of the motivation of people, the right kind of communication with them, and of a social structure which permitted people to utilize such opportunities.

Thus, when the development economist turned away from his textbooks and learned about underdeveloped countries, he was driven back toward the earlier position, namely, that those queer fish and lesser breeds — sociologists, anthropologists, psychologists, etc. — had after all a lot to contribute to the problems of economic development. So we were back to the earlier position but with an important difference: the economists no longer said, "The subject does not interest us; it can be left to the sociologists, etc." This time they said, "The social aspects of development are too important to be neglected by us and left to the sociologists. The problem interests us too much to leave it to them. We must move in and find a broader basis for an understanding of the problems and approaches to policy." The discussion of social aspects of development has become the very thing which every stock-exchange investor or broker is looking for — a growth sector within the general growth sector of concern with the economic development of the poorer countries.

The tendency to think of development as an economic process is due to the fact that all development requires an emphasis on increasing the output of each producer. Keeping also in mind that until the present day the measurement of "how a nation is doing" or "where it is moving ahead and where it is falling behind" are very much discussed in terms of economic indicators, this tendency to think of development as an economic process was perhaps the only alternative. Having at hand all this information that consists of basic financial data on the volume and composition of national production, the level and distribution of national income, and the use of various goods and services for consumption and development, a nation considered that it had an approximation of the picture of its standing. However, national economic accounting itself includes a large amount of statistical error and guesswork (as Oscar Morgenstern has cogently pointed out in *The Accuracy of Economic Observation*). The producers of such data should have done more to publish their margins of error. Economists and other social scientists are now experimenting with methods of social accounting that will go beyond economics. The new methods will include cultural, technological, biophysical, institutional, and political information, to reflect better the complexities of the modern world.

As Bertram Gross wrote in a recent article,

monetary data and "guesstimates" have serious shortcomings because they:

(a) rarely deal with either unemployment or the depletion of natural resources;

(b) usually ignore investment in people and institutions;

(c) arbitrarily calculate the output value of government services (such as public education) in terms of their input costs, thereby understating the contribution of many expanding sectors of society;

(d) ignore changes in quality not reflected in price changes, thereby understating the rate of growth in many countries;

(e) base international comparisons on exchange rates of doubtful validity.

Gross continued by saying, "The economic accounts exclude the social, cultural, and political instruments needed to promote economic growth. They exclude the fundamental changes in social structure that are both the prerequisites for, and the consequences of, the significant economic changes." Social changes are essential to economic advance but are often more difficult of achievement because they affect those deeply-rooted relationships in which people have formerly found their security and satisfaction.

This new insight has been made possible by a shift in our whole thinking about the problem of growth and development. The fundamental problem is no longer considered to be the creation of wealth, but rather the creation of the capacity to create wealth. Once a society has acquired this capacity to create wealth, the creation of wealth itself becomes almost incidental; it follows quasi-automatically.

What is the capacity to create wealth? Essentially, it resides in the people of a country. It consists of brainpower; it is based upon the application of systematic research to the problems of production and of the best organization of the economic institutions of a country — research systematically pursued and systematically applied. The history of the postwar years has shown that given this underlying capacity and systematic application of research, economies can make up for gaps or destruction in their physical capital equipment in a surprisingly short time. The history of the postwar era also shows that systematic application of brainpower seems to transcend in its importance for economic growth the distinctions between different economic and social systems, however important and fundamental these differences may be in other respects.

One facet of this development of research and brainpower as a built-in growth element is the systematic expenditure of about 1.5 to 2 percent of national income on research and development. Where this is done in a society in which a willingness and capacity to apply the results of this expenditure exists and where the educational level of the population makes this application with its necessary adjustments possible, this level of expenditure seems to be sufficient to create a flow of new investment opportunities that can maintain the productivity of new capital accumulation at a high level, even though capital accumulation itself proceeds at the high rate of 15 to 20 percent of the national income, that is, ten times the expenditure on research and development (not counting the cost of education itself).

In the underdeveloped countries, total new capital formation is presently of the order of magnitude of about $15 billion per annum, but it ought to be of the order of magnitude of $25 billion per annum to convert them into progressive economies. This means that preinvestment expenditure on the creation of new investment opportunities in the underdeveloped countries (not counting the cost of education) should be of the order of magnitude of about $2.5 billion per annum. The actual figure is only a fraction of this sum and so are the international resources available to aid the underdeveloped countries in this purpose.

Development is a total process in which not one aspect of human life, education, health, and aspiration can be ignored. It deals directly with a consciously projected forward movement of the total society; in other words, it is assumed that an upcoming generation will be prepared to maintain the gains already made and carry forward the process of development.

Therefore, it is obvious that every developing society must do the best it can in preparing its youth for their future roles as workers, citizens, and parents. Many efforts will have to be made towards that end, and a heavy investment will be required. Investment in the younger generation always has been the main and the crucial channel of development investment, although economists over a long time have failed to perceive this.

Children and young people are the main potential agents and beneficiaries of all economic development programs, the fruits of many of which will not be evident for at least a generation. In their early years, however, young people are also a major burden on current resources for development. Children are consumers, not producers, and the greater the scope of further educational facilities available for young people, the longer their entry into productive employment will be delayed. In many developing countries where children are viewed as a supplementary source of income for the individual family, there may be strong pressures in favor of putting them to work as young as possible, but it is essential to potspone immediate utilization of youthful labor in favor of "investment" in its development if the full potential of the younger generation as a resource for development is to be realized.

This practical view of children and young people as an underdeveloped or undeveloped resource, requiring investment to develop its potentialities, does not conflict with the view that children have certain basic human rights: the right, first of all, to survive, and also the right to improved standards of health and nutrition, the right to education and the right to a job that is both personally satisfying and useful to the community at large. In considering the needs and role of the younger generation during the development decade, it is necessary to examine not only questions of education and training but also the provision of health, nutrition, and welfare services, and vocational guidance and training for children and young people.

While the economics of investment in programs of education, social welfare, health, nutrition and other programs aimed at improving the quality of labor and human-resources utilization has attracted the interest of scholars, the economic aspects of housing investment have received scant attention and analysis. One reason for this oversight is that the provision of good or adequate housing has fairly consistently been regarded as a social target, necessary as an adjunct to industrial development but contributing inherently little to economic growth.

According to the findings of the *Case Study of a Cost-benefit Analysis of Improved Housing,* by Leland S. Burns, which was prepared for the Meeting of Experts on Cost-benefit Analysis of Social Projects, organized by the UN Research Institute for Social Development in Rennes, October 1965, "the customary measure of evaluating only direct returns (received from a project) — which in this case accounted for a meager seven percent of the total stock of benefits — seriously underestimates by excluding important social economic gains."

The anticipated benefits are obviously many, and there is no way as yet that we can account them exactly, one by one. No attempt has been made to order the benefits listed in a systematic causal chain or to eliminate possible redundancies.

The notion of economic and social growth can be expressed more precisely and purposefully by a succession of models characteristic of the different modes of approach. We may start off with Model I which we may call the classical puritan model of growth. In this model consumption is reduced, the saving is invested in productive capital, the productive capital produces both more productive capital and more consumption goods so that ultimately the cut in consumption can be restored. In this model, as will be seen, at any given time economic growth requires a cut in consumption — that is why I call this model puritan — although in the end result an increase in consumption may result.

Next came the Keynesian Model II, distinctly less puritan. Under this model, consumption and capital formation grow and decline together, tied together by the multiplier and the accelerator. In the Keynesian Model II underemployment gnaws at the vitals of the economy, and sets up vicious circles of depression — unemployment — lack of investment — loss of output — more unemployment — more depression, etc., ad infinitum.

The new Model III, which I would call the human-investment model, is based on the basic notion of human capital and its role in the development process. It has obviously some attractive features: it combines the necessary emphasis in Model I on the importance of capital accumulation with the emphasis in Model II on the need to increase consumption. But it has also great weaknesses: above all, it treats human welfare as an instrument, while it treats the increase of GNP or the accumulation of physical capital as a final value. Thus, the apparent beautiful simplicity of Model III in combining the useful elements for underdeveloped countries from the two previous models is bought at the high price of inverting, or perverting, the true relationship between human welfare and national income or physical capital.

There is something not only degrading but also misleading and leading to wrong policy approaches in the notion of human investment, or human capital. The misleading nature of this approach lies in the fact that any improvement in human welfare which leads to an increase in income or capital will be called productive investment, while any increase in human welfare which does not do this will be called consumption. But this is obviously unreal: the whole purpose of the former "productive" type of increase is also that it should lead in its turn to increased consumption or welfare. Hence on policy grounds there is no general case for a priority of the productive expenditures which lead indirectly, that is, via higher incomes and increased resources, to higher levels of living, as compared with other expenditures, labeled consumptive, which do so directly without a detour through higher incomes. Moreover, by establishing this sharp dichotomy between these two types — human investment, on the one hand, and consumptive welfare, on the other hand — Model III deprives policy-makers of the common standards or measurements by which to allocate total resources among these different purposes.

Thus, while gratefully accepting Model III as a useful stepping stone on our journey, it is not what we really need and want. Or rather, it is only an ingredient of the Model IV which we need. We can say something about the main features of Model IV, if it is to be relevant to the underdeveloped countries of today. The clue of our basic thesis comes from the publication, *UN Development Decade,* which notes that "the problem of the underdeveloped countries is not just growth, but development. Development is growth plus change; change, in turn, is social and cultural as well as economic, and qualitative as well as quantitative."

The very concept must be the improved quality of people's life. This is a notion that combines both growth and change. Improvements in the quality of people are at the same time consumption and investment; objective and instrument; demand for resources and supply of resources. Health measures are the instrument for improving the quality of people — but better health is also the desired result and in turn a source of increased productivity which provides the necessary resources for further health expenditures. Better food is the instrument, but better nutrition is also the objective. Better education and training are instruments of change, but the better-educated man is also the objective. Better housing is the instrument but it is also the objective. The same is true of social security, of improvements in land tenure, and other social indicators of levels of living.

And in providing the initial resources for the better health, better education, better nutrition, better housing, greater social security, etc., which are the keys to growth, we must make people aware of the possibilities of improving the quality of life: we must make people aware of the possibilities of better health and find means of communication with them to utilize the existing facilities to improve their health conditions and adopt better health habits; as also with nutrition, education, better housing, and all the other factors discussed. Because of this importance of communication, the problems of education and ignorance are particularly important even though in the debate so far they have perhaps been too much singled out at the expense of other factors involved.

In a formal sense it is clearly possible to accommodate three new insights and developments in thinking within the structure of an economic model. In the Harrod-Domar model, for instance, it would be quite possible to lay a lot more emphasis on the capital-output ratio (the second determinant of economic growth) rather than on the rate of physical investment (which is the first determinant). It would be possible, when considering the capital-output ratio, to bring in many of the factors, such as the higher productivity of healthier people, the higher productivity of literate or better-trained people, the higher productivity of people working under better-regulated conditions of employment and social security, and the greater productivity of people in whom the proper motivation and incentives for accepting change have been awakened. It would be formally possible to introduce all these factors into a model based on physical capital investment as a primary determinant. But it would be unnatural. It would be a case of the tail wagging the dog.

What we need is the development of a new approach in which social factors and social policies take their proper place as chief determinants alongside such economic factors as the rate of saving and investment, the availability of foreign exchange through exports and aid, and the proper technical selection of productive projects and necessary fiscal, monetary, and trade policies. We need an approach and a model which sets alongside these such factors as the motivation of people; their willingness to innovate or at least accept change; their effectiveness as producers; investments in their health, education, training, and housing; and the raising of a new generation through interrelated policies. That is the kind of approach and model in which the dog will be wagging the tail, at last!

A development model must take into account that raising the level of living is both the objective of development and also its instrument. Improvements in people's level of life can be achieved both directly ("social development") or indirectly via income and economic resources ("economic development"). But a rational development policy must be able to look at these two things as a single entity; where they are taken apart for analytical or descriptive purposes, they must be put together again in policy as well as in the final analysis. Thus, such a model must include provision for common measurements of improvements in quality of levels of living, according to its main relevant components, whether they are labeled economic or social. It must contain transformation curves of expenditures into improved levels of living, whether by the direct route or the indirect route. It must contain provision for a feedback process in which improved levels of living lead to higher productivity and higher productivity in turn leads to higher levels of living. It must incorporate the four types of relevant movements: (1) the direct improvement of levels of living and its value to itself; (2) improvement leading to growth, that is, the translation of higher levels of living into increased productivity; (3) growth leading to improvement, that is to say, the use of resources for improvement in levels of living; and (4) growth by itself, the predominant concern of economists in the early phase, as represented by the Harrod-Domar model, which may now be seen to take its place as one element — but only one element — of what is sought.

During the last twenty years, as I have put it before, the wheel has come full circle, but we are not back where we were before. We are further forward and are at a new point of departure from which a new journey can begin. This is the road ahead which the Dutch government perceived and for which with farsighted generosity they provided the vehicle. This is the journey on which the new UN Research Institute for Social Development has set out. This Institute which started its work in July 1964 for an initial period of three to five years "is conducting research into problems and policies of social development and relationships between various types of social development and economic development during different phases of economic growth." It is hoped that the findings of the Institute will help the United Nations, its specialized agencies, and the governments to relate the action in various social fields to economic development and vice versa. It would thus also help the developing countries in their efforts towards a balanced overall development.

The three major areas of research of the institute are

1. The study of the interrelationships between economic and social factors in the development process. By social factors the Institute means the factors such as health, education, housing, nutrition, social welfare, social security, etc. As the relationships between these social factors and the economic factors probably differ according to the state of development, the Institute will also try to make an analysis of the patterns of social-economic development and of the specific relationships between economic and social factors at different levels of development.

2. The study of the methods of social planning as a means of influencing the development process. An examination of the meaning of social concepts, of the possibility of measuring social factors, and of their interrelation with economic factors has been undertaken. It is to be followed by an examination of the actual planning practice in the social field. All this work is intended as a contribution towards an improvement of the methods of planning for development.

3. The study of methods and problems of social development

and planning at the social level. This area covers first of all the study of the methods to induce social and economic change at the local level. It may, however, also include the problem of the social effects of national or regional development plans on local populations and how to deal with them.

Although the work of the Institute has just begun, it would perhaps be invidious to stay entirely in the arid area of problems, research programs, and models. In early 1966 the Institute's first finished project came out: the interrelation of economic and social factors in development. It is now possible to bring together some of the tentative findings of this pilot study and to look at the wider implications of the results.

According to the findings, it was shown that changes in social-economic profile during 1950–1960, that is, changes in the relative levels of economic and social development, are the results of a number of distinct but interrelated structural and functional relationships between economic and social factors. It is understood that all these findings should be regarded as necessarily provisional, and they are subject to further study and confirmation.

There is a tendency for the intracorrelation of economic and social indicators, both in 1950 and in 1960, to be stronger than the intercorrelation between economic and social factors. Enrollment rates tend to form a cluster, and there appears to be a close relation between education levels and infant mortality rates. First of all, in 1950 levels, primary school enrollment ratio has a correlation coefficient of .87 when correlated with the secondary school ratio; .76 when correlated with vocational school; and .72 when correlated with the higher education ratio. This strong intracorrelation among social factors is continued up to 1960 with the following correlations: primary with secondary have a correlation coefficient of .85; primary with vocational .77; and primary with higher .82. Another significant correlation we would also note is the correlation between primary school and infant mortality rate. The 1950 coefficient is .73 and in 1960 is .63.

Medical services, however, are more closely related to economic levels than to health levels. In 1950, we have a correlation coefficient of .65 and .57 respectively between per capita energy and inhabitants per physician and per capita energy and hospital beds per inhabitant. In 1960 the coefficients for the same correlations are .83 and .62. This is the relation between medical services and economic levels. As far as the health levels go, their correlation with medical services is insignificant. In general, the findings confirm the existence of a "social profile" made up of social components more strongly related among themselves than with economic levels.

It is suggested that lack of consistency between economic and social indicators may be more marked among less-developed countries than among developed countries.

It has been the main thesis of this project that a favorable social-economic profile influences economic growth and in turn is influenced by economic growth. In other words, a high level of social development tends to be a favorable precondition for more rapid economic growth as measured by per capita GNP. The evidence of correlation is unmistakable. Some part of this correlation may be due to the fact that the more fortunate of the underdeveloped countries (of the type of Japan, Israel, Greece, Mexico) tend to achieve economic growth faster than the poorer among the under-developed countries. This is the first law of development: "To him who hath shall be given." However, in the light of our first results we could reformulate the first law of development slightly differently: "To him who has assembled the social preconditions and who has reached a certain critical social level shall be given." The first law of development thus reformulated would suggest and explain a correlation between higher levels of social development and more-rapid growth.

While it has been shown that favorable social levels are associated with more-rapid economic growth, the study has confirmed that the opposite is also true, that more rapid economic growth tends to bring about higher levels of social development. This seems to show that social improvement accelerates economic growth — the accelerated economic growth provides resources for further social improvement — this, in turn, creates preconditions for new economic growth, etc. From this point of view, the debate about whether the social factors are preconditions for economic growth or vice versa, turns out to be a rather academic question.

It is worth noting that the influence of economic growth on subsequent social levels is clearly higher than the influence of economic growth on 1960 economic levels or of social growth on 1960 social levels. However, it is seen that economic growth appears to influence social levels indirectly through social growth.

In addition to the interdependence of economic and social factors, it is clear that social development has a dynamism of its own which cannot be ignored in the total picture. The social components are linked among themselves by a network of functional and structural relationships. There is in addition a strong tendency for countries ranking high under social levels in 1950 to rank high under social levels in 1960. There is evidence of strong stability in the social profile.

Another clear and interesting finding relates to the question of the critical level. This can be pictured either in terms of income or, perhaps more significantly, in terms of social development. In the latter sense, it can be shown that there are certain critical levels of, say, infant mortality: as long as a country is still above (that is, on the wrong side of) the critical level of infant mortality, improvements in infant mortality can occur without much association with rising per capita incomes; the income elasticity of social improvements at that stage is low. But once the critical level of infant mortality is reached and the country moves beyond it and achieves lower rates of mortality, the associated rise in per capita income shows a big jump at the critical level and much higher elasticity than before subsequent improvements. One has a picture of the social improvement forming a kind of infrastructure which by itself has only limited immediate feedback effect on per capita incomes; but once the infrastructure has been completed — that is, the critical level reached — its existence makes possible a much more rapid increase in per capita incomes, and the subsequent necessary further additions to this basic infrastructure are comparatively modest.

On all such matters, however, we can only speculate at the moment. However, the high degree of stability found, as well as the general consistency of the results obtained, has tended gradually to strengthen confidence in the statistics with which we have been operating. This is not in any way to minimize the case for data improvement or for further broadening and deepening of the statistical basis by intensive country research; both these are high up on the list of plans for the immediate future but to vindicate our decision to proceed on the basis of available data with an immediate pilot study, in order to obtain provisional hypotheses which can then subsequently be tested.

The Problem of Quantification

Few would quarrel with the importance Hans Singer gives to social factors in economic development. Nor would anyone hesitate to support attempts to seek handy coefficients by which to judge their impact. Yet, attempts like Singer's to quantify qualitative social factors have long eluded the social scientist. As a consequence we have tended to deal with their (or at least what we impute to be their) overt effects — GNP or per capita GNP growth; investment as a percent of GNP; rising marginal-savings ratios; and so on. The further we move into the causal foundations for the behavior of some of these variables — which may for particular purposes be treated as independent but which in the final analysis are all dependent — the more apologetic becomes the qualifying language we use with our estimates and forecasts. Even the application of Harrod-Domar or Cobb-Douglas, Arrow-Chenery-Minhaus-Solow functions and relationships have gotten some of us, who must come up with pragmatic guidelines and policies, into embarrassing discussions and defense postures.

The instability of some of these handy models, including the well-worn incremental capital output ratio is due partly to the unpredictable or unmanageable or immeasurable behavior of critical social factors we have not yet been able to include in our formulations. Singer's ex poste analysis may help us to produce more accurate ex ante prescriptions.[1]

The usual criticism of these models or attempts at quantifying social relationships is that (1) the data is either imperfect or the yield probabilities immeasurable, (2) many relevant variables are perforce neglected, which leaves the job far from complete (for example, some will argue strongly for the value in the nonproductive aspects of education);[2] and (3) the distinction between private and social costs and yields is important but is often impossible to quantify within even order of magnitude range. Singer's correlations are, however, less open to these weaknesses, because they constitute fairly straightforward ratios of infant mortality, inhabitants per physician, literacy percentage of population, and school enrollments.

My skepticism does not apply so much to the correlations nor to most of the inferences drawn from them, although others in this field question them and rather stress the inconstancy and the scope of the diffusion effects of social factors.[3] I question whether they will lead to effective means for distinguishing cause from effect, and to locating the basic social or cultural bottlenecks to more rapid growth in the less-developed countries. I am also concerned about the long time lags involved in some major social indicators like education, nutritional programs, and the like. While work in these fields must go on, we simply do not have the time in today's urgent atmosphere to focus excessively on forces of only glacial movement but must stress both economic and social factors which will bring quicker results.

This kind of criticism, I realize, is common, and Singer would no doubt reply that it is too early to know what solutions will emerge from these explorations but that that is the purpose of examining his correlations for meaning.

Singer (and even more so, perhaps, Harbison) may be aware of the recent Corazzini and Bartell[4] complaint against Hector Correa's linear and nonlinear programming applications to the public costs and private yields to be expected from general and vocational education.[5] The criticism in that case is the opposite of the concern we regard most crucial in our own more individualistic society. Correa compared the public costs of general vocational education against yields in each instance. We are often more concerned, in our affluent environment, with the private costs and only the ex poste yields to society. This may be because we assume private interests have undertaken their own cost-benefit analysis and have assumed their undertaking to be personally or commercially beneficial for a variety of reasons. This applies to both business and education. We are, it is true, more concerned with social costs and benefits than we used to be but still far less so than the less-developed countries can afford to be. The scarcity of resources in the presence of a marginal existence for the vast majority in the less-developed countries necessitates a thorough review of the total use of resources and the cost-benefit considerations for both individuals and society, while for the status and mores of our environment Correa's assumptions may be valid.

The relatively abundant resources and individualistic bent prevalent in our society may also explain in part why we are so late in attempting to measure more precisely the impact of the social factors Singer talked about. We have been so successful in our growthmanship and in areas affecting the social indicators to have had to bother much with them. The fact that capital formation was more important in earlier decades of America's growth, while the major contribution of education and some other social factors has been felt in more recent decades, may also account in part for our neglect of these indicators.[6] Moreover, we have in the past regarded many of the social and cultural factors as the concern of the individual or the family and not of society and its statisticians. Even where private yield estimates were high only because the social costs were high, we have been slow historically to rectify the imbalance. We have also allowed private units to introduce large doses of subjective judgment in determining their own MRP-MC ratios, irrespective of either their private or social consequences. The less-developed countries cannot afford the luxury, and those of us who work at locating the key elements of growth struggle more with the social and cultural factors than anything else, for it is in this area that we lack formulas and techniques of procedure.

My own view is that there will always be some social factors that will escape the ratios and will only yield to careful and detailed description. I say this as one who spends much of his time quantifying everything in sight.[7] I am reminded of a typical example of one such factor in Edward Banfield's *The Moral Basis of a Backward Society*[8] — a study produced by the Research Center at the University of Chicago. A nine-month survey and study of factors contributing to the depressing lack of aspiration or "n-achievement"[9] in a particular village in underdeveloped southern Italy produced the conclusion that the extreme poverty and backwardness was due largely to "the inability of the villagers to act together for their common good or, indeed, for any end transcending the immediate, material interest of the nuclear family."[10] This inability, he contends, arises from an ethos which he called amoral familism, which in turn depresses economic advance. For example, community welfare or effective political administration is of no concern in the village unless the effort pays off somehow for individuals or for the family; officials are corrupt because it is expected, and the public is itself indifferent; selfishness precludes joining group activity which might help start certain growth elements; officials and professional people alike work for private ends only; anyone who tries to organize for a social purpose will be suspect and ignored. The author lists seventeen characteristics in all of amoral familism. And this regressive amoralism exists in spite of the spirit and precepts which are laid down by the church and the villages' religious leaders. Both Banfield in his view of the poverty of southern Italy, and Geertz, in recording the results of his long labors in analyzing Indonesian village transition, could accept the conclusion, "With every shake of the kaleidoscope the past seemed further back and the future further ahead."

The essence of Banfield's study is that lack of morality in its broader sense was the heart of the problem, keeping the vicious circle intact, and while the social ratios may have recorded the results, they would not have necessarily located the intangible causes.[11]

Raymond Vernon emerged from his Mexican research with other nonquantifiable problems.[12] In this instance, the bottleneck — as it is in other less-developed countries — is in the inability or unwillingness of government officials to establish unpopular taxes; prices; balance-of-payments constraints; or import-liberalization, foreign-investment, or other policies which would produce a surge forward in the pace of development.

Still others have blamed the "tendency to shirk the seeking of constructive solutions to problems"[13] or the lack of courage or willpower to carry out fiscal and monetary reform measures.[14] Geertz's penetrating Indonesian studies traced the impact of social change upon economic progress and concluded, too, that "a cultural paradigm is in fact paradigmatic — an operative force — showing that it in fact orders behavior."[15]

These attitudes or qualitative criteria, to a significant extent, make the numbers we work with in many less-developed countries what they are, instead of what they should be or would become. One might also say that the presence of these and other factors make the difference, very often, between actual and our so-called shadow prices or between the actual and the possible absorptive capacities in the less-developed countries.

The point I am making with respect to Singer's paper is that the measures of correlation between his social indicators and economic growth will be valuable to us, but the task of getting at fundamental causal factors in the set of vicious circles with which we contend, and to some of which I have referred, yields essentially to pragmatic and descriptive effort — or to what has been called the documentary method[16] — and otherwise eludes our handy list of quantified ratios. In fact, the ratios become themselves useful descriptive elements but leave unresolved the matter of locating and focusing on cultural or other noneconometric causal attributes, which keep the vicious circles in their grooves and the gaps ever widening.

Harbison, too, whose correlations are widely known,[17] is familiar with the argument made by others that a high level of economic development is essential to a high level of manpower training rather than the other way around, as he believes — that is, the environment for the cultural attitudes conducive to developing a broad base of high-level manpower will not exist in the absence of the environment they seek to achieve and that the education-output ratios, for example, of Western countries have no relevance for less-developed countries, particularly in Africa, which have either no relevant or drastically different histories.[18] This seems to be in support of one of Singer's conclusions that in general social components within his "social profile" are more strongly related among themselves than with economic levels and that there is a lack of consistency between economic and social indicators in less-developed countries which is not so marked in developed countries.[19] In this respect, Singer's attempt to determine more accurately how much economic growth produces social growth or economic growth or how much social growth produces economic growth or social growth may yield some very fruitful rules of the road.

The dynamic area of continued concern, I feel, is still in the feedbacks he has referred to and in the influence which can be brought to bear by factors like determination, political attitude, moral purpose, skill in organizing, dedication to individual and social betterment, vision and willingness to implement policies which run counter to deeply rooted cultural and political attitudes, and other indicators not mentioned by Singer but which take a lot of our time to resolve. These are our hidden values, and they have a tremendous effect on the whole process, often in a shorter time span than other, more obvious social indicators can effect.

Notes

1. Hans W. Singer, "Social Development: Key Growth Sector," *International Development Review* (March 1965), p. 3 ff.

2. Webster Cash, "A Critique of Manpower Planning and Educational Change in Africa," *Economic Development and Cultural Change* (Oct. 1965), pp. 33–47.

3. Mary Jean Bowman and C. Arnold Anderson, "The Role of Education in Development," *Development of Emerging Countries,* (Washington, D.C.: Brookings Institution, 1962).

4. Arthur Corazzini and Earnest Bartell, "Problems of Programming an Optimum Choice Between General and Vocational Education," *Kyklos,* XVIII, fasc. 4 (1965), p. 700 ff.

5. Hector Correa, "Optimum Choice Between General and Vocational Education," *Kyklos,* XVIII, fasc. 1 (1965), p. 107 ff.

6. Gerald Mier, "Investment in Human Capital," in *Leading Issues in Development Economics* (New York: Oxford University Press, 1964), p. 270. Singer has countered this point by insisting that investment in education is also capital formation, although it is still counted in national accounts as consumption and that this would be a substantial investment in our earlier development.

7. Attempts to quantify in two complex areas are reflected in R. Ward, "Forecasting with Computers: A Commodity Case," *Engineering Economist* (Spring, 1965); see also chap. 19.

8. Published by the Research Center in Economic Development and Cultural Change, (Chicago: Free Press, 1958).

9. To use McClelland's adaptations: *The Achieving Society* (New York: Van Nostrand, 1961).

10. Banfield, p. 10.

11. Another factor which has moral implications is the effect of "fatalism" upon birthrates in both Latin America and the Far East, particularly among the lowest income groups of India. It derives from poverty, in part, but in turn perpetuates it through child marriages and indiscriminate procreation. See Albert Nevett, S.J., in "People and Resources in India," *Christian Responsibility and World Poverty* (Westminster, Md.: Newman Press, 1963).

12. Raymond Vernon, *The Dilemma of Mexico's Development,* (Cambridge, Mass.: Harvard University Press, 1963).

13. John P. Gillin, "Some Signposts for Policy," in *Social Change in Latin America Today* (New York: Vintage, 1960), p. 46.

14. Peter Franck, *Afghanistan: Between East and West* (National Planning Association, 1960).

15. Clifford Geertz, *The Social History of an Indonesian Town,* (Cambridge, Mass.: M.I.T. Press, 1965), p. 153.

16. A. Garfinkel, "Common Sense Knowledge of Social Structures; The Documentary Method of Interpretation," in Jordan Scher, ed., *Theories of the Mind* (New York: Free Press, 1962).

17. Frederick Harbison, "High Level Manpower for Nigeria's Future," *Investment in Education: The Report of the Commission on Post-School Certificate and Higher Education in Nigeria, Lagos* (Federal Ministry of Education, 1960). Also his and Charles Meyer's, *Education, Manpower and Economic Growth* (New York: McGraw-Hill, 1964); *High-Level Manpower Resources: Country Studies,* (New York: McGraw-Hill, in press).

18. Webster Cash.

19. Nancy Baster and Muthu Subramanian, *Aspects of Social and Economic Growth,* U.N. Research Institute for Social Development (October 1965).

Part 2

Development Problems
for This Decade

6　The Growing Income-Inequality Problem in Developing Countries

In human society extremes of wealth and poverty are the main sources
of evil. . . . Where a population is divided into the two classes of the
very rich and the very poor, there can be no real state; for there can
be no real friendship between the classes, and friendship is the essential
principle of all association.

Aristotle

Research on income-distribution trends in the less-developed countries has been relatively limited. However, attention to the problem
seems to be increasing. The Brookings Institution devoted one of
its recent panels (28 January 1969) to a discussion of "income inequality issues" for which this article provided a basis of discussion.
Events in Pakistan which led to President Ayub's resignation are
said to have been due in part to growing awareness of social
inequalities. It is periodically said that aid (or development) is
making the rich richer and the poor poorer, that it operates only
on the "trickle down" theory, or that it is unnecessarily exacer-

bating social cleavages.[1] The Brookings seminar posed the question What are the facts and what, if anything, should be done about the situation? In addition to the studies referred to in this chapter a UN study indicated its view that there was an "urgent need" for studies on income distribution in Latin America, though attention to the problem has increased considerably in recent years. It complained that little progress had been made on empirical research or analysis of causal factors or of remedies and concluded that "from now on it will be very hard to imagine a development program which does not analyze explicitly the existing distribution of income and its evolution within the objective of the plan."[2]

This article attempts to deal with some of the findings of a number of studies, primarily related to India and Pakistan. Simon Kuznets and other references are used to make comparisons between the developed and underdeveloped world as to progress in reducing inequality during the course of economic development. This is but a brief review of a complex but inadequately explored field. The aim here is to invite more attention to the problem and, it is hoped, to promote more research in this decade, when the issue will likely become crucial for many countries.

Income-Distribution Trends

Data developed by Simon Kuznets offer perhaps the best basis for making comparisons and for indicating where research might be done to verify or elaborate on inequality issues. These data support the conclusion that inequality of income distribution in the less-developed countries is more pronounced than in developed countries but no more so than it was in the present developed countries prior to World War I. Kuznets also finds, as do others, that inequality tends to increase in the early stages of development, because of the advantages the early entrepreneurs get in terms of high returns and consequent high savings for reinvestment. Only the top group is able to save significantly and therefore to invest. Over time, however, as development proceeds, the gap in inequality of income declines substantially.[3]

Some of the data and conclusions developed by Kuznets may be summarized as follows:[4]

1. Shares of upper-income groups are distinctly larger in underdeveloped countries (all after tax).

Table 6.1: Percent of Income Earned by Income Groups
(Late 1940's–Early 1950's)

	Income Group			
	Top 5%	Top 10%	Top 20%	Bottom 60%
Underdeveloped	30	40–45	50–60	21–32
Developed	20–25	30–35	40–50	29–33
India (1950)	33	43	55	28
India (1955/56)	24	33	47	34

The data seem to indicate that the recent development process in India has had some effect in reducing income inequality from 33 percent of the income earned by the top 5 percent of the income units in 1950 to 24 percent in 1955/56.

2. The concentration of urban income in the less-developed countries is more pronounced than concentration of rural incomes and more pronounced than the urban income in developed countries. This may partly be true because "urbanization has grown considerably faster than industrial employment in underdeveloped countries."[5]

3. The studies consulted indicate that the upper-income brackets — the top 10 percent — do nearly all the saving in a free-market investment economy, particularly in the underdeveloped world. This may be expected, but it obviously aggravates income inequality.

4. Shares of the income pie gained by the lower-income groups as between developed and underdeveloped are not significantly different, although the absolute levels of living in this group in the less-developed countries and developed countries differ widely. This helps explain why growthmanship in the recent past has become a more dynamic issue than the distribution problem.

5. The income inequality in developed countries in the early

Table 6.2: Percent of Income Earned by Upper-Income Groups

U.K.	1880	1913	1938	1957
Top 5%	48	43	24	14
Top 20%	53	59	46	38

Germany	1929		1941	1944–59
Top 5%	22	29.5	21.5	18
Top 20%	n.a.	54	47	44

Denmark	1908	1925	1955
Top 5%	30	26	17.5
Top 20%	55	53	44

U.S.	1913–19	1929	1929–38	1944–48	1955–59
Top 5%	22	—	24	14 (Kuznets)	18 (Com.)
Top 20%	n.a.	54 (Com.)	—	46 (Com.)	45 (Com.)

years (pre–World War I) was about the same as it is in the less-developed today. The top 5 percent received roughly 30 percent of the total income, the top 20 percent about 55 percent. Absolute per capita income was, however, higher for the pre–World War I developed countries than for some of today's less-developed countries.

6. The degree of inequality in income shares (all after tax) has declined significantly over time in the developed countries.[6] Note that this process began only after World War I in the developed countries after a long period of relatively little change.

Aspects of the Indian Experience

The income-inequality issue has not received much effective attention in India in terms of tax-policy reforms. One should, however, consider the very considerable outlays for health, education, and various forms of welfare and subsidy pricing for food which has helped the poor classes and which are not included in the income data. Since these data are also excluded from income data of the advanced countries, the comparisons may not be distorted significantly, if at all.

An October 1965 IBRD study showed that between 1955/56 and 1961/62 national income in India increased 50 percent whereas revenue from personal income tax increased only 42 percent.[7] Even this increase in income tax was achieved only by broadening the tax base, not by making it more progressive. The report also indicates that:

1. Although there are 20 million nonfarm households, there are only 1 million which have had tax assessments.

2. The number of taxpayers assessed in the top income brackets in India ($40,000–over $100,000) actually declined between 1955/56 and 1961/62 from 740 to 640.

3. At the same time the amount of assessed income they represented declined from 6 percent to 2.5 percent.

4. The decline in assessees and assessable income is not due to a marked change in income received at the top of the income scale but, the report concludes, a reflection of increased evasion of taxation.

5. By comparison with other countries India's income tax burden is low, as Table 6.3 indicates.[8]

In 1960, Prime Minister Nehru announced plans for an inquiry "to find out how the additional national income in the last two Plan periods had spread over the population."[9] The Planning

Table 6.3: Burden of Taxes on Income in Selected Countries in Recent Years

Country	Level of income up to which no tax is paid (stated as a multiple of average per capita income)	Income taxes paid on income at various income levels — taxes paid as a percentage of earned income to be			
		10	20	50	100
		times the per capita national income			
India	11.5	—	2%	9%	23%
U.K.	1.9	28%	44%	67%	78%
U.S.A.	1.3	23%	35%	54%	69%
Japan	3.4	11%	19%	31%	39%
Burma	19.0	—	—	4%	11%
Malaya	9.8	—	4%	12%	21%

Annual Income in Rupees Converted at Official Rate of Exchange	Tax as Percentage of Income		
	India	Japan	Israel
4,500	0.6	5.9	5.9
6,000	1.8	8.8	12.1
9,000	3.0	12.5	20.2
12,000	6.1	15.6	25.4
15,000	8.3	17.2	29.3
20,000	11.8	20.4	34.7

Commission appointed a committee of distinguished economists and officials, headed by P. C. Mahalanobis. The committee was to look into distribution of income and wealth, ascertain the extent to which the operation of the economic system had resulted in concentration of economic power and look into changes in levels of living from 1950 to 1960. Not until 1964 did part 1 of the report get produced; part 2 has not yet been published.[10]

The report points out that (1) while mining and factory workers seemed to have kept ahead of the growth of average income for employed persons, agricultural laborers, especially the half of the rural population who own no land or who have holdings of less than an acre, were and remained in desperate straits; (2) government controls, ties between firms, relations with foreign investors, and controls over newspapers resulted in a high and still growing concentration of power in the hands of the few; and (3) the strategy of development should give more attention to social goals to reduce income inequality, since the country and its planning was pledged to reducing concentration of economic power in private hands.

Income-Inequality Issues in Pakistan

A former Norwegian economic advisor to the Pakistan Institute of Development Economics, Ashjorn Bergan, undertook a study of

Table 6.4: Distribution of Households by Income Group

Cumulated Percentage of Total Number of Households 1963/64

Monthly Income Per Household		East Pakistan			West Pakistan			All Pakistan		
		Rural	Urban	Combined	Rural	Urban	Combined	Rural	Urban	Combined
Rs.	$									
Up to 50	10.42	9.0	5.0	8.8	5.4	1.7	4.6	7.2	2.5	6.9
Up to 100	20.84	42.8	28.3	41.5	28.5	15.7	25.7	35.6	18.6	34.3
Up to 150	31.26	66.7	52.6	66.0	54.0	38.4	50.5	60.6	41.7	59.0
Up to 200	41.68	82.2	65.3	81.3	71.8	57.4	68.5	77.1	59.2	75.5
Up to 250	52.10	90.0	73.7	89.1	82.3	69.7	79.4	86.2	70.6	84.7
Up to 300	62.52	94.2	80.8	93.5	89.3	78.4	86.5	91.8	78.9	90.3
Up to 400	72.94	97.2	85.7	96.6	95.2	87.0	93.6	96.2	86.6	95.3
Up to 500	83.36	98.6	90.2	98.2	97.1	91.7	96.0	97.5	91.3	97.2
Up to 700	93.78	99.5	94.7	99.2	99.1	95.5	98.4	99.3	95.3	98.9
Up to 900	104.20	99.8	96.7	99.6	99.6	97.3	99.1	99.7	97.2	99.4
Up to inf.	Above	100.0	100.0	100.0	100.0	100.0	100.0	100.0	100.0	100.0

Source: Bergan article

Table 6.5: Cumulated Percentage of Total Personal Income, 1963/64

Cumulated Percentage of Households	East Pakistan			West Pakistan			All Pakistan		
	Rural	Urban	Combined	Rural	Urban	Combined	Rural	Urban	Combined
Lowest 5% get	1.0	0.7	1.2	0.8	1.0	0.8	1.1	0.9	1.0
Lowest 10% get	3.5	1.5	2.7	2.3	2.5	2.3	2.5	2.2	2.5
Lowest 20% get	8.0	5.0	7.0	6.8	6.0	6.5	6.5	6.0	6.5
Lowest 30% get	13.0	9.0	12.0	12.0	11.0	11.5	12.0	10.0	11.5
Lowest 40% get	18.5	13.5	18.0	18.0	16.0	17.5	18.5	15.5	17.5
Lowest 50% get	26.0	19.0	24.5	26.0	21.5	24.5	26.0	21.0	24.5
Lowest 60% get	35.0	25.5	33.5	34.5	29.0	33.0	34.0	28.0	33.0
Lowest 70% get	45.0	33.0	43.5	44.5	38.5	43.0	44.5	37.0	42.5
Lowest 80% get	57.0	43.0	55.5	57.0	49.0	54.5	57.5	48.0	55.0
Lowest 90% get	73.0	59.5	71.5	72.0	63.5	69.5	72.5	63.0	70.0
Lowest 95% get	82.5	70.5	81.5	83.0	74.0	80.0	82.0	74.0	80.0
Lowest 100% get	100.0	100.0	100.0	100.0	100.0	100.0	100.0	100.0	100.0

Source: Bergan article

99

Pakistani income distribution for 1963/64.[11] The author heavily qualifies his conclusions with apologies for the small size of the sample (2,614 households used instead of the 10,710 planned and selected) and for the great uncertainties in all of the data. Some conclusions from the Bergan article indicated the following (also see Tables 6.4–6):

1. If 100 rupees a month is regarded as the "lower limit of subsistence," over one-third of all households in Pakistan (5.5 persons per household) lie below the subsistence level. The percentage below subsistence is higher in the rural areas than in the urban.

2. East Pakistan is worse than West; 41.5 percent households get 100 rupees or less in the East, 25.7 percent get 100 rupees or less in West Pakistan.

3. Only 0.6 percent of the households receive over $104 a month ($1,248 a year).

4. Only 5 percent of households receive about 20 percent of personal income.

5. A much higher degree of inequality exists in urban areas. This agrees with Kuznets's data.[12]

6. Since income inequality is greater in urban than in rural areas, to the extent that urbanization is likely to be a concomitant of development, overall income inequality could increase unless incomes in other sectors and welfare or tax measures counter the trend.

7. Pakistan's degree of income inequality is worse than India's. If this is true, it would appear that India's inequality had decreased further from 1955/56 (Kuznets's data), although data comparability may not be precise as to the degree of difference in the two countries.

8. Pakistan's income inequality is not as marked as Germany's, Mexico's, Ceylon's, Italy's, while India is not as bad as the U.S. However, the comparisons between less-developed and developed countries are not very meaningful.

Table 6.6: Rough Concentration Ratios[14]
(After Tax)

Mexico, Ceylon, Puerto Rico (1950–1953)	0.47	—, 0.41, —
West Germany (1950)	0.45	—
Italy (1948)	0.48	—
Sweden	0.44	0.41
Denmark	0.44	0.40
Pakistan (1963/64)	0.38	—
United States (1950)	0.35	0.32
India (1953/54–1956/57)	0.34	0.33
United Kingdom (1951/52)	0.33	0.29

Bergan quotes a somewhat controversial study done by P. S. Ojha and V. V. Bhatt on India to make intercountry comparisons.[13] The measure used is the concentration ratio — the area between the Lorenz curve and the diagonal divided by the total under diagonal.

Despite the mass poverty in Pakistan, the Bergan study indicates an overall gross domestic savings rate of 12.5 percent of GNP, all but 1.7 percent of it private and 75 percent of it from rural areas. This is partly based on an estimate of private hoards in the form of precious metals.

That more equality in income distribution may not, in fact, have occurred in Pakistan, at least from recent growth, may be borne out in data developed by A. R. Khan.[15] Some conclusions from that study are as follows:

1. From 1954 to 1964 real wages in all industries declined from 966 rupees per worker per year to 871 rupees per worker per year.

2. The difference between real wages in agriculture and in industry in both East and West Pakistan is small ("in the situation of general surplus labor one does not expect the industrial wages to be disproportionately greater than the average wage in the traditional agricultural sector"). The gap between urban and rural incomes in East Pakistan is greater than in West Pakistan because the tenancy system in East Pakistan gives the laborer some stake in the land which requires a higher inducement in wages to bring him to the city.

3. A very large majority of rural population in both East and West Pakistan is better off than the average industrial worker. For example, in West Pakistan, only about a quarter of the rural population had lower than the average income of a wage-earning family in industry.

4. Real wages have on the average been about 25 percent higher in West Pakistan than in East Pakistan, without making an adjustment for regional differences in purchasing power. However, preliminary investigation indicates that the prices of wage goods in East Pakistan are on the average 10–15 percent higher than in West Pakistan; therefore, the discrepancy would be somewhat higher than the 25 percent.

5. From 1954 to 1964, per capita income increased in Pakistan, particularly in the urban areas. Thus income distribution over this period must have changed unfavorably for the working class, and in particular urban income distribution "must have become more unequal." This effect was more pronounced in West Pakistan than in East Pakistan, since per capita income increased impressively

in West Pakistan even while real wages in industry declined somewhat.

Gustav Papanek points out that in 1959 seven individual families or foreign corporations (through over 3,000 firms) controlled 25 percent of all private industrial assets in Pakistan. Only 24 owning units controlled nearly 50 percent of all private industrial assets. Also, only 15 families owned 75 percent of all shares in banks and insurance companies.[16] At the same time, Papanek points out that those in control of industries used collusion, price agreements, and other practices to ensure monopolistic markets and consequent high profits. Similar concentration exists in the United States (one-half of 1 percent of all U.S. firms account for 50 percent of all manufacturing assets), but ownership is more widely spread through stocks, and U.S. income tax is more progressive and more effectively collected.

The problem of inequality of income and concentration of economic power and wealth is clearly an important one in Pakistan. It applies to farmers in the rural sectors, parallel to the advantage that industrial newcomers gain from investment of their savings and reinvestment of their profits. The wealthier land cultivators, the "kulaks," who produced cash crops were, unlike the poorer peasants and landless laborers, able to invest in tubewells, fertilizer, and new seeds and to call upon the extension service for advice in improving techniques. Papanek stresses the importance of perspective in judging the impact of inequality on the development of Pakistan. The case he makes includes the following:

1. Concentration of income in agriculture or industry produces high savings which are reinvested. The wealthier and more enterprising peasants sank the tubewells which increased agricultural output.

2. High profits were necessary to create industry and industrialists in a high risk environment.

3. The output of this reinvestment means cheaper food, clothing, and supplies of all kinds for the bulk of the people.

4. After five or ten years of industrial growth, the profit rate need not be so high and inequality can decline.

5. If income had been more equally distributed in Pakistan's early period of development, the rate of growth would have been less and, therefore, the lower-income groups worse off in absolute terms, though better off relatively.

6. As the greatest inequality can be between those who have jobs and those who are unemployed, it is the formerly unemployed who have benefited most from the phenomenal growth of industry in Pakistan. (Papanek also believes overall real wages increased

in the 1960's, contrary to Khan's conclusions about wages of industrial workers.)

7. High incomes in Pakistan have been socially acceptable because they have been used chiefly for investment rather than consumption. Controls over foreign trade helped reduce consumption, especially of the rich relative to the poor and of luxury goods relative to necessities.[17]

Papanek is quick to qualify the apparent impact of some aspects of inequality by stressing the long-term effort required to bring about a significant rise in Pakistan's per capita level of income. The country will remain among the poorest in the world for about two decades. Meanwhile, to quote Papanek, "the growth process has allowed serious economic inequality to remain between areas (East and West Pakistan) and groups," and it will take a long arduous effort to increase internal savings on a broad basis. Nevertheless, he believes that full employment is now a reasonable long-term goal for Pakistan, and if it is achieved, this will be its most important step toward moderating income inequalities.

Inequality is being moderated to some extent in Pakistan by the government of Pakistan's own efforts. In the middle of the 1960's, the government took measures to discourage investment by the dozen or so largest families through investment-sanctioning procedures. (This is not the "right" approach; permitting investment, then taxing its yield is obviously preferable, but it does reflect a growing concern.) At the same time, the government reduced direct controls to make it easier for smaller entrepreneurs to enter trade and industry. In a further effort to reduce the concentration of industrial control, government credit agencies helped newcomers and medium-sized industries to expand. The government also undertook the Rural Works Program and housing, health-services, and educational programs.

The "Socio-Economic Objectives of the Fourth Five Year Plan, 1970–75" dwells on the inequality issue. Several additional proposals are made in the Plan: a review of protection policy and tax-collection machinery; a ban on the ownership of banks and insurance companies by industrial groups; a ceiling on the proportion of total advances of a bank to any one particular industrial group; reserving new, simpler consumer-goods industries for newcomers; greater encouragement of the Pakistan Industrial Credit Investment Corporation, the Industrial Development Bank of Pakistan, and the Investment Corporation of Pakistan to provide new investment capital; reforms in the present managing-agency system; and introduction of a rational wage policy.

Income Tax in Less-Developed Countries

As economic growth advances and the base of investment is broadened most advancing countries have increasingly supported measures which tend to narrow income inequality. The progressive income tax is one of the most obvious measures used, but progressivity is evident in other forms of taxes. It is, of course, common knowledge that the income tax provides but a relatively small share of government revenues in most less-developed countries.

While efforts to increase returns from income taxes may have met with some success in terms of improved tax structures or internal administration, the fundamental situation in this area does not seem to have improved much if income-tax revenue as a percent of total is the criterion for judging progress. For example, Pakistan's income tax represented about 20 percent of domestic revenue in 1958, 16.7 percent in 1962, 13.5 percent in 1966, 12.9 percent in the 1967 revised budget, and 12.1 percent in the 1968 budget. In India, income tax represented about 22 percent of domestic revenues in 1958, 23.1 percent in 1962, 19.5 percent in 1966, 17.5 percent in the 1967 revised budget, and 17.1 percent in the 1968 budget.[18]

The decline of income taxes (personal and corporate) as a proportion of domestic revenue in India over the past ten years results in part from the fact that agricultural income has been exempt from the central-government income tax, although nine of seventeen states levy such a tax. There was a net shift of resources into the agricultural sector during India's first three development plans, but because of the exemption the yield of the central government's income tax did not benefit appreciably from the resultant growth in agricultural productivity and income. The central income-tax base has become narrower over the years, greater reliance having been put on indirect taxation through a pattern of increased rates. A 1965–1967 recession, coupled with reductions in personal income tax rates and some concessions to the corporate sector, intensified the declining importance of the central income tax. Failure of national income to grow significantly during those two years kept central income taxes from growing, while other types of revenue continued to increase. A similar rationale could explain in part the trend in Pakistan. The ratio of income tax to total domestic revenues for the central government in Turkey has remained around 29–30 percent, both actual and in recent budgets. In all of these cases the absolute amount of income tax revenue collected has increased over the last five or six years but not nearly as much as revenues from sales and other domestic revenues sources.

It should be said at this point that the yield of income tax to central budgets in less-developed countries is not a particularly good indicator of the redistributive effect of taxes, because the people who pay the income tax in these countries are not the wealthy, that is, industrialists, merchants, and big farmers, who are not effectively taxed and who find many ways of evading the taxes which are supposedly due on their incomes; rather civil servants, employees of banks and large corporations, and others in middle-income brackets pay the bulk of taxes.

The problem is complex and much has been written and discussed, in taxation conferences and elsewhere, on the issues.[19] The following are the classic prerequisites put forward for use of income taxation as a major revenue source:[20]

1. Where nonmonetized activity in the rural sector is large, the real income is almost impossible to tax. Thus a predominantly money economy is essential to a successful income tax.

2. Where illiteracy or semiliteracy is high, even among wage earners, craftsmen, or small shopkeepers, complying with instructions, keeping records, or making out forms is difficult. Thus, broader literacy is necessary.

3. Where businessmen keep no books, few records, or several sets for varied reasons, the administration of a tax is thwarted. Therefore, improved literacy, more training in record-keeping, and more administrative help in enforcing compliance is badly needed.

4. Where there is no tradition of massive compliance or no moral stigma attached to avoidance, collections are small. It takes a long period of improvement in formal and informal relations with officials, agencies, and government requirements to build respect for government.

5. Where wealthy groups in society have political power or influence to block tax measures, progressive taxes are difficult to legislate and even more difficult to collect. The will toward voluntary compliance is lacking in less-developed countries. Excessive pressure on this group can also meet with their stiffening resistance. Some method of inducing compliance and getting to the social consciousness of the well-to-do is needed.

6. Where honest and efficient administration is lacking, minimum acceptable standards — needed for income tax more than for any other tax — are hard to come by.

Goode counters the argument that high incomes (and savings) are needed to promote investment by the rich, by suggesting that investment of savings is more common in an expanding, more-developed, capitalist economy than in the less-developed countries. To the extent that high-income groups can be persuaded to invest more in productive enterprises, the progressivity of taxation might be postponed with benefit to the economy. Goode has also suggested elsewhere that where indirect taxes are significant and imposing income taxes too difficult, more attention should be paid to the progressivity or regressivity of the indirect taxes.[21]

Influence of Foreign Aid

To the extent that foreign aid contributes to the growth process it has a constructive effect on the income problem. Briefly stated, the objectives of U.S. assistance, for example, have been to broaden participation, especially by the private sector, in private industrial production; to help the aid recipients liberalize their import systems, reduce trade-inhibiting administrative controls, utilize capacity more fully, and encourage production for export; to promote a more broadly based agricultural prosperity; to encourage works projects for unemployed; to help when requested with family planning programs; and to expand educational opportunities.

The trade liberalization and decontrol measures that the U.S. Agency for International Development has supported and the substantial volume of spare parts and raw materials that U.S. aid helps finance enables more entrepreneurs in the private sector to participate. This promotes competition and to some extent erodes monopolistic profits and prices. These expectations are similar to Papanek's. Foreign-aid support of agricultural inputs helps the efficient large landowner considerably, but it also enables the enterprising smaller farmer to buy inputs and increase his returns. There is a net competitive gain in this process and encouragement of enterprise and innovation. To the extent that the relatively well-to-do are already involved in the last two areas of assistance, aid efforts in these sectors should benefit the poorer classes more.

At the same time, there is the danger that foreign aid which promotes private entrepreneurship and investment may advance the welfare of the few in farming and industry and therefore increase income inequality. The socialists make this claim and urge that their national governments manage capital formation and investment to avoid the injustices the free-market system generates.

It may not be clear whether foreign aid has had these effects in a given period in a particular country, but U.S. aid policy argues that the welfare of more people has been improved and the opportunity enhanced for the countries receiving foreign assistance to realize social objectives. It is to be expected that the more enterprising will take advantage of the opportunities and therefore reap the rewards, but this process, it is believed, will eventually involve a sizable middle class who otherwise would remain among the mass poor. The argument that socialist systems reduce income inequality is so interwoven with the growth issue that definitive statements are not very helpful. To the extent that freer market economies have fostered more rapid investment and growth, producing a more rapidly expanding total pie, the income inequality may not have declined rapidly, but the lower-income classes may be better off than the middle classes of a socialist society in which growth has been slower.

General Comments and Policy

It is difficult to sum up or to generalize on the basis of such uncertain and sometimes conflicting data. A few generalizations may however, be restated: There appears to be agreement that there is greater inequality in income distribution in the less-developed than in the developed countries. Kuznets argues that over a long period of time in the course of development, income distribution may widen, then stabilize, and finally narrow. Some countries, especially India and Pakistan, may still be in the inequality-widening stage. Kuznets, Papanek, and Myrdal seem to agree with what might be the expected result, that in the earlier stages of development those who have resources to invest reap large profits which accentuate their ability to invest further; this increases inequality. The scarcity of supply of talent adds to the special advantage of the few. On the other hand. Myrdal argues that the Kuznets hypothesis may not apply to less-developed countries. He would opt for more aggressive and direct approaches to reducing income inequality.

Western experience, Myrdal claims, is not relevant to the less-developed nations, particularly to India.[22] He points out there is far less opportunity to break out of the social framework (that is, the caste system), and the abhorrence of manual labor permeates the Indian philosophy, thereby perpetuating poverty, poor health, and low productivity. With mass malnutrition and poor health, productivity is extremely low. Yet if measures are taken to elevate the lower-income groups through intensive transfer of resources via the income tax, it is not at all clear as to how the development process will show a net benefit. By taxing the high-income group or corporations heavily serious inroads are made into the investment function which these groups influence. Investment in favor of consumption is discouraged in order to get longer-range increases in productivity. But how the transfer of capital to industry is achieved through tax or other incentive policies has at best a complex and at worst an indeterminate impact on social welfare. For example, higher transfers to the government sector from high-income groups may be achieved only to reveal that resources which the high-income groups might have invested effectively are poorly or inefficiently invested by the government. Similarly, a welfare program might raise living standards for lower-income groups to perpetuate poverty and stultifying dependence on welfare incomes.

Ceylon is an example where there have been large flows in the form of welfare payments to individuals, but this has increased consumption considerably without demonstrating any clear positive effect on investment and growth.

One might conclude that a successful development effort over a sustained period may be the best guarantee of progress on income inequality.[23] With greater general participation in education, training, involvement in economic enterprises, and an expanding total GNP, the middle class itself should increase in size. At the same time, social responsibility along with effective monetary and fiscal policies should succeed in striking an equitable balance between investment and consumption goals, so that more people have rising incomes and savings, thereby duplicating the experience of Western countries.

The critical issue is that time is running short in efforts to remedy the serious inequalities which now exist throughout the less-developed world. The growing unemployment problem further exacerbates the social distinctions. The 1970's should provide a more urgent atmosphere for action on this issue.

Notes

I am indebted to a number of persons for comments, particularly Ed. Cohn, Alex Lachman of AID, and Alan Strout of the Brookings Institution. Maurice Williams, assistant administrator of the Planning Bureau for Near East South Asia provided invaluable comments.

1. This was the subject of a series of articles in the *Washington Post* in December 1968 by Stanley Karnow on the Philippines, which aroused congressional interest in the subject. The issue is expected to receive increasing attention in U.S. foreign-aid discussions.

2. United Nations, *The Economic Development of Latin America in the Post-War Period,* part 2, chap. 2.

3. However, overall inequality in the proportions of earners included in various personal income brackets has not changed much since World War II. Cf. Economic Commission for Europe, *1956 Economic Survey of*

Europe (Geneva: UN, 1957), chap. 9, and *Income in Post-War Europe: A Study of Politics, Growth and Distribution* (Geneva: UN, 1967).

4. Derived from Simon Kuznets, "Quantitative Aspects of the Economic Growth of Nations: Distribution of Income by Size," *Economic Development and Cultural Change* (January 1963), Table 3, p. 13. Kuznets uses data based on other Indian studies. His footnotes are a good source for additional references. Other Kuznets studies consulted for some of these conclusions are "Quantitative Aspects of the Economic Growth of Nations: Long Term Trends in Capital Formation Proportions, *"Economic Development and Cultural Change* (July 1961); "Quantitative aspects of the economic growth of nations: The Share and Structure of Consumption," ibid. (January 1962); "Economic Growth and Income Inequality," *Studies in Economic Development,* Okun and Richardson, eds. (New York: Holt, Rinehart, Winston, 1962); *Economic Growth and Structure* (New York: Norton, 1965).

5. UN, ECAFE, *Economic Bulletin for Asia and the Far East* (December 1959), quoted in Gunnar Myrdal, *Asian Drama,* 3 vols. (New York: Pantheon, 1968), I, p. 468.

6. Adapted from Kuznets, op. cit., Table 16. The U.S. data for 1929, 1944–1948 under the top 20 percent and 1955–1959 are Department of Commerce estimates, quoted by Kuznets.

7. IBRD, "India's Economic Development Effort," (Bell Economic Mission), 1 October 1965, p. 13.

8. UN, *Economic Survey of Asia and the Far East,* 1960, quoted ibid., p. 16, and Indian Planning Commission, "Annual Plan 1963–1964: The Fiscal Task," also quoted in Bell report, p. 17.

9. Myrdal, II, p. 758.

10. Government of India, Planning Commission, *Report of the Committee on Distribution of Income and Levels of Living,* part 1 (New Delhi, 1964).

11. Ashjorn Bergan, "Personal Income Distribution and Personal Savings in Pakistan, 1963–1964," *The Pakistan Development Review* (Summer 1967).

12. But not with data collected for Chile, Ecuador, Mexico, and Venezuela. The rural sector is said to have greater inequality in these countries because of great concentration of landownership and to heavy investment in cattle, which requires few workers from the plentiful supply relative to the capital investment (UN, *The Economic Development of Latin America in the Post-War Period,* part 2, chap. 2, p. 63).

13. "Patterns of Income Distribution in an Underdeveloped Economy: A Case Study of India," *American Economic Review* (September 1964).

14. Eva Mueller and L. Sarma, *American Economic Review* (September 1965), pp. 1173–1178, complain that Ojha and Bhatt used household expenditures instead of household income data which they claim seriously biased their results. There are numerous conflicts between researchers in this field over the data, methodology, assumptions, and conclusions. However, most economists accept Kuznets's conclusions that less-developed countries have more inequality. Nevertheless, differences reflect the serious measurement problems.

15. "What Has Been Happening to Real Wages in Pakistan," *Pakistan Development Review* (Autumn 1967).

16. *Pakistan's Development* (Cambridge, Mass.: Harvard University Press, 1967), pp. 67, 68.

17. ". . . tax, tariff, and direct-control measures . . . impinged most severely on the consumption of the upper-income groups" (Papanek, p. 235).

18. AID, Statistics and Reports Division data, provided for this paper, 29 January 1969.

19. R. Bird and O. Oldman, eds., *Readings on Taxation in Developing Countries* (Baltimore: Johns Hopkins Press, 1967); *Problems of Tax Administration in Latin America,* Joint Tax Program, OAS, IDB, ECIA, Papers of Buenos Aires Conference, October 1961, (Baltimore: Johns Hopkins Press, 1965).

20. Richard Goode, "Reconstruction of Foreign Tax Systems," Bird and Oldman, p. 122ff.

21. Elaborated in the Brookings Institution panel where an earlier version of this article was presented, 28 January 1969.

22. Myrdal has a wealth of references on income distribution. See *Asian Drama* (paperback), I, chap. 12, "Levels of Living and Inequality"; II, chap. 16, "Equality and Democracy"; III, Appendix 14, "Estimation of Overall Income Inequality." Also numerous references in footnotes of these chapters.

23. It is clear that more detailed information is needed in specific countries on the degree to which growth has, in fact, affected income distribution. Recent growth in a number of countries now "graduated" from U.S. concessionary assistance compares well with long-term performance of the developed countries, but additional studies are needed to ascertain the impact on income inequality in specific countries. Recent growth trends are indicated in AID, Statistics and Reports Division, "Gross National Product, Growth Rates and Trend Data," 25 July 1968, and long-term trends in Simon Kuznets, *Modern Economic Growth, Rate, Structure and Spread* (New Haven: Yale University Press, 1966), pp. 64, 65. Also Kuznets, *Economic Growth and Structure,* pp. 307, 315; and Kuznets, Wilbert Moore, Joseph Spengler, *Economic Growth: Brazil, India, Japan* (Durham, N.C.: Duke University Press, 1955), pp. 121, 128. Also in Kuznets, *Six Lectures on Economic Growth* (Glencoe, Ill.: Free Press, 1959), p. 25; Harry Oshima, "Food Consumption, Nutrition and Economic Development in Asian Countries," *Economic Development and Cultural Change* (July 1967), p. 393. AID is supporting a study on the Philippines by Harvey Averch of the RAND Corporation which should also, when completed, enlighten us on this issue. Richard Weisskoff has in process a doctoral dissertation on "Income Distribution and Economic Growth in Puerto Rico," Harvard University.

7 The Burden of Debt Service for the 1970s

The Burden of Debt Service for the 1970's

Frequently, the debt-service ratio (debt payments as percent of export earnings) is used as an indicator of the seriousness of the repayment burden facing a country. However, while a significant indicator, it does not tell the whole story. Mexico and Israel have had debt-service ratios of 39 percent and 26 percent respectively without these countries calling for reschedulings. Australia and Canada have had similar experiences. On the other hand, other countries have defaulted with much lower debt-service ratios (Bolivia, Brazil, Colombia, Cuba, Peru, and Uruguay, in 1931–1933). With a high level of foreign-exchange earnings relative to import demand or with good credit standing in international markets, high debt ratios can be maintained.

The More-Serious Cases

The several factors which reflect the seriousness of the debt-service burden for a particular country include growth or fluctuation in export earnings relative to imports, the ratio of imports to GNP or national income, the feasibility of checking certain imports, the level of reserves, the growth of total debt service, and the amount and terms of debt relief or new aid. A study by Frank, Clive, and Gewecke dealt with all of these factors in an attempt to develop a composite index reflecting vulnerability.[1] Whatever the index, India and Pakistan are facing more-serious debt-service burdens in the years ahead. This chapter uses the debt-service ratio and other indicators (Tables 7.1–10) to help gauge the significance of debt service to the aid requirements for developing countries.

Table 7.1: Turkish Debt and Debt Service[1]
($ millions)

	Out-standing	Of Which Principal Not Utilized	1968	1969	1970	1971	1972
Multilateral Creditors	377.2	94.6	28.0	55.4	65.4	37.7	27.0
EMA	95.0	—	13.5	22.9	27.0	26.0	15.2
IMF	51.6	—	3.1	21.5	27.0	—	—
IDA	80.7	29.0	0.5	0.5	0.5	0.5	0.5
IBRD	34.3	5.7	5.3	4.2	4.5	4.5	4.5
E.I.B.	98.3	69.1	2.9	3.4	3.5	3.6	3.8
Other	17.3	9.2	2.7	2.9	2.9	3.1	3.0
Bilateral Creditors	1,418.7	338.1	96.4	97.9	90.9	79.4	86.1
France	85.9	30.4	17.2	15.2	12.6	9.6	9.2
Germany	304.9	32.4	21.1	30.0	28.3	27.1	27.3
Italy	72.3	30.9	11.2	8.8	7.7	7.0	7.1
United Kingdom	114.7	2.6	11.1	12.0	12.6	10.3	11.0
United States	729.3	196.3	25.1	22.1	20.4	16.4	22.4
Other	111.6	45.5	10.7	9.8	9.3	9.0	9.1
Total Debt Service	1,795.9	432.7					
a. No New Aid[2]			124.4	153.3	156.3	117.1	113.1
b. DAC Estimates[3]			152	171	181	151	158
c. Frank Study (Constant Gross Aid)			152	(160	170	140)	126

1. Debt incurred up to December 1967. In 1968, Turkey acquired approximately $30 million in debt relief. The Frank study does not take into account the 1968 debt relief but assumes constant gross and constant net aid alternatives, arriving at $126 million in 1972 with constant aid.

2. This is an OECD projection, exclusive of new aid assumptions.

3. This is based on continuation of consortium terms and following new gross aid series, 1968–1972 ($ millions): 228, 239, 241, 198, 193. (OECD, Consortium/Turkey 67/24, 24 November 1967, Part II, Table 5.) However, this series does not have a donor breakdown nor include the 1968 debt relief. Therefore, the actual debt service by 1972 would be less than the $158 million but more than the $113 million. If terms soften, the service will be still less. Thus, the Frank figure of $126 million for 1972 may not be far off. The years 1969–1971 against the Frank study are estimates, since they were not given in the study. They are lower than the DAC estimate by the 1968 debt relief and a somewhat lower-terms assumption.

Table 7.2: India's Debt-Repayment Schedule[1]
($ millions)

Existing Debt[2]	1967/68	1968/69	1969/70	1970/71	1971/72
IBRD/IDA	85.04	58.47	72.61	73.16	66.72
United States	27.84	85.15	67.98	78.72	74.97
United Kingdom	50.14	36.88	39.15	30.60	37.01
West Germany	52.35	40.00	45.32	47.85	49.03
France	7.16	13.05	13.96	13.72	12.49
Italy	6.76	4.63	10.55	10.53	12.00
Japan	35.38	36.30	45.52	52.75	50.37
USSR	85.79	73.03	87.72	85.35	97.28
Other bloc	—	26.19	33.26	41.01	46.72
Total existing	443.75	373.70	416.04	433.69	446.59
On new debt[3]	—	10.00	40.00	50.00	70.00
Total debt service[4]	443.75	383.70	456.04	483.69	516.59

1. The table excludes Soviet Bloc debt service of about $100–115 million (in 1968/69).

2. Ministry of Finance, India. On debt existing as of 3/31/68.

3. IBRD estimate, based on expected utilization of new debt after 3/31/68.

4. This represents an increase in service of over 10 percent a year from 1968/69–1971/72. The drop in 1968/69 over 1967/68 is attributable to the rescheduling undertaken in that year.

Within a range of from 4 percent to 8 percent per year growth of exports to 1972, and extrapolating import growth from recent trends,[2] Turkey's debt-service burden should decline; India's will increase gradually; and Pakistan's will increase rapidly (debt-service payments by creditor are shown in Tables 7.1, 7.2, and 7.3 for Turkey, India, and Pakistan, respectively). For Turkey, the debt-service ratio could decline from about 20 percent to 14–17 percent, depending on whether the upper or lower export projection is used, but for India it is likely to increase from about 23 percent to about 28 percent if exports grow at only 4 percent or to slightly above the current level even if exports grow at 8 percent a year to 1972. For Pakistan, the ratio increases sharply from 11 percent in 1967 and 13.9 percent in 1968 to over 20 percent in 1972, even if exports grow at 8 percent a year, or to nearly 24 percent if exports grow at only 4 percent a year (the comparisons are summarized in Table 7.4).

The Pakistan debt situation is in the process of more-rapid change. One tends to think of Pakistan as less vulnerable than India because of its more-favorable export performance, yet the rate of growth of its debt service is nearly double India's, while Turkey's debt service increases up to 1970 and then declines (Table 7.5). The squeeze on Pakistan's net foreign exchange (after debt service) will increase even if exports grow at 8 percent a year to 1972 (with imports at 6.5 percent a year). World Bank data underestimates this debt service when large portions of debt are excluded or no assumptions are made about future aid flows (see note to Table 7.3).

Table 7.3: Debt-Service Payments, Pakistan, FY 1967–FY 1972
($ millions)

Country or Agency	FY 1967	FY 1968	FY 1969	FY 1970	FY 1971	FY 1972
United States	9.3	12.1	23.4	32.4	35.3	41.1
Exim Bank	(5.4)	(5.9)	(7.4)	(14.4)	(17.7)	(21.1)
Other	(3.9)	(6.2)	(16.0)	(18.0)	(17.6)	(20.0)
IBRD/IDA	23.1	26.3	32.4	42.1	50.4	58.5
Germany	13.7	17.5	20.9	23.3	25.3	26.6
Japan	8.0	11.6	17.5	22.4	25.2	27.7
United Kingdom	11.4	12.6	9.8	9.0	9.9	10.9
Canada	1.1	1.9	2.5	4.8	7.5	9.1
Belgium	—	—	—	—	—	0.1
France	0.2	0.3	0.3	0.5	0.8	1.3
Netherlands	0.1	0.5	0.9	1.0	1.3	1.7
Italy	—	0.2	1.1	2.0	2.1	2.6
Total Consortium	66.9	83.0	108.8	137.5	157.8	179.6
Denmark	—	—	—	—	—	0.1
Sweden	—	—	—	0.3	0.5	0.8
Other Free World	—	—	—	0.3	0.5	0.9
Yugoslavia	2.0	3.5	3.6	3.9	4.3	4.8
Eastern Governments	2.3	4.5	8.3	10.2	11.0	11.8
All Other	4.3	8.0	11.9	14.1	15.3	16.6
Suppliers Credit	5.9	16.3	16.9	17.3	17.9	21.5
Other Privately Placed Credit	3.3	4.5	4.9	5.7	4.7	3.2
TOTAL	80.4	111.8	142.5	174.9	196.2	221.8

Source: IBRD Reports, April 1967, 1968. (See notes.)

Notes to Table 7.3

This represents the medium-aid-level case indicated by the U.S. Pakistan Aid Mission, which has gross aid increasing by 6.8 percent a year. This is a high growth expectation for aid, but the result is about the same as Frank's assumption of constant gross aid.

The data includes estimated external medium and long-term public debt outstanding and repayable in foreign currency including undisbursed as of 31 December 1966 with reported additions to 31 December 1967 and estimated addition to 1972.

The IBRD Report (1968) has shown debt outstanding, amortization, and interest on calendar-year basis. These have been adjusted to fiscal-year basis by making a July–December/January–June division, assuming equal increase or decrease, as the case may be, during each half of a particular year.

The IBRD Report (1968) takes into account loans signed through 17 November 1967. Additions for the period 18 November 1967 through 1972 have been made on the basis of existing average terms and USAID estimates of loan commitments during this period. The terms where not available in the IBRD Reports have been taken from the *Budget-in-Brief*, 1967/68, pp. 43–45.

The IBRD figures do not cover the following loans for which the terms were not available:

Suppliers Credits	$ 64,694,000
Private Bank Credits	29,903,000
Loans from Germany	20,998,000
Loans from Yugoslavia	15,804,000
Loans from USSR	13,688,000
	$145,087,000

The IBRD Report (1968) shows no debt outstanding, amortization, and interest for Italy. I have taken the figures for Italy from the last year's IBRD schedule and have added them to this year's IBRD totals after making adjustments for additions during 18 November 1967 to 30 June 1975. These should, however, be considered as suppliers credits, as has been recently clarified by the IBRD.

The average terms on half the debt omitted above is assumed to be high (suppliers and private bank credits) — three to five years, 6–8 percent, and an average ten-year grace on the others. However, new aid is not taken into account in the IBRD data, which on these two counts (omitting $145 million of debt and estimates of future aid) produces low estimates of debt service from 1968–1972. The increasing aid assumed in the Mission data compensates somewhat for the omission of the $145 million in the IBRD data, so that the net result is a debt-service series which approximates that of the Frank study with a constant gross aid assumption.

Table 7.4: Comparative Debt-Service Ratios,
India, Pakistan, Turkey, 1968–1972
(Percent)

	1968	1969	1970	1971	1972
At 8% growth					
Inda	27.8	22.2	24.4	24.0	23.8
Pakistan	13.9	16.4	18.7	19.4	20.3
Turkey	19.1*	22.8	22.5	17.2	14.3
At 4% growth					
India	27.8	23.1	26.4	26.9	27.6
Pakistan	13.9	17.1	20.1	21.7	23.6
Turkey	19.9*	24.7	25.2	19.9	17.3

*Turkey's exports projected from 1967.

Table 7.5: Growth of Total Debt Service, 1968–1972
($ millions)

	1968	1969	1970	1971	1972	Growth Per Annum 1968–1972
Turkey	124.4	160	170	140	126	neg.
Percent annual change		+28.6	+ 6.2	—18.0	—10.0	
India	443.8	383.8	456.0	483.7	516.6	10.4*
Percent annual change		—14.0	+18.8	+ 6.1	+ 6.8	
Pakistan	111.8	142.5	174.9	196.2	221.8	18.8
Percent annual change		+27.5	+22.7	+12.2	+13.0	

*From 1969 following rescheduling. The rate is 3.8% a year from 1968.

Debt Service and Export Performance

As debt service over this limited period is already predictable, the impact of export earnings (or debt relief) on net earnings available for imports is critical. For example, if India's exports grow at 4 percent a year instead of at 8 percent a year, the difference in terms of net earnings (after debt service) would be over $300 million by 1972. For Turkey and Pakistan, the difference would amount to over $150 million, with similar consequences for the net aid flow. Put another way, if export earnings grow at only 4 percent, the net export earnings of Turkey would finance 16 or 17 percent less of its imports and the net earnings of India and Pakistan would finance 11 or 12 percent less of their imports (Table 7.6). A lower export growth rate could undermine the early or mid-1970 U.S. assistance completion goal for Turkey or alternatively impair Turkey's economic-growth momentum.[3] The impact on the net aid flow to India and Pakistan could resemble the impact of a withdrawal of all U.S. program assistance.

The chances of the impact being so severe are less for Turkey and Pakistan because their export earnings performance is likely to be above 4 percent a year, but a higher annual growth of imports than projected (5.5 percent for Turkey, 6.5 percent for Pakistan) could keep the pressure up. India's exports showed little growth through the 1960's until the India fiscal year 1968/69, when they increased over 9 percent, but the India Mission projects a 5–6 percent rate of increase through 1972. No assurance exists that this rate will be achieved or maintained through the 1970's, so that a 4 percent annual growth is still possible.

The alternative export growth rates of 4 percent and 8 percent combined with debt service already anticipated (omitting future reschedulings) obviously will affect the capacity of net export earnings to finance imports, as indicated in Table 7.8. Even with an 8 percent export growth, net earnings after debt service will finance a lower percentage of imports for Pakistan in 1972 than they did in 1968; this is not true for India and Turkey with an 8 percent export growth rate, because their debt service is not growing so rapidly. However, if India's imports grow at 7 percent instead of at 5 percent, net earnings as a percent of import needs would decline even if exports grew at 8 percent (Table 7.8).

Indian imports, excluding food imports financed by foreign aid, have increased at a very low rate in the past. The rate of growth between 1961/62 and 1968/69 has been less than 1 percent (see Table 7.7). Even the prewar growth 1961/62 to 1965/66 was only 3.4 percent a year. Moreover, in projecting imports (again excluding food

Table 7.6: The Impact of Export Performance on Debt-Service Burden,
India, Pakistan, Turkey, to 1972

	1967	1968	1969	1970	1971	1972	Percent Growth Per Annum
Turkey							
Export earnings ($ millions)							
At 8% growth	600[1]	648	700	756	816	881	8.0
At 4% growth	600	624	649	675	702	730	4.0
Debt-service ratio (%)							
(Payments/export earnings)							
At 8% growth	—	19.1	22.8	22.5	17.2	14.3	—
U.S. share of foreign exchange	—	3.9	3.1	2.7	2.0	2.5	—
At 4% growth	—	19.9	24.7	25.2	19.9	17.3	—
U.S. share of foreign exchange	—	4.0	3.4	3.0	2.3	3.1	—
U.S. share of debt service	—	20.2	14.4	13.1	14.0	19.8	—
Net earnings[3] ($ millions)							
At 8% growth	—	523.6	540.0	586.0	676.0	755.0	9.0
At 4% growth	—	499.6	489	505	562	604	5.0
Difference	—	24.0	51.0	81.0	114.0	151.02	
Imports ($ millions)	685	723.0	762.0	804.0	848	894 (961)	5.5 (7.0)
Difference as percent imports		3.3	6.7	10.1	13.4	16.9 (15.7)	
India							
Export earnings ($ millions)	1,558[4]	1,598					
At 8% growth			1,726	1,864	2,013	2,174	8.0
At 4% growth			1,662	1,728	1,797	1,869	4.0
Debt-service ratio (%)		27.8					
(Payments/export earnings)							
At 8% growth	—		22.2	24.2	24.0	23.8	—
U.S. share of foreign exchange	—	1.7	4.9	3.6	3.9	3.4	—

118

	1967	1968	1969	1970	1971	1972	Percent Growth Per Annum
At 4% growth	—	—	23.1	26.4	26.9	27.6	—
U.S. share of foreign exchange	—	1.7	5.1	3.9	4.4	4.0	—
U.S. share of debt service	—	6.3	22.2	14.9	16.3	14.5	—
Net earnings ($ millions)	—	1,154.2					
At 8% growth	—		1,342.3	1,408.0	1,529.3	1,657.4	9.3
At 4% growth	—		1,278.3	1,272.0	1,313.3	1,352.4	4.0
Difference	—		64.0	136.0	216.0	305.0	—
Imports ($ millions)5	2,770						
Including food	2,770	2,246	2,358	2,476	2,600	2,730	—
Excluding aid-financed food	2,200	—	2,426	2,620	2,830	3,056	7.0
Difference as percent nonfood imports	—	—	2.7	5.5	8.3	11.28 10.09	—
Pakistan							
Export earnings ($ millions)6	752	803	—	—	—	—	—
At 8% growth	—	—	867	936	1,011	1,092	8.0
At 4% growth	—	—	835	868	903	939	4.0
Debt-service ratio (%) (Payments/export earnings)							—
At 8% growth	10.7	13.9	16.4	18.7	19.3	20.3	—
At 4% growth	10.7	13.9	17.1	20.1	21.7	23.6	—
U.S. share of foreign exchange (8% growth)	1.2	1.5	2.7	3.5	3.5	3.8	—
U.S. share of debt service	11.6	10.8	16.4	18.5	18.0	18.5	—
Net earnings ($ millions)	671.6	691.2					
At 8% growth			724.5	761.1	814.8	870.2	5.8
At 4% growth			692.5	693.1	706.8	717.2	.9
Difference			32.0	68.0	108.0	153.0	—
Imports7 ($ millions)	1,108	1,098	1,169	1,245	1,326	1,412	6.5
Difference as percent imports	—	—	2.7	5.5	8.1	10.8	—

Table 7.7: Projection of Indian Imports
($ millions)

	61/62	62/63	63/64	64/65	65/66	66/67	67/68	68/69	61/62–65/66	61/62–68/69	71/72
Food-grains	245.4	302.9	377.2	592.4	649.2	893	710	575	—	—	—
Nonfood imports	2043.7	2073.1	2190.8	2241.1	2273.9	1877	2040	2246	2.6	1.3	—
Total	2289.1	2376.0	2568.0	2833.5	2923.1	2770	2750	2821	6.2	3.0	—
Minus PL 480 and other food aid	-192.0	-258.0	-390.0	-466.0	-520.0	-573	-550	-594	—	—	—
Total self-financed imports	2097.1	2118.0	2190.8	2367.5	2403.1	2197	2200	2246	3.3	.9	33251 27302 30563

Source: Adapted from USAID/India data.

1. 5 percent per annum 1965/66–1971/72.
2. 5 percent per annum 1967/68–1971/72.
3. 7 percent per annum 1968/69–1971/72.

Notes to Table 7.6

1. Based on USAID data from Turkey.

2. Imports increased an average of 5.7 percent a year from 1956–1966, reaching $718 million in 1966, an estimated $685 million in 1967. If projected roughly at this rate to 1972, it would mean that by 1972 a growth in export earnings of only 4 percent a year would finance about 17 percent less imports than a growth in earnings of 8 percent.

3. Export earnings minus debt-service payments. Import growth: 6.5 percent, 1961–1965; 7.4 percent, 1961–1966 (USAID data).

4. Based on USAID data from India mission.

5. Indian imports (including food) grew by about 6 percent a year between 1961/62–1965/66 (imports including food were $2.9 billion; excluding food $2.3 billion in 1966) but dropped by nearly 6 percent in 1966/67 and dropped slightly further in 1967/68. Nonfood-grain imports, however, increased by only 2.6 percent a year over the period 1965/66 but dropped about 17 percent in 1966/67 and then increased by 9 percent in 1967/68. If nonfood imports are projected to FY 1971/72 at the average growth rate of about 5 percent a year from 1968, the difference of $305 million in the 8 percent and 4 percent export growth rates would represent about 12 percent of nonfood imports. Put another way, the absolute difference would exceed recent U.S. aid levels to India.

6. Data from USAID/Pakistan. Export earnings in 1966 were $713 million.

7. USAID/Pakistan, *Statistical Fact Book,* Table 8.4 and other USAID/Pakistan data.

8. At 5 percent import growth.

9. At 7 percent import growth.

Table 7.8: Net Earnings After Debt Service as Percent Imports (At 8% and 4% Growth of Export Earnings)*

	1968	1969	1970	1971	1972
At 8% growth					
Turkey	72.4	70.9	72.9	79.7	84.5 (78.6)†
India					
At 5% import growth	51.4	56.9	56.9	58.8	60.7
A 7% import growth	51.4	54.2	51.4	50.5	49.5
Pakistan	63.0	62.0	61.1	61.4	61.6
At 4% growth					
Turkey	69.1	64.2	62.8	66.3	67.6 (62.9)†
India					
At 5% import growth	51.4	55.3	53.7	54.0	54.2
At 7% import growth	51.4	52.7	48.5	46.4	44.3
Pakistan	63.0	59.2	55.7	53.3	50.8

*Based on Table 7.6. The numbers fluctuate somewhat due to the variation in debt service from year to year. The growth rate of net earnings in Table 7.6 is averaged over the period. For Turkey 1967 was used as base year, for India and Pakistan, 1968.

†Using a higher alternative on import growth rate of 7 percent per annum (See Table 7.6).

imports financed by foreign aid), the U.S. aid mission to India showed import growth at 2.5 percent a year between 1965/66 and 1969/70. However, increases from 1966/67–1967/68 or 1968/69–1969/70 have been projected at 7–9 percent a year. Projection of a 5 percent per year growth from 1965/66, the year before the serious drought, produces a postdrought self-financed import growth between 1968/69 and 1971/72 of about 11 percent, which is high. Therefore, a 7 percent growth in imports from the 1968/69 estimate to 1971/72 is more realistic. If we assume that most of a declining food-import requirement will be met by foreign aid in the early 1970's, export earnings will be released for nonfood imports.

With growth in exports of only 4 percent a year, net earnings after debt service will finance a lower percentage of imports for all three countries, but significantly lower for Pakistan. In fact, Pakistan's net earnings after debt service, should exports grow at only 4 percent, would increase less than 1 percent a year (Table 7.6), while imports are likely to grow at least by 5 or 6 percent a year. Imports in Pakistan have increased an average of over 8 percent a year between 1961 and 1967. (The predrought rate was 14 percent a year from 1961 to 1965.) Since 1968 represented a resumption of more normal growth, while 1961 was low, the 1963–1968 growth reached 6.5 percent a year. This is the rate of increase used in the projection to 1972 (Table 7.6). If higher foreign-loan aid were to materialize, the debt-service burden would become still more of a constraint as service payments on additional loans accumulated.

Beyond 1972, the situation for India and Pakistan, according to the Frank Report, will continue to worsen whether constant gross or net aid is assumed. Even with exports growing at 8 percent a year and gross aid rising at 3.5 percent a year (a constant net-aid assumption) India's debt-service ratio will be well over 30 percent by 1977 and nearly 50 percent if exports rise at only 4 percent a year. For Pakistan, the ratio would rise to near 25 percent even with 8 percent growth in exports, whether gross or net aid is constant. If export earnings rise only 4 percent, debt service will take over 40 percent of Pakistan's export earnings by 1977 or so.[4] Turkey's longer-term debt-burden situation is better, but would again rise to around 20 percent as a proportion of foreign exchange earnings if exports increase at only 4 percent a year. With a 6 percent or 8 percent growth in export earnings, Turkey's debt service need not have a serious impact on a rising import demand.

Debt Service and Reserves

Reserves are a marginal indicator in that they serve a vital purpose in time of crisis. For this reason, reserves to support four or five months of imports is sometimes indicated as an adequate safeguard to cover such crises. In this regard, India's reserve position fell short of this requirement with just over three months of reserves at the end of 1968, while Pakistan and Turkey fell further below the requirement (Table 7.9). However, the export performance of Turkey and Pakistan has been and is likely to be better than India's, so that a two-month reserve is supportable, barring crises. Yet, a drift downward in the reserve position for these countries is likely to lead to import and fiscal policy restrictions — both possibly detrimental to growth momentum. Since 1962, India's reserves have increased in absolute terms and those of Turkey and Pakistan have declined, producing the results shown in Table 7.9. If reserves are projected at the 1968 level to 1972 and imports increase as projected in Table 7.6, India's safety margin will decline to two and one-half months, that of Pakistan and Turkey to less than two months. If the four-month safeguard criteria were to be applied to the reserve level of 1972, India would need $281 million more in reserves, Pakistan $264 million, and Turkey $176 million (or $198 million if Turkey's imports grow at 7 percent instead of 6.6 percent a year). Whether an "adequate" level is two, three, or four months of imports, a low reserve level may not be critical, except as an inhibitor to import liberalization and internal public investment policy.

Finally, if a change in income elasticity of imports were warranted from past trends (a parabolic rather than linear trend), then imports would increase at a growing, rather than a constant, rate as assumed in Table 7.6. However, there is little expectation of a pronounced change in the ratio of imports to national income, if the recent past is a valid indicator. The ratio has not changed enough since 1961 to warrant unusual change in elasticity assumptions relative to the period to 1972. If anything, the ratio appears to decline somewhat (Table 7.10), but a slight reduction in the growth-rate assumptions would eliminate the decline.

The Terms Impact

Minimum terms of AID have stiffened from 2.5 percent interest, forty years maturity, and 1 percent interest during the ten-year grace period, to 3 percent interest, forty years maturity, and 2

Table 7.9: Comparison of Reserves as Related to Imports,[1]
India, Pakistan, Turkey, 1962–1968, 1972

	1962	1963	1964	1965	1966	1967	1968	1972
Reserves ($ millions)								
India	512	607	498	599	608	662	7002	700
Pakistan	280	308	244	221	200	161	207	207 (Nov)
Turkey	189	178	141	141	131	119	122	122 "
Reserves as percent imports								
India	21.8	24.6	17.4	20.5	26.9	23.7	26.9	20.9
Pakistan	38.1	34.9	24.4	21.3	22.4	14.7	18.9	14.7
Turkey	30.4	25.8	26.0	24.4	18.1	17.2	16.2	13.6 (12.7)
Reserves/one month's imports (months of imports)								
India	2.7	3.0	2.1	2.5	3.2	2.8	3.1	2.5
Pakistan	4.6	4.2	2.9	2.6	2.7	1.8	2.3	1.8
Turkey	3.6	3.1	3.1	2.9	2.2	2.1	2.0	1.6 (1.5)
Added reserves needed to reach four[3]								(With constant[4] reserves)
Months imports ($ millions)								
India	273	—	—	—	—	268.4	216.8	2815
Pakistan	0	—	—	—	—	205.0	159.0	264
Turkey[6]	18	—	—	—	—	111.2	128.0	176 (198)
Total needed		—	—	—	—	584.6	503.8	721 (743)

1. IMF, IFS data, Bulletin of January 1969.
2. IMF Report SM/69/11, Supplement No. 1, 29 January 1969.
3. Stated as adequate "safeguard," OECD "Consortium for Turkey," 30 November 1967 ("A Study of Turkey's Long Run Foreign Debt Position"). The report suggests four to five months as a "good" safeguard.
4. Using import projections of Table 7.6, reserves constant at 1968 level.
5. Imports including food projected from 1968 ($2750 million) at 5 percent. However, India USAID data gives $400 million decline in food imports which is subtracted from 1972 total imports.
6. 1972 shows difference between a 5.5 percent and 7.0 percent growth of imports over the period.

Table 7.10: Imports as Percent of National Income, Turkey, India, Pakistan, 1961–1967, 1972[1]

	1961	1962	1963	1964	1965	1966	1967	1972
Turkey	10.9	10.8	10.4	7.6	7.6	8.2	7.1	6.9 (6.2)[2]
India	7.6	7.4	6.7	6.7	6.6	7.1	—	5.7[3]
India	—	—	—	—	—	—	—	8.1[4]
Pakistan	9.4	10.3	11.7	12.4	·11.7	9.3	9.7	9.3[5]
Pakistan	—	—	—	—	—	—	—	10.3[6]

1. IMF, IFS data, January 1969.
2. Based on projection of IMF 1967 NI at 6 percent a year 1967–1972 and import projections, Table 7.6.
3. Based on projection of IMF 1966 NI at 5 percent a year 1966–1972, import projections, Table 7.6.
4. Based on projection of IMF 1966 NI at 4 percent a year 1966–1972, import projections, Table 7.6.
5. Based on projection of IMF 1967 NI at 6 percent a year 1966–1972, import projections, Table 7.6.
6. Based on projection of IMF 1967 NI at 5 percent a year 1966–1972, import projections, Table 7.6.

percent interest during the ten-year grace period. Over half the total aid to India is on terms closer to what are regarded as hard terms, averaging over 4 percent interest, about fifteen years, and 4 percent interest during a 3-year grace period. Terms vary considerably, with commercial credits of 6 percent or above for nine years, and a one-year grace period at 6 percent interest to 0.75 percent, fifty years maturity and a ten-year grace period (terms provided by the International Development Association of the World Bank).

The significance of the difference in terms may be better appreciated by considering the following, drawn and adapted from an AID report:[5]

1. To maintain a $100 million annual net flow, it takes 30 percent more aid in five years on hard terms (5.5 percent, thirteen years, a three-year grace) than on soft terms (2.5 percent, forty years, a ten-year grace at 1 percent). It would take 230 percent more aid to maintain the constant net flow of $100 million over 10 years and 300 percent more aid to maintain it for fifteen years.

2. Considered in dollar terms, if a $1 billion annual net aid flow requirement over a ten-year period is assumed (India being a plausible case), it would take eleven years and $10.4 billion to affect the flow on low terms (0.75 percent, fifty years, a ten-year grace without interest); fourteen years and $10.8 billion on terms of 2.5 percent, forty years, a ten-year grace with 1 percent interest; forty-five years and about $45 billion on terms of 3.5 percent, twenty years, a three-year grace; and an indefinite number

of years and beyond $150 billion to effect the $1 billion net flow on hard terms of 5.5 percent, three years, a three-year grace.

Terms on reschedulings and new aid have a significant impact on the amount of aid required to get the job done. By providing a total annual aid package to India at terms of 3.5 percent interest, twenty years, a three-year grace (assuming the $1 billion annual requirement for ten years), instead of at 2.5 percent, forty years, a ten-year grace at 1 percent interest, we are quadrupling both the gross aid required and the time span to achieve the target, two perhaps critically scarce factors in both political and economic terms. The donors may increasingly resist giving aid this long, and the people of India may not remain quiescent during such a long, slow growth evolution. It is doubtful, given the magnitudes and political realities involved, that the entire task of relief in terms of an essential net aid flow can be achieved by reschedulings on better terms unless these are combined with considerably better terms across the board on new aid. Commercial credits, which are on the hardest terms, might better be tied separately by some formula to either export performance or reserve levels.

U. S. Policy Implications

The U.S. share of total debt-service payments to India and Pakistan is rising more rapidly than that of any other donor (Tables 7.2–3). Although it was the sixth largest on the Indian repayment schedule in 1967/68, the U.S. share became number one in 1968/69 (the Soviet share became first in 1969/70). At the same time, all bloc debt service combined will be nearly double U.S. debt service to India by 1972. The already high debt-service claims of Japan and Germany will also be rising. These factors will bear importantly on the structure of future debt reschedulings. The Frank study concludes that very liberal debt rollovers on a grant or near-grant basis will be desirable and inevitable as rising gross aid becomes less politically feasible in donor countries. On the other hand, some donors believe repeated reschedulings can only undermine confidence in the recipient economy. The resistance to them will probably increase.[6] Rollovers may postpone the critical squeeze on net aid, but even on softer terms, the problem will intensify. At the same time, the chances of increasing gross aid considerably seem slim. This leaves the terms on new aid and export performance as the two prime factors in easing the debt of recipient countries. This gives force to the recommendation of the Development Assistance Committee (DAC) "Working Party on Financial

126

Table 7.11: Foreign U.S. Indebtedness Issues
($ millions)

	Exports[1]	Aggregate Indebtedness[2]	Interest & Dividends[3]	Net Internat. capital movements[4]	Interest & Dividends as % Exports[4]	U.S. Investment abroad[5]	Foreign Investment in U.S.[5]	Foreign Invest. in U.S. as % U.S. Invest. abroad
1820	64	−87	4.8	1.0	7.5	—	—	—
1840	132	−266	11.9	−31.0	9.0	—	—	—
1860	400	−379	25.1	104.4	6.3	—	—	—
1869	—	—	—	—	—	100	1500	1500
1870	451	−1256	75.4	99.4	16.7	—	—	—
1880	853	−1603	96.2	29.4	11.3	—	—	—
1890	710	−2907	174.4	192.6	19.2	—	—	—
1897	—	—	—	—	—	700	3400	486
1900	1499	−2491	149.4	−296.4	10.0	—	—	—
1908	—	—	—	—	—	2500	6400	256
1914	2532	−3700	200.0	−72.0	7.9	3500	7200	206
1919	8528	+3700	130.0	−2,712	1.5	7000	3300	47
1930	4013	+8800	295.0	−700.0	7.4	17200	8400	49
1957	20,989	+20100	653.0	−3,442.0	3.1	54200	31400	58

1. U.S. Dept. of Commerce, *Historical Statistics*, Colonial Times to 1957. Includes gold, silver, merchandise.
2. Douglas North, "The U. S. Balance of Payments, 1790–1860," *Studies in Income and Wealth*, vol. 24.
3. Matthew Simon, "The U. S. Balance of Payments, 1861–1900," ibid. After 1900, Dept. of Commerce Historical Statistics, ser. V, 168–192, U. S. Balance of International Payments, 1790–1957.
4. Simon.
5. Dept. of Commerce, *Historical Statistics*, ser. V, 168–192. The net here differs from col. 2 due to estimating procedures of individual researchers.

Aspects of Development Assistance," that members should provide 60 percent of total aid as grants or grantlike aid or as loans at "no harder than" thirty-year maturity with 2 percent interest and a ten-year grace period.[7] Export performance also becomes a most vital long-term means for alleviating the burden. Excessive reliance on export credits and repeated reschedulings are not the answer.[8] Therefore, U.S. aid efforts should give even greater stress to lower terms on new aid and increased focus on export-oriented policies, while considering debt-relief exercises as essential interim aid supplements.

The decade of the 1970's will bring the debt-service question into critical focus for a number of important countries in the less-developed world. Solutions will not easily present themselves. This chapter provides some of the basic considerations which bear upon this problem.

Addendum: U.S. Long-term Indebtedness

The data attached reflect the fact that even the United States experienced sizable capital inflows during the nineteenth century and consequent debt service amounting to over 19 percent of its export earnings at the peak deficit year of 1890. This ratio is not unlike the ratios now experienced by India, Pakistan, and Turkey, as we have seen. However, with ratios already near or above the U.S. nineteenth-century experience, the debt-service ratios of both India and Pakistan are still rising.

It is also of interest that between 1816 and 1819 the United States defaulted on $100 million of its international indebtedness, which was almost one-third of the value of its total export earnings over the same period. There were defaults by the U.S. government also in 1842, and in many different years on private debt owed to foreigners.

The U.S. experience indicates that whether developed or otherwise, countries experience periods of large capital inflows during their formative stages, which in turn leads to repayment problems and even default. Such an historical perspective is essential in judging the performance of some of the less developed economies today which require foreign capital, but encounter difficult repayment problems.

Notes

1. USAID data corrected for reschedulings or other recent factors were available only for years up to 1972. Trends beyond that year have been developed and analyzed by Frank, Cline, and Gewecke, in "Debt Servicing Problems of Less Developed Countries and Terms of Foreign Aid: With

Special Reference to United States Policy," August 1968 (unpublished AID document). However, the data in the Frank report do not include the 1968 debt rescheduling for India and projects exports at levels of exports that were significantly affected by the droughts in southern Asia. These two factors produce debt-service ratios that exaggerate the case in some instances, but the essential message is the same. As new debt is incurred, future projections require revision, but again the basic conclusions remain valid that debt service will remain a critical problem in this decade.

2. See notes of Table 7.7 for assumptions on import trends not referenced in this text.

3. However, see Table 7.6 and note 2 for assumptions concerning Turkey's export and growth trends and projections.

4. The Frank study shows that if gross aid to India, Pakistan, and Turkey were to remain constant for an extended period of time, with no change in terms or reschedulings, net aid would be zero in each case by 1984.

5. USAID Report, "Summary Report of a Study on Loan Terms, Debt Burden and Development," April 1965, p. 6 and charts C and D.

6. The Canadian Delegate to the Working Party on Financial Aspects of Development Assistance held in Paris, 22 January 1969, said that with respect to reschedules he thought "everyone will agree that the fewer the better."

7. DAC/FA (68) 12, 24 December 1968, para. 8.

8. This is supported by the Pearson Commission Report, *Partners in Development,* (New York: Praeger, 1969), p. 156ff.

8 Growth Performance of the Less-Developed World

Whether there are elements of isolationism creeping into our national psyche may be hotly debated, but it hardly seems questionable when foreign aid is mentioned. The Congress reflected the national mood in its views and action on the U.S. fiscal year 1970 appropriations for economic assistance to the underdeveloped countries. Little sense of urgency was exhibited in getting the foreign-aid bill through the congressional-hearing process. The hearings were postponed more than once on short (it seemed peremptory) notice, yet without recorded complaint from the White House or AID. In fact, each postponement seemed to be accepted with relief — as though a reprieve from some dire fate had been achieved. The mood has also been prevalent in AID itself. Competent personnel have been drifting from the agency to more encouraging challenges, and the many competent officials who remain seem destined to strive through a period of limbo until study groups — for example, the Pearson Commission — and congressional committees produce new assessments and aid directions of more

*Appeared as "Long Think on Development," *International Affairs*, January 1970.

appeal. Development economists outside of the operations of foreign-aid programs have cooled too, if not in their convictions, then in applying themselves to the aid business. Much of the fight for renewed vigor and bold *New Think*[1] in aid strategies seems to have faded from what was only lately a vibrant romance in the field of economic growth. Top advisers to foreign-assistance administrators and organizations come and go now, when they do at all, more unobtrusively and with less confident eagerness.

The mood, in a word, is one of doubt. There is doubt about what has been achieved with the resources we have poured into Latin America and Asia, doubt as to whether it is worth the cost in terms of domestic priorities, doubt as to whether the aid recipients give a fig, and doubt concerning the future as to whether it makes any difference how much assistance flows to the underdeveloped world — be it half as much as in the past, twice as much — or none. The inevitable mental logic to such pessimism is as follows: If it doesn't really matter, or appears not to matter, then why struggle to provide any? Why borrow energy and leverage from other important quests?

Gunnar Myrdal added impressive if ponderous respectability to the view that outside influences have but little ultimate effect on the development processes within the underdeveloped economies. He, too, has weakened the basis of our convictions by blaming "Western approaches" and the abstractions of Western economists for misleading the Indians, the governments or institutions they represent, and themselves into believing that the plans and priorities prescribed in their models had any relevance to the indigenous development process.[2] By downgrading the rationalization process by which in the United States we have tried to justify to the public and the Congress the substantial commitment of resources. Myrdal has contributed to the current hesitancy about support of foreign-aid initiatives. At the same time, his plea for an institutional emphasis in place of market-oriented inducements and strategies — a reversal of current focus — has given support to critics against the professionals and produced additional clutch-slipping in purpose and momentum. His conclusion, if taken to heart by dedicated developers, is simple but devastating: "The participation of outsiders through research, provision of financial aid, and other means is a sideshow of rather small importance to the final outcome."[3]

The war in Vietnam has put the cap on this mixture of gall and doubt, adding pressure to the ferment. The traumatic effect has produced a gnawing erosion of belief that we could induce or guide any foreign country to do anything we think right and has even raised doubts in our own minds as to the correctness in our approaches to foreign problems of any kind.

Historical Perspective Essential

In such a time of skepticism and ennui there is a genuine need for historical perspective concerning world development. It would be presumptuous to try to deal with all of these doubts about development, and our ability to promote, inspire or hasten it in a brief chapter. Nevertheless, I am not alone in concluding that the doubters, including Myrdal, are too pessimistic.[4] The doubters have failed to grasp the significance of the transformation that has taken place in the developing world in the last decade or two, relative to its long, relatively stagnant history. The critical task now is to determine how to sustain the momentum in increasing output of goods and services and how to create conditions leading to restraint on population growth. Myrdal's investigations on India ended, unfortunately, in the midst of southern Asia's devastating droughts, and the faulty impressions concerning an incipient green revolution in Asian agriculture were not caught even in his brief "Postscript," in which he concluded that, even in June 1967, "the problems remain fundamentally unchanged". Apparently unknown to Myrdal and his researchers, India farmers had dramatically, yet unobtrusively, been increasing their use of fertilizers, miracle seeds, and pesticides, responding like economic man to the high returns thereby generated. Fertilizer use increased from virtually none in the early 1960's to well over a million tons during 1967, when Myrdal wrote his postscript, and now exceeds 2 million tons. Even as Myrdal was writing his afterthoughts, Pakistan was actually in the process of doubling fertilizer consumption, having already increased consumption fourfold since 1964. The miracle seeds were also spreading the abundance by doubling and tripling yields. The two successive years of bad drought had hidden the effects of these extraordinary changes, which had been going on quietly for years. All this in agriculture, while private-sector industry was being revitalized with incentive-oriented trade liberalization and administrative decontrol policies.

What does the long-term view tell us about agriculture? The fact is that throughout the fifty-year period up to the end of World War II, India and Pakistan experienced a deadening downward drift in annual food-crop production. The average annual production of food crops in India in the years 1893/94 to 1895/96 was 74 million tons. The average for the ten years before World War I was about the same, while the average for the twenty-year period beginning in 1926 was less than 70 million tons. During this whole period population had increased nearly 40 percent.[5] The result, therefore, was a significant decline in food-crop output per capita, exceeding 30 percent.

On the other hand, the output of food-grains in India reached 100 million tons in the good monsoon year of 1967/68, and was close to this level even in the more normal monsoon year of 1968/69, producing a sharply rising food-crop output per capita for the third year in a row. These levels are 8–10 million tons above the previous all-time record level of 89 million tons in 1964–65, before the two successive years of severe drought interfered.[6] Chapter 1 outlined the dimensions of the green revolution and how it might be consolidated in this decade.

McKim Marriott, an American anthropologist, returned in the middle of the 1960's to a once isolated Indian village after an absence of sixteen years to find in the midst of this new prosperity a new acceptance of innovative change and progress which has slowly but effectively been permeating village life. People now have three meals a day instead of two; electric mills instead of primitive and wasteful hand power to grind the grain; other machines in place of hands to increase productivity and release children for schooling. There were no teachers sixteen years ago, the tape relates; in 1968 there were nine. There was better clothing, and radios, bicycles, and good tools, virtually absent sixteen years before, were everywhere.

All this appears to have been missed by Myrdal's sweep of history and also by many disheartened erstwhile proponents of foreign aid. The fact that self-sufficiency in food — and even surpluses for export — has now become "the problem" (that is, surpluses–storage–marketing–price–crop-diversification dilemmas),[7] instead of the famine the Paddocks talked about and Lord Snow and others echoed, is all too cavalierly overlooked by some of the detractors.

Historical perspective is as essential as calculated prophecy about the future, considering the complexity of the progress of nations. Besides the more current evidence of progress which many believe is before our eyes, the drift of economic history seems definitely to have accelerated the progress of change. Mechanical indicators do not convey the whole story, but they imply a great deal. Simon Kuznets, one of our most noted statistical economic historians, has said that "the provision of more goods to satisfy human wants, individual and collective, is necessarily general, but describes as well the economic growth of Periclean Athens, Augustan Rome, medieval France, modern United States, and even India and Egypt in some centuries."[8] A per capita product (or income) growth measure, accounting as it does for both gross income and population growth, is not merely a mechanical measuring rod but implies welfare progress in its many ramifications. It is worth having Kuznets's words on this measure to help revive some confidence in its utility in the face of some of the skepticism prevailing:

> The emphasis on a sustained and substantial rise in per capita product is particularly important because of its implications for the structure and conditions of modern economic growth. Given the structure of human wants, a cumulatively large rise in a country's per capita product necessarily means a shift in relative proportions of various goods demanded and used — and hence major changes in combinations of productive factors, in patterns of life, and in international relations. Modern economic growth implies major structural changes and correspondingly large modifications in social and institutional conditions under which the greatly increased product per capita is attained. Yet for the purpose of measurement the changing components of the structure must be reduced to a common denominator; otherwise it would be impossible to compare the product of the economy of the United States with that of China, or the product of an advanced country today with its output a century ago before many of the goods and industries that loom so large today were known.[9]

What the Facts Show

Accepting these premises on behalf of the per capita product measure of progress, let us review and compare in brief the progress of certain developed and underdeveloped nations in the course of recent history. Kuznets has been emboldened by his logic of extrapolation from recent growth performance to conclude that backward rates of increase similar to those experienced in recent years "would yield impossible levels [of living] in earlier times because life could not have been maintained at such low levels."[10] In other words, if India has a per capita income of $100 today and had been growing at 2 percent a year for a thousand years, life could not have been supported for the mass of Indians at the level such a backward extrapolation would derive. Therefore, recent rates of per capita growth could not have prevailed, say, before 1800, which suggests that living standards for the masses stagnated for thousands of years previous to more-recent history.[11] The case for ancient history, with its flashes of glorious and prosperous civilizations here and there, is more obscure and perhaps immeasurable. Nevertheless, the significance of these statements and this picture will be more vividly appreciated when we review the table of comparative and relative per capita performance.

Table 8.1 summarizes historic per capita growth rates of a number of developed and underdeveloped economies, plus such rates for a few of the countries which had been U.S.-aid recipients for some years but which no longer need concessional (low cost) U.S.

assistance. The conclusions drawn from this data are, I believe, surprising. From 1950–1968, the per capita product (or income) growth of the underdeveloped countries the United States is assisting has equaled and in many instances surpassed that of the developed countries in any decade since 1870, and in the whole ninety-year period up to 1960. The comparison does not change on the whole when viewing the growth rates of developed countries from 1870–1913, when their development might have been in a stage more comparable to the present stage of the underdeveloped countries. In a number of underdeveloped countries receiving U.S. assistance (Korea, Philippines, Turkey, pre-June 1967 Jordan, Peru), per capita income growth since 1950 has been about double that of some developed countries (United Kingdom, France, Italy, Belgium) throughout modern history. The average annual growth in gross product or income of the eleven underdeveloped countries indicated (omitting Jordan) including all of Latin America from 1950–1960 is more than twice the rate (5.1 percent per year), at which the developed countries progressed from 1870–1960 (or two and one-half times in the 1913–1960 period). The comparison is even more startling when the growth performance of some recent aid graduates, or countries no longer in need of U.S. low-cost aid, are listed beside the historic growth rates of developed countries. The growth of the aid graduates has exceeded historic growth of the developed economies by factors of three and four. The average of the gross per capita growth rates of the seven developed countries shown is 2.6 percent in the pre–World War I period, 2.1 percent in the post–World War I period (compared to 8.2 percent a year growth for the five recent aid graduates from 1960–1968) and appears not much different over the whole period, 1950–1968. As the difference between the gross and per capita product rates equals the population growth rates, it is clear that historic population growth rates are also much less than recent population growth rates.

There is so much by way of implication in such figures, especially when the hypotheses of Kuznets, Gerschenkron,[12] Rostow, and other economic historians are taken into account, that one chapter could not suffice to deal with them. In fact, there is as much to be said explicitly as there is hidden implicitly in these numbers. We therefore have space to pursue further but a few implications.

Per capita growth of 2 percent a year doubles the average living standard per person in about thirty-six years; a 3 percent growth in per capita product or income does it in twenty-four years, a 4 percent per year growth doubles the average living standard per capita in about eighteen years. What this suggests is that while a

Table 8.1: Comparative Historic Average Annual Growth Rates of Total Product

	1870–1913 Gross	1870–1913 Per Capita	1913–1960 Gross	1913–1960 Per Capita	1870–1960 Gross	1870–1960 Per Capita
Developed Economies[1]						
U.K.	2.2	1.3	1.9	1.4	2.1	1.4
France	1.6	1.4	1.5	1.3	1.6	1.4
Germany (1871)	2.9	1.7	2.5	1.6	2.7	1.7
Italy (1890)	1.9	1.4	2.3	1.6	2.1	1.5
U.S.	4.2	2.2	3.0	1.7	3.6	2.0
Belgium	2.7	1.7	1.4	1.0	2.1	1.4
Sweden	2.9	2.2	2.4	1.8	2.7	2.0
LDC Countries[2]	1950–1960		1960–1968		1950–1968	
Asia and Near East						
Korea	4.4[3]	2.1[4]	8.5	5.6	6.5	3.9
India	4.2	2.2	4.2	1.6	4.2	1.9
Pakistan	2.7	.7	6.0	3.2	4.4	2.0
Philippines	6.6	3.5	5.8	2.3	6.2	2.9
Turkey	5.8	2.9	5.4	2.9	5.6	2.9
Jordan	9.0	6.0	10.0	7.0	10.0	7.0
Latin America						
Brazil	5.8	2.8	4.6	1.8	5.2	2.3
Colombia	4.7	1.6	4.5	1.1	4.6	1.4
Peru	5.2	2.8	5.7	2.5	5.5	2.7
Chile	3.6	1.2	4.4	2.1	4.0	1.7
Ecuador	5.0	1.9	4.5	1.1	4.8	1.5
Latin America[5]	5.2	2.3	4.7	1.7	5.0	2.0
Recent Aid Graduates[2]						
Iran	n.a.	—	7.9	4.7	8.0	5.5
Greece	5.9	4.9	7.4	6.6	6.7	5.8
Taiwan	8.1	4.6	10.0	6.9	9.1	5.8
Israel	9.0	5.2	8.5	5.1	8.8	5.2
Cyprus	n.a.	—	7.0	5.8	—	—

1. Simon Kuznets, *Modern Economic Growth* (New Haven: Yale University Press, 1966), p. 352. This is gross domestic product, at constant prices.
2. AID, Statistics and Reports Division, *Gross National Product* (Bulletin), 25 April 1969. GNP at constant 1967 prices.
3. 1955–1960.
4. 1953–1960.
5. 18 LA countries.

Table 8.2: Recent Performance of Developed Economies
(Percent per year)

| | | 1950–1968 | |
	Gross	Per Capita	Percent Population Growth Per Year
United Kingdom	2.9	2.3	.6
France	5.0	3.8	1.2
West Germany	6.1	5.4	.7
Italy	5.4	4.9	.5
United States	4.5	3.0	1.5
Belgium	4.2	3.6	.6
Sweden	4.2	3.5	.7
Average	4.6	3.7	.8

Table 8.3: Population Growth Rates of Table 8.1
(Percent per year)

	1870–1913	1913–1960	1870–1960
Developed Economies	.9	.7	.8
	1950–1960	1960–1968	1950–1968
Asia and Near East	2.5	2.9	2.7
Latin America	2.9	3.0	3.0
Recent Aid "Graduates"	2.8	2.4	2.6

population explosion is taking place, largely due to a rapid reduction in the death rate, an equally impressive explosion has occurred in the ability to generate high real growth rates in gross output or income — more so, it appears, than at any time in the past. This does not mean that either the income or population growth rates can be maintained at the levels implied in the tables forever, thus resolving our worries and efforts. There are relative absolutes to deal with — in the world's resource and space capacity. There appears, however, to be no such limitation in man's ability to innovate. Over 150 years ago Malthus expressed the fear that the earth would soon be inadequate to the resource demand. Even early in the present century, when the first conservation movement was at its height in the United States, a conference convened in 1908 predicted the exhaustion of coal, iron ore, and other mineral deposits in a number of years. Yet, more-recent appraisals remain optimistic on this score.[13]

The record of the developed economies on population growth also offers some encouragement. While the average annual population growth rate of seven developed countries shown from 1870–1913 was less than 1 percent a year (0.93), it was slightly less from

1950–1968 (0.8). The population growth rate of the United States since 1950 (1.5 percent a year) has gone down slightly over the long-term growth from 1870–1960 (1.6 percent a year) and compares to the growth rate between 1870–1913 of 2 percent a year. Thus, development itself should create over time what I have called elsewhere a preoccupation effect on population growth. People get diverted from marriage and from pastoral boredom to education, careers, urban and many other distractions, so contributing, with artificial and other birth-control influences, to reduce the birthrate. There is thus some hope that if we can keep the gross income or product rates up, current population-control programs will be greatly assisted in time by modernization influences.

Some Intractable Problems

These encouraging comparative patterns of growth in the under-developed world admittedly hide much that remains to be done, even some things that seem never can be done. One of these is the gap in per capita income levels between rich and poor. Even if India were to grow at a per capita growth of 4 percent while the United States, for example, grew at 2 percent per capita, the ab-solute levels would continue to widen. To illustrate, a 4 percent growth would increase an income per capita of $100 to $104 in one year — or by $4, while a 2 percent increase on a U.S. per capita income of $4000 generates an increase of $80, twenty times the Indian increase. The widening gap problem has not been considered seriously in U.S. foreign-aid programs, because it is not only in-tractable to practical solution but is regarded as irrelevant to the development process as an average income earner who expects to achieve Rockefeller wealth status in his lifetime. Instead, it is growth that is emphasized — that is, a better living standard this year than last rather than a gain on Western living standards every year. This may not be an adequate approach, but it is understandable when one considers that even at a 4 percent per capita growth, highly optimistic for India, it would take nearly 200 years to in-crease a $100 per capita income to $2,500, by which time Western relative standards will have shot still further ahead in absolute terms. Thus, a widening gap between rich nation and poor appears inevitable until we find catalysts hitherto unknown to man to pro-duce innovative surges in growth in the less-developed world. To what extent cognizance of the internationally widening gap affects political and social stability in the underdeveloped countries, theory offers little insight.

We can, however, be sure that progress brings unrest in its wake and accentuates internal frictions concerning internal income inequality, as chapter 6 described. It is all the more urgent when high rates of gross product reflect rapid economic change, wherein extended family monopolies accumulate fortunes quickly while propertyless workers observe with growing frustration the invidious status comparisons thereby generated.

Conclusions

What conclusions can one draw from the above? One is that in an historical context the underdeveloped countries should not be faulted for their performance in terms of generating material growth; they are doing as well or better than the developed did or have been doing.

Another is that, given the population explosion, the underdeveloped countries could not afford to grow less — they need to grow more rapidly. They have, and with man's ability to innovate and change, there is no need to join the pessimists of history and prophesy impending future chaos. The world, as Barbara Ward has said, is, to be sure, lopsided, but the quickening processes of change are more likely to work for even faster gross product growth paths in the future than in the past.

A third conclusion is that these rapid changes in material well-being must increasingly be transferred to the masses if the development effort is to have meaning. President Ayub Khan's difficulties in Pakistan may well have stemmed from neglect of the social-inequality issue. In all Asia, Africa, and Latin America, a keen sensitivity to this issue and a heightened purpose to work at tax administration and equitable capital mobilization for investment is critically necessary.

A fourth conclusion is that with both growth in well-being and better distribution of the fruits of development, we must be prepared for more unrest. We have apparently accepted this as an axiom of progress. It is probably so, but has this not always been true — anywhere? We must expect the turbulence that accompanies budding maturity and try to cope with it, even as we continue to work at building the basic economic foundations of more stable societies. We can only surmise, although it is a safe bet, that chaos and turmoil in the underdeveloped world, without the kind of historic growth patterns we have dealt with here, would have produced catastrophic consequences for even a partial world peace.

Finally, foreign assistance to the underdeveloped world is not necessarily responsible for most of the growth of the underdeveloped countries discussed here. But it has opened the door to a flood of technical, economic, administrative, and every other kind of advice needed to help unequipped societies change. The United States, Western European countries, the World Bank, the International Monetary Fund, the United Nations, and numerous other organizations — including Communist-bloc countries — have joined in the effort to bridge the widening chasm with flows of educational, professional, and material assistance. Given the size of the planet, the feverish pursuits and competitive drives of its diverse inhabitants, the progress already made and potential progress to be made, we must conclude that continued, if not enhanced, dedication to world development in this decade must seem to reasonable men to be less the sideshow Myrdal describes than the essence of perspective as well as prophetic wisdom.

Notes

1. Edward De Bono's mind-opening book, *New Think.* (New York: Basic Books, 1967); English ed., *The Use of Lateral Thinking* (London: Cape, 1967).

2. Myrdal also appeared before a congressional seminar, chaired by Charles Goodell of New York, attended by this author, in the early spring of 1968, to expound his views.

3. *Asian Drama,* 3 vols. (New York: Pantheon, 1968), I, p. 34.

4. Gustav Papanek of the Harvard Advisory Service, author of a book on Pakistan, and other reviewers of Myrdal's volume were highly critical.

5. Daniel Thorner, "Long Term Trends in Output in India," in Kuznets et al., *Economic Growth* (Durham, N.C.: Duke University Press, 1955), pp. 121, 123.

6. See Lester Brown, "The Agricultural Revolution in Asia," *Foreign Affairs,* July 1968.

7. Clifton Wharton ably covered these in his "The Green Revolution: Cornucopia or Pandora's Box?", *Foreign Affairs,* April 1969.

8. Simon Kuznets. *Six Lectures on Economic Growth* (New York: Free Press of Glencoe, 1959), p. 13.

9. *Economic Growth,* pp. 14–15.

10. Ibid., p. 25.

11. There were exceptions in time and place, and those who make these measurements are well aware that people in different societies and in different countries and ages have different values about material goods.

12. Alexander Gerschenkron, *Economic Backwardness in Historical Perspective* (Cambridge, Mass: Harvard University Press, 1962).

13. Hans Landsberg, *National Resources for U.S. Growth* (Baltimore, Maryland: Johns Hopkins Press, 1964), contains projections to the year 2000 by the Resources for the Future, Inc.

9 Foreign Aid and Trade Balances

Additionality is a term used currently, particularly by donors of foreign aid, to identify the effect of aid on the donor's normal export trends. When aid is tied to the donor's exports, as most of it is, recipients must use that aid to purchase donor-country commodities. In this way, foreign aid has a minimal adverse effect on a donor country's balance of payments. However, the donor country is interested in whether the aid it provides to an underdeveloped country promotes more permanent growth in markets for its exports after aid is reduced or terminated. Additionality also seeks to prevent developing nations from using aid funds for U.S. goods and services they already have been purchasing or would purchase, commercially. This chapter deals with the effectiveness of additionality as a tool and some of the problems it creates.[1] As the balance-of-payments problem in the United States and the pressures of certain industry groups for protectionist policies continue, this issue will remain vital in this decade. This chapter seeks to promote understanding of the issue and show the impact of its practice in the past. It concludes with the hope that it will take a more rational direction in the future.

Tables 9.3–8 summarize commodity exports financed by AID under project and program loans to India, Pakistan, and Turkey. While there are difficulties and important qualifications associated with the data in matching these commodity flows with calendar-year totals of U.S. exports of the same commodities to these countries

143

and in drawing definitive conclusions without further verifications of magnitudes, concepts, and conclusions, the material suggests a selective commodity method of assisting the U.S. balance of payments.

One of the more serious lacks at present is that of specific commodity-flow data which would facilitate judgments about the United States as the normal competitive source for AID-financed commodities. Would AID-financed commodities be purchased from the United States by the developing countries in the absence of AID-financing? Ceteris paribus reasoning on additionality may afford us some satisfying sequences in logic, but in the end there is the disappointing reawakening to the fact that in the real world there is no ceteris paribus. An examination of the actual trade data should help answer the key questions or point the way to an improved empirical approach in the 1970's.

Even if there are margins of error in the data, it seems evident that there is already a considerable element of additionality in U.S. aid itself, without which the volume of U.S. exports to India, Pakistan, and Turkey would be substantially less than it is. Of the sixty-five separate code listings of commodities for these three countries, the United States is the major supplier for only about fifteen of the listings, suggesting that by and large most of the items on the U.S. export list would shift away from the United States as a source in the absence of U.S. aid. At the same time, some additionality might be obtained, perhaps without significant effect on the developing countries but with a meaningful assist to the U.S. balance of payments, if items in which the United States appears to be competitive were dropped from the AID-financed eligibility list (that is, items for which AID finances but a small percentage of the total U.S. exports to the less-developed countries).

What the Data Suggest

Accepting the fact that we are dealing with difficulties in the data, matching of AID-financed commodity flows against total exports and worldwide imports to less-developed countries of the same commodities in India, Pakistan, and Turkey produces the following implications:

1. Most U.S. exports to less-developed countries are AID-financed. On the whole, U.S. exports of commodities which are also AID-financed under project and program loans are about 70 percent AID-financed in India, over 80 percent AID-financed in Pakistan, and about 90 percent AID-financed in Turkey. Roughly the same results were obtained for India and Pakistan in each of two methods tried by researchers working independently. In one case (Table 9.1) program and project commodity data was obtained

Table 9.1: AID-Financed Exports Compared to Total U.S. Exports to India, Selected Commodities, 1963–1965*

(Calendar Years)

AID Code	Commodity Description	Financed by Program Loans ($000)	Financed by Project Loans ($000)	Total Loan Shipments ($000)	Total U.S. Exports Incl. Loans ($000)	Program Loans as % Total U.S. Exports	Project Loans as % Total U.S. Exports	Total Loans as % Total U.S. Exports	Worldwide Indian Imports ($000)	U.S. Exports as % of Worldwide	AID-financed as % of Worldwide
234 237/891	Fertilizer ($NH_4 PO_4$)	33906	7514	41420	57610	58.9	13.0	71.9	181996	31.7	22.8
696	DDT, rubber, tin	24006		24006	33477	71.7		71.7	171891	19.5	14.0
370	Drugs (antimalaria)	169	2274	2443	12543	1.4	18.1	19.5	68866	18.2	3.5
390	Chemicals	24716	8169	32885	33334	74.1	24.5	98.6	603256	5.5	5.4
540	Yarn (tire cord)	11098		11098	14446	76.8		76.8	NA	NA	NA
542	Misc. textile products	166	164	330	407	40.6	40.0	80.6	982945	nil	nil
591	Pulp, paper, paper products	34961	777	35738	NA				109979		32.5
621	Lubricants and petroleum coke	51776		51776	53142	97.4		97.4	639685	8.3	8.1
640	Nonmetallic minerals	30376		30376	41422	73.3		73.3	110879	37.4	27.4
660	Iron and steel	119098	20788	139886	141402	84.2	14.7	98.9	170357	83.0	82.0
690	Nonferrous metals	143966	10511	154477	153325	93.4	6.9	101.0	509076	30.0	30.3
691	Alumina	966		966	9828	9.8		9.8	39307	25.0	25.0
700	Machinery and machine tools	63300	237562	300862	529651	12.0	44.8	56.8	781492	67.7	38.5
820	Autocomponents and spares	44911		44911	58775	76.4		76.4	350084	16.8	12.8
880	Scientific and professional instruments app., supplies	18	1255	1273	6654	.3	8.9	19.2	54454	12.2	2.3
881	Lab equipment and supplies	1		1	1424	.1		.1	16008	8.9	
891	Synthetic rubber	21772		21772	NA	NA		NA	NA		
950	Ocean transportation	1984		1984	18108	11.0		11.0	23067	78.5	
		607190	289014	838694	1,215,548	50.0	23.8	69.0	4,813,860	25.3	17.4

Source: Borrower's Shipping Reports as of 30 September 1965.

*The commodities included in Program and Project Shipments were provided under five loans as follows: $200 million (eligibility period 21 June 1962; terminal date for disbursements 30 September 1965); $225 million (eligibility period 1 April 1962; terminal date for disbursements 30 September 1965); $240 million (eligibility period 1 April 1963; terminal date 30 June 1966); $50 million (eligibility date 1 April 1964; terminal date for disbursements 31 December 1966); $150 million (eligibility period 1 April 1964; terminal date for disbursements 31 December 1966). Diversified classification in Indian and U.S. Dept. of Commerce produces inaccurate totals for pulp and synthetic rubber. The data provided were therefore omitted in the totals for pulp and rubber. AID, Operations Reports show AID-financed synthetic rubber of $9.2 million.

Table 9.2: Trends in AID-Financed and Total U.S. Exports to India, 1962–1964
(Calendar Years)

Code	Description	AID Expenditures for Commodities Procured in the U.S. ($000)			U. S. Exports by Commodity ($000)			AID-financed Exports as a Percent of Total U.S. Exports		
		1962	1963	1964	1962	1963	1964	1962	1963	1964
230	Nitrogenous fertilizers*	5300	4511	7832	6242	7627	8261	84.9	59.1	94.8
540.8	Man-made fibers and yarns*	3922	9326	4812	10516	7765	4407	37.3	120.1	109.2
660.8	I&S—tinplate, terne, blackplate									
691	Aluminum, incl. scrap*	2309	5903	3086	5688	3774	3316	40.6	156.4	93.1
695	Nickel, incl. scrap*	1857	10510	4283	10551	5566	4447	17.6	188.8	96.3
697	Zinc, incl. scrap*	17	2	1	224	136	284	7.6	1.5	.4
710	Generators, motors, and parts	4288	7337	5302	7182	6647	3479	59.7	110.4	152.4
730.8	Engines, turbines, and parts	13459	11248	18063	3967	30600	34127	339.3	36.8	52.9
740.8	Construction, mining and conveying equipment, and parts	12602	16400	7829	26383	18254	27295	47.8	89.8	28.7
761.9	Metalworking machinery and parts	5856	9681	17197	35436	40736	39885	16.5	23.8	43.1
778	Textile machinery, acc., and parts	4106	11894	17017	9630	27611	34628	42.6	43.1	49.1
790	Industrial machinery, acc. parts, NEC	916	1250	1928	14067	6890	9525	6.5	18.1	20.2
820	Motor vehicles, engines, parts, NEC	14499	35444	27152	14609	23789	26203	99.2	149.0	103.6
18/0	Trucks, buses, chassis	5315	14217	16634	17445	23249	29824	30.5	61.2	55.6
3&2	Passenger autos and chassis	3583	6758	8773	7300	10172	18820	49.1	66.4	46.6
3&5	Motor-vehicle engines, parts	—	19	618	638	420	286	—	4.5	216.1
850	Railroad transportation equipment and parts	3038	7336	7654	9507	12657	10718	32.0	58.0	71.4
		32639	33913	12966	28967	34359	16418	112.7	98.7	79.0
		113706	185754	161147	208352	260252	271923	54.5	71.3	59.2

Source: Operation Report, AID; Market Share Report: India, 1962–64. U.S. Dept. of Commerce.
*Does not include commodities with an SITC commodity index below 500.

Table 9.3: AID-Financed Exports Compared to Total U.S. Exports to Pakistan, Selected Commodities, 1963–1965 (Calendar Years)

AID Code	Commodity Description	Financed by Program Loans[1] ($000)	Financed by Project Loans ($000)	Total Loan Shipments ($000)	Total U.S. Exports Incl. Loans ($000)	Program Loans as % Total U.S. Exports[1]	Project Loans as % Total U.S. Exports	Total Loans as % Total U.S. Exports	Worldwide Pakistan Imports ($000)	U.S. Exports as % of Worldwide	AID-financed as % of Worldwide
230 233 235 236	Nitrogenous fertilizers, Potash fertilizers, Phosphate fertilizers, Pesticides[2]	3181	2981	6120	4756	66.8	60.5	128.6	30029	15.9	20.4
370	Drugs and medicines	12447	2407	14854	15748	79.0	15.3	94.3	42846	36.7	34.6
390/393	Chemicals	10320	3195	13515	34003	30.4	9.4	39.7	87261	38.9	15.4
500/510	Excess property	3022	—	3022	NA	NA	—	—	—	—	—
540	Yarns and threads	182	1296	1478	1275	14.2	101.0	115.0	1785	71.4	82.8
591	Pulp, paper, and products	462	68	530	679	68.1	10.0	78.0	1982	34.3	26.7
621	Petroleum nonfuels	13860	4903	18763	16040	86.4	30.6	116.9	90042	17.8	20.9
640	Nonmetallic minerals	107	827	934	2703	3.9	30.5	34.5	8298	32.6	11.3
650	Nonferrous ores	554	—	554	601	92.1	—	92.1	3849	15.6	92.2
660/680	Iron- and steel-mill Products	174342	101673	276015	236128	73.8	43.0	116.9	337839	69.8	83.4
690	Nonferrous metals, products	3781	963	4744	3984	94.9	24.2	119.0	39934	10.0	118.8
700/720 740/770 790	Industrial machinery and equipment	7844	31704	39548	85676	9.2	37.0	46.1	576991	14.8	6.9
820/822	Motor vehicles, engines, parts	19671	13010	32681	52422	37.5	24.8	62.3	104123	50.3	31.4
833/835	Tractors	1737	501	2238	14580	11.9	3.4	15.3	16441	88.6	13.6
840	Aircraft and parts	1605	—	1605	13233	12.1	—	12.2	16629	79.6	9.7
850	Railroad transport equipment	1814	13660	15474	28526	6.4	4.8	54.2	132552	21.5	11.7
880	Scientific and professional equipment	939	—	939	1644	57.1	—	57.1	17299	9.5	5.4
891	Rubber and rubber products	2571	—	2571	8866	29.0	—	28.9	31875	27.8	8.1
950	Ocean transportation	1505		1505	NA						
	Totals	254439[3]	177188	431058[3]	520864	49.9	34.0	83.0	1539775	33.8	28.1

1. Source for program-loan data: Final Procurement Report on USAID Loan 390-H-056, 31 October 1965 and Final Progress Report, 31 March 1966; Quarterly Progress Report on USAID Loan 391-H-066, July-September 1965; Quarterly Progress Report on U.S. AID Loan 391-H-080, October-December 1965; Quarterly Progress Report on USAID Loan 391-H-096, October-December 1965.
2. Not available separately.
3. Ocean transportation omitted in total.

Table 9.4: AID-Financed and U.S. Commercial Exports to Pakistan, 1962–1964

AID Code[1]	Commodity Group and Item[2]	AID Expenditures on Commodities Procured in the U.S. ($ Millions)[3]			U.S. Commercial Exports (Total, AID Financed) ($ Millions)[4]		
		1962	1963	1964	1962	1963	1964
230	Nitrogenous fertilizers, chemicals and products	5.34	3.66	—	—4.42	—.95	—
236-237	Pesticides & agric. chem. spec., incl. DDT	1.61	4.09	1.30	1.28	.30	.28
370	Medical & pharmaceutical preparations	2.43	7.52	4.32	1.04	—.54	.08
390.1	Coal-tar products, excl. dyestuffs	.10	.13	.13	—.04	—.06	.02
390.3	Pigments, paints, varnishes	.14	.64	.28	.25	.11	.23
390.6	Industrial chemicals, excl. alcohol N.E.S.	.90	3.50	.62	1.87	1.48	2.25
390.8	Raw materials for plastics	.54	1.13	.47	.26	.50	1.22
540.8	Man-made fibers and yarns	—	1.25	.08	.06	—.80	.35
570	Lumber and manufacturers	.02	1.16	—	.99	—.77	.52
591	Pulp, paper products, excl. newsprint	—	.34	.19	.28	.10	.06
640	Nonmetallic minerals and products	.06	.23	.30	.68	.59	.54
660	Iron- and steel-mill products						
660.1	Pig iron	2.74	4.42	7.27	—.84	—.90	—.10
660.8	Tinplate, terneplate, blackplate	4.22	6.79	16.05	—.99	.21	.59
661.1	Crude & semifinished steel	18.02	23.51	28.72	—3.35	—4.21	2.74
661.3	Bars & rods, structural shapes	.13	4.75	3.70	3.54	—2.50	—.64
661.5	Plates, sheet, skelp, etc.	26.89	27.77	41.63	—9.39	—10.08	—11.62
670.1	Railroad track materials	10.38	7.46	2.37	—2.99	—1.01	.54
670.5	Wire and products	2.34	2.25	2.09	—.20	.19	.44
671.4	Tubes, pipes, fittings	1.99	5.16	7.07	1.24	.87	—.08
690	Nonferrous metals and products						
691	Aluminum	.10	.18	.95	.68	.42	.05
692	Copper	.06	1.02	1.10	.04	.14	.35
700	Machinery and equipment						
710	Generators, motors, parts	.35	1.23	2.45	2.43	1.80	3.89
720	Electrical apparatus & parts	1.68	2.21	6.69	.91	2.21	—.79
730	Engines, turbines, parts	.37	.68	1.61	3.56	3.55	3.69
740	Construction, mining conveying equipment	1.52	1.19	1.94	22.97	14.47	10.55
761	Metal-working machinery, machine tools	.29	1.16	.98	1.60	1.17	1.24
770	Agriculture equipment, parts, excl. tractors	.02	.32	.42	.25	.32	—.16
778	Textile accessories, parts	—	.03	.01	1.57	2.50	4.10
790	Industrial machinery N.E.S.	1.43	3.05	4.36	4.86	5.39	4.81
820	Motor vehicles, engines, parts						
820.1 820.9	Trucks and buses	2.61	11.79	4.39	4.29	.87	2.19
820.3 820.5	Engines and parts	1.67	5.51	.83	5.45	4.94	4.92
833	Tractors and parts	.09	.85	1.05	15.20	4.56	1.14
840	Aircraft, accessories, parts	.11	.18	1.30	10.50	1.48	—.16
850	Railroad-transportation equipment, parts	Loan 7.85 Data Not Available	7.69 3.24	2.70 3.95	Loan —1.55 Data Not Available	14.09 14.35	.52 .82
850.2	Locomotives (all types)						
858	Vessels and equipment	—	—	.45	.25	.11	.50
880	Scientific and professional equipment	.07	.21	.30	1.65	2.00	1.68
891	Rubber and products	1.27	2.84	1.45	.67	1.23	3.28
891.3	Tires, tubes, repair material	1.05	2.61	1.43	.61	.94	2.58
	Totals	98.39	146.75	150.52	63.31	37.74	37.72
	Combined total		$395.66	plus	$138.77=Total exports		
	Total U.S. exports				$534.34		
	AID-financed as % U.S. Exports				$395.66=74 percent		
					$534.43		

148

Notes to Table 9.4

1. The AID code for a given commodity group is found in AID, Statistics and Research, *The Commodity Code Book*. While AID commodity classifications differ from those of the Standard International Trade Code (SITC), *Commodity Code Book* indicates which SITC commodities comprise a given AID commodity group. When translating AID codes to SITC, the 1965 AID code book must be used rather than the 1963 edition, which translates to Bureau of the Census "Schedule B" code in *U.S. Exports*. Not until 1965 was this later code brought into conformity to the SITC.

2. The following listing of commodities that have been financed partially by AID (1962–1964) is based on AID Statistics and Reports listings in *Operations Reports*. For this study December and June issues (December 1961–December 1964) were used, especially the tables entitled "AID Expenditures for Commodities Procured in the U.S. During . . . By Commodity Group, Region, and Country or Destination." We have omitted some of the items on the *Operations Reports* lists either because they were financed for Pakistan in insignificant amounts (e.g., cotton fabrics) or because data were not available on the amount of total exports of the commodity to Pakistan. Some items have been combined (e.g., pesticides and DDT; bars and rods and structural shapes) and the title of one group changed (blooms, billets, slats, etc., to crude and semifinished steel) for convenience and accuracy in translating between the different code systems. Detailed commodity descriptions at the above SITC are found in the Standard International Trade Classification, Revised, U.N. Statistical Papers Series M.N. 34. Also, *Market Share Reports 1962–1964, Pakistan* lists commodities exported to Pakistan in the SITC codes and gives the dollar value and percentage of U.S. exports to Pakistan, the dollar value of the total exports to Pakistan of fourteen developed countries, and the dollar value of exports of several individual countries out of these fourteen.

3. AID *Operations Reports* based on fiscal years. Data are corrected for calendar years by using the June and December issues. Data is for AID expenditures in the U.S. only. As most all AID loans are tied to purchase of U.S. goods, the data represents the great bulk of all AID expenditures for exports to Pakistan.

4. Commodity figures for U.S. commercial exports are computed in the following manner: the dollar values of U.S. exports to Pakistan are taken from the *Market Share Reports,* the SITC items are summed to get the dollar value of the AID commodity group, and the figure for AID expenditures for each group is subtracted from this sum. It should be noted here that some of the figures derived from the *Market Share Reports* are to an extent incomplete for one of two reasons: (1) No data is available for SITC commodities below code 512, where an AID commodity group consists of SITC commodities above and below 512, (e.g., nonmetallic minerals and products), the figure for U.S. exports of the group is the sum of all data above 512; however, the bulk of the commodities in this study are manufactures and the effect of this limitation of data is probably fairly insignificant. (2) Data for "special category" items, which are listed on the front page of *Market Share Reports,* is incomplete due to the security significance of the item (e.g., aircraft). Also when a four-digit SITC item contains larger-digit items that in a more exact, detailed study belong under more than one AID commodity group, the major composition of the four-digit item is the criteria used for including it in the sum value of the AID group.

In some cases this sum also includes the value of items which are not financed by AID, but are similar to those that are and fall within the general description of the AID group (e.g., the value of scientific and professional investments includes the value of photographic equipment which is not AID financed). Possibly the use of broader data than indicated in the AID code book will balance out the limitations on market-share figures.

Where U.S. commercial exports are reported as negative, AID expenditures on a particular good exceeded total exports in a given year. This discrepancy results from figures in *Market Share Reports* being based on shipping data (i.e., recorded f.o.b. when the item leaves the U.S.), while *Operations Report* data are on a payments basis (i.e., are recorded when documents are presented for payment after the shipment reaches Pakistan). Payments may take place several months after shipment (and this is generally the case for nonperishable goods as those in this study), and thus the AID expenditure figure for one fiscal year may represent payment for a good shipped in the previous fiscal year. While the above explains most negative values for commercial exports in a given year, it may not explain a high negative value for three years (see figures for plates, sheets, skelp, pig iron). Such figures will require further checking. Sources used in this study have their limitations, but alternative sources are equally troublesome. Export data in U.S. exports for 1962–1964, for example, are based on Schedule B, and it would be extremely difficult to translate the figures into AID commodity data.

from borrowers' shipping reports and, with an adjustment for shipping, these were matched with the broad SITC categories of U.S. Bureau of the Census export data in the FT-420 series. Tables 9.2 and 9.4 match the more detailed AID-financed commodity breakdowns provided in the AID Operations Reports and Market Share Reports, with important qualifications indicated in the notes to Table 9.4. AID-financed exports as a percent of total U.S. exports of the same commodity to India are in each case roughly within the 65–75 percent range. For Pakistan (Tables 9.3 and 9.4), the range is from about 75–85 percent, although a further correction for shipping would reduce the lower figure some. This would seem, in turn, to suggest that a very substantial proportion of U.S. exports in these commodities in the aggregate would not be purchased from the United States in the absence of AID-financing. It would be extremely difficult to ascertain definitely to what degree this would be so.

2. The rest of the world is the source of most imports of AID goods to less-developed countries. That AID-financing has been essential to these exports would appear to be particularly true in view of the fact that AID-financed commodity flows represent less than 25 percent of worldwide imports of these commodities into India, Pakistan, and Turkey, indicating in the main that the United States is not competitive in most of its exporting to these countries. There may be supply reasons for importing from the United States

which must be sorted out. In some cases, other world sources may not be adequate even though lower priced.

3. Some AID goods are competitive. On a selective, rather than aggregate, commodity basis, however, some AID-financed exports appear to be competitive, where AID-financing for the commodity represents but a small proportion of the total commercial purchases from the United States. Where the U.S. export percentage still represents a small proportion of worldwide imports of the commodity into the less-developed countries, it may be that supplies are limited relative to the needs of the developing country. More specific knowledge regarding U.S. and the rest of the world supplies and prices are required for confirming these conclusions. The schema suggested below encompasses some possibilities. Further qualification is necessary where continued import of the U.S. commodity by the less-developed countries is based on specifications which have to be met on U.S. manufactured capital units or processes for which continued U.S. maintenance inputs are essential.

4. To increase additionality without significantly impairing the aid efforts, commodities might be singled out for which AID-financing represents but a small percentage of total U.S. exports of that commodity. It would depend on what percentage is selected below

Table 9.5: Significance of Various U.S. Export Market Shares*

AID-financed exports as percent of total U.S. exports:	U.S. Share of a Country's Import Market	
	Low	High
Low	Either indeterminate or U.S. commodities are not competitive, but world supplies	U.S. commodities are highly competitive even without AID-financing
High	U.S. commodities noncompetitive unless AID-financed	Either (1) U.S. commodities are competitive or (2) U.S. commodities are not competitive, but AID-financing has been used to create a market

*Omits commodity comparability or homogeneity considerations within a commodity class.

Table 9.6: AID-Financed Exports Compared to Total U.S. Exports to Turkey
Selected Commodities, 1963–1965[1]
(Calendar Years)

AID Code	Commodity Description	Financed by Program Loans ($000)	Financed by Project Loans ($000)	Total Loan Shipments ($000)	Total U.S. Exports Incl. Loans ($000)	Program Loans as % Total U.S. Exports	Project Loans as % Total U.S. Exports	Total Loans as % Total U.S. Exports	Worldwide Turkey Imports ($000)	U.S. Exports as % of Worldwide	AID-financed as % of Worldwide
050	Fats and oils	(Not available separately)[2]		55	51816	(Not available separately)		.1	92663	55.9	.1
215	Gums and resins			7826	10167			77.0	10500	96.8	74.5
236	Pesticides			84	89			94.6	8305	1.0	1.0
370	Drugs, Medicines			1716	4411			38.9	28046	15.7	6.1
390/393	Chemicals, dyestuffs			22325	33153			67.1	177334	18.7	15.5
470	Hides and skins			4718	6581			71.7	15052	43.7	31.4
540/590	Yarn, thread, man-made fibers			23209	27802			83.5	50632	45.9	38.3
543	Textiles			74	77			96.6	264008	.0	.0
591	Pulp, paper, paper products			4458	4480			99.5	37168	12.1	12.0
621	Petroleum nonfuels			22788	26087			87.4	201741	12.9	11.3
640	Nonmetallic minerals			1197	3926			30.5	6661	58.9	18.0
660	Iron- and steel-mill products			32972	38838			84.9	226481	17.1	14.6
680	Misc. Iron- and steel-mill products			549	1799			30.5	14385	12.5	3.8
690	Nonferrous metals, products			6251	7692			81.3	51611	14.9	12.1
696	Tin and tin alloys, products			3874	5474			70.8	6264	80.4	61.8
700	Industrial machinery, equipment			121519	160105			75.9	523516	30.6	23.2
770	Agricultural equipment, excl. tractors			4667	14229			32.8	40558	35.1	11.5
778	Textile machinery			243	2259			10.6	121381	1.9	.2
820	Motor vehicles			26111	41989			62.2	288507³	14.6	9.1
822	Misc. vehicles, parts, and acc.			1619	9564			16.9	21000³	45.5	7.7
880	Scientific and professional instruments and appliances			443	4412			10.0	64750	6.8	.7
890	Misc. commodities			2250	6403			35.1	37582	17.0	6.0
891	Rubber and rubber products			18161	22573			80.5	73729	30.6	24.6
	Totals			307109	339926			90.3	2371874	14.3	12.9

1. Borrower's shipping reports for India and Pakistan had summary tables in which total AID-financed commodities and program-loan finance of commodities were available. These summaries were not available for Turkey.
2. See notes, India table.
3. This figure is questionable. The 1963 total was $137,000; 1964, $10,800,000; 1965 is assumed to be the same as 1964.

Table 9.7: Additionality with Roughly a 25 Percent Rule
(Illustrative Case)

	Percent of U.S. Exports AID-Financed	Additionality Saving for U.S. Balance of Payments Cumulative 1963–1965, Now AID-Financed
		$000
India[1]		
1. Alumina	9.8	966
2. Scientific and professional equipment	19.2	2,177
3. Drugs	18.1	2,443
4. Textile machinery, parts	14.9	4,094
Total savings		9,380
Pakistan[2]		
1. Tractors	15.3	2,238
2. Aircraft and parts	12.2	1,605
3. Textile accessories, parts	.1	40
4. Construction, mining, conveying equipment	8.5	4,650
5. Engines, turbines, parts	24.1	2,660
Total savings		11,193
Turkey[3]		
1. Textile Machinery	10.6	243
2. Miscellaneous vehicles, parts	16.9	1,619
3. Scientific equipment	10.0	443
Total savings		2,305
Grand cumulative total		22,878

1. Items 1–3 from Table 9.1; item 4 from Table 9.2. For textile machinery the flow in 1962, 1963, 1964 assumed to be equal to the flow 1963, 1964, 1965.

2. Items 1 and 2 from Table 9.3; items 3, 4, 5 derived from Table 9.4; totals for 1962, 1963, 1964 taken as the same as totals for 1963, 1964, 1965.

3. A more detailed commodity breakdown might uncover more eligible commodities.

which AID chooses not to finance the commodity. To illustrate, if there is a 25 percent limit for the India list, additionality might include drugs, alumina, and scientific and professional equipment, which grossed about $3 million annually over the three-year period. There is no way to be certain, however, that India would continue to purchase these commodities in the same amounts as in the past if they were to be taken from the list. Still, 90 percent of the alumina item, 80 percent of the drugs, and 80 percent of scientific and professional equipment was purchased by India in the U.S., presumably with its own funds. For Pakistan, similar additionality savings might be possible on a number of products where AID financed about 25 percent more or less of the total U.S. export of such commodities. Assuming Pakistan would have added this amount to its regular purchases, the total saving could have meant about $3.7 million annually over this period. In the Turkey case (Table 9.6), three items come under the 25 percent or less rule: textile machinery, miscellaneous vehicles and parts, and scientific equipment. These could conceivably have produced additionality savings of about $800,000 a year. If a 35 percent rule had been invoked below which Turkey would have had to purchase the commodity on its own, U.S. exports might have increased another $2.7 million annually. On these assumptions the grand total for the three countries would have been $7.6 million annually. The lists are indicated in Table 9.7.

As there is an implied assumption that because AID-financing of these commodities is relatively low compared to total U.S. exports of these commodities, they are competitive or preferred for a variety of reasons, there should be less concern that these countries were being forced to buy with their own resources high-cost items they otherwise would not purchase without U.S. aid. AID funds released on these items might, however, be used to purchase other U.S. high-cost items.

Where AID finances most of the export in a particular commodity (for example, chemicals to India) and where U.S. total exports of this commodity to the less-developed countries represents a small percentage of worldwide imports of the item into the less-developed countries (again, chemicals for India), this may be fairly conclusive evidence that in the absence of the AID-financing none of this commodity would be exported from the United States to the less-developed countries. The U.S. item in such cases is noncompetitive.

Other Considerations

While the implications drawn above are probably valid despite data problems, there are obviously too many instances where the data produce erroneous aggregates. These discrepancies are too important to be hidden in a footnote. Tables 9.2–4 in quite a few instances show the combined total of project and program loans exceeding the U.S. total export figure — an impossibility. While part of this in Tables 9.2 and 9.4 is due to the fact that AID-financed shipments are recorded on a payments basis and the U.S. total exports are f.o.b., the size of the indiscrepancies suggests that other factors are involved. Matching the aid flows with calendar-year exports is particularly hazardous, and much more time-consuming scrutiny of shipping documents is involved in eliminating this discrepancy.

Table 9.8: AID and SITC Codes Matched

AID Commodity Group	AID Code	SITC
Nitrogenous fertilizers	230	561.1
Pesticides and agricultural chemical specialties	236⎱	599.2
DDT, 20 percent or more	237⎰	
Medical and pharmaceutical preparations	370	541.1, 541.3–541.7, 541.9
Coal-tar products, excl. dyestuffs	390.1	521.1, 521.3
Pigments, paints, varnishes	390.3	533.1–533.3, 513.5, 513.27
Industrial chemicals N.E.S.	390.6	512.1–512.9, 513.1, 513.3, 513.4, 513.6, 599.7, 599.9
Raw materials for plastics	390.8	581.1–581.3, 581.9
Man-made fibers and yarns	540.8	651.6, 651.7
Lumber and manufactures	570	631.1, 631.2, 631.4, 631.8, 632.1, 632.2, 632.4, 632.7, 632.8, 821.0
Pulp, paper, and products	591	641.2–641.7, 641.9, 642.1–642.3, 642.9
Nonmetallic minerals and products	640	661.1–661.3 661.8, 662.3, 662.4, 663.1, 663.2, 663.4–663.9 664.1–664.3, 664.5–664.9 665.1, 665.2, 665.8, 666.4–666.6 667.1–667.4
Pig Iron	660.1	671.2, 671.3
Tinplate, terneplate, blackplate	660.8	674.7
Crude and Semi-finished steel	661.1	672.1–672.9
Bars and rods, structural shapes	661.3	673.1, 673.2, 673.4, 673.5
Plates, sheets, skelp, etc.	661.5	674.8, 675.0
Railroad track materials	670.1	676.1, 676.2
Wire and products	670.5	677.0, 693.11
Tubes, pipes, fittings	671.4	678.1, 678.2, 678.3–678.5
Aluminum	691	684.1, 684.2
Copper	692	682.1, 682.2
Generators, motors, parts	710	722.1
Electrical apparatus	720	722.2, 723.1, 723.2, 724.1, 724.2, 724.9, 725.0, 729.1–729.3, 729.6, 729.9

Engines, turbines, parts	730	711.1–711.3, 711.5–711.8
Construction, mining, and conveying equipment	740	718.4, 718.51, 719.21, 719.3
Metal-working machinery, machine tools	761	715.1, 715.2
Agriculture equipment, parts, excl. tractors	770	712.1–712.3, 712.9
Textile machinery, accessories, parts	778	717.1
Industrial machinery N.E.S.	790	714.1–714.3, 714.9, 717.2, 717.3, 718.52, 719.1, 719.22, 719,23, 719.5–719.9, 729.5
Trucks and buses	820.1 820.9	732.2, 732.3
Motor vehicles, engines, and parts	820.3 820.5	729.4, 732.8
Tractors and parts	833	712.5
Aircraft, accessories, parts	840	711.4, 734.1, 734.9, 899.98, 899.99
Railroad transportation equipment	850	731.2–731.7
Locomotives	850.2	731.2, 731.3
Vessels and equipment	858	735.3, 735.9
Rubber and products	891	621.0, 629.1, 629.3, 629.4, 629.9
Tubes, tires, repair materials	891.3	629.1
Scientific and professional instruments	880	726.1, 726.2, 861.1–861.9

Furthermore, as Table 9.8 shows, matching of AID commodity codes with the Standard International Trade Code (SITC) is a complex task and fraught with potential mismatching. Some SITC categories might have been omitted in a particular AID-code category, thus producing a U.S. commercial export figure below what it should be. On the other hand, where SITC categories should have been omitted, the AID-financed portion would have been higher than shown. Compensating errors of this kind probably reduce the discrepancies, but others of disturbing magnitude remain. The data derived from the shipping reports and Bureau of the Census seem more consistent (Tables 9.1, 9.3, 9.6) than the Market Share Reports, for reasons requiring further research. Finally, the data here exclude the effect of supporting assistance and development grant funds.

To promote a rational policy on a commodity basis, it is important to establish reliable data and firm ratios on AID-financed percentage of total U.S. exports for each commodity. For example, drugs become an additionality item in the Indian figures, but clearly not in the Pakistan figures, while the Turkey percentage is between the two. The notes to Table 9.4 reflect in detail the complex problems encountered in implementing a selective additionality policy.

Additionality as a Policy

Promoting additionality on a selective basis may, nevertheless, do relatively little harm to the less-developed countries, while providing some assistance to current U.S. balance-of-payments strains. Yet, a massive attempt to force additionality, as many others have argued, could be costly to the recipients. It could also be costly to the donors. Costs to the recipients may rise in the form of higher debt servicing as high cost maintenance inputs call for higher internal and external prices to cover costs, thereby lowering internal and external sales potential. The cost to the donor increases in terms of covering less ground with the aid dollar, thereby adding pressure for more aid to make up for the high-cost development inputs. There are also hidden costs in the inflationary effect of the added U.S. exports in the nearly fully employed U.S. economy, when resources are diverted from producing for the domestic market and in foreign-trade multiplier effects. This, in turn, raises costs in all industries, including those producing for export, thereby making U.S. exports less competitive. At the same time, other countries lose the trade we have tied, which in turn, in some cases (Europe), reduces their capacity to buy imports from the United States. U.S. consumers, too, pay higher prices for higher-cost domestic production. While it would be difficult to determine on balance what the final effects of these movements are, it is entirely possible that, when the tallies are all in, tied aid has a more negative effect on the U.S. balance of payments than untied aid would.

Overriding U.S. balance-of-payments considerations may dictate maintaining a tied-aid policy, even though it is against U.S. basic trade principles and in the long run is counter to a more soundly based U.S. balance-of-payments position. It is hoped that the new directions aid-giving is experiencing in this new decade will continue to resolve the conflicting issues implicit in U.S. policy with respect both to tied aid and additionality.

Notes

1. Since this chapter was written, the U.S. additionality policy, but not tied aid, was suspended (as of 20 June 1969), largely as a result of the heated opposition of Latin America, where it had its most irksome effect. As the United States is Latin America's largest trading partner in regular trade, it had been much more difficult to find new trade items to add to the list through a deliberate additionality technique than in India, for example, where most of the U.S. imports are aid-financed. Promotion of U.S. exports may, however, call for identification of new goods to be marketed abroad.

10

Myrdal from the Inside

A number of reviews have been written of Myrdal's three-volume *Asian Drama*. Working within an aid donor-recipient relationship for some years, both in less-developed countries and in Washington, and witnessing daily the programs and policy debates, the areas of progress and of disappointment in the process, one feels uneasy that the picture is different in many respects than depicted by Myrdal and much also is left unsaid by his reviewers. Hence, the reason for this longer appraisal.

Whether "inside" or "outside" of the aid business, readers will undoubtedly view Myrdal's assessment and prescriptions differently. Most reviewers are agreed that this work is a landmark in development literature and is therefore must reading for developers concerned with Asia. No one review can deal with all the issues raised in such a (2,200-page) monument of words. The issues dealt with here, therefore, cover selective ground, largely on economic rather than political aspects of the *Drama,* and reveal some of the flavor and problem areas as seen by one involved in administering and planning aid programs. For reasons of space, numerous sections deserving high praise have not received attention. The volumes should be read and the appendices studied; and that compliment, con-

*Reprinted from the *Indian Economic Journal* 17, no. 1, (July-September 1969).

sidering the length of this work, should balance any critical comments made in this assessment.

An "insider's" opposing reactions to Myrdal, which went undetected by other reviewers, might well be summarized at the outset as follows:

1. Contrary to Myrdal's low opinion of Western approaches to less-developed countries, these approaches have provided the catalysts to whatever development has been achieved — catalysts forthcoming from no other source.

2. The contributions of other disciplines which Myrdal deems essential, as do all of us in the business, have been too unstructured to have made adequate operational impact on programs and policies in the less-developed countries.

3. Political ideologies or systems need not, as Myrdal contends, determine or decisively constrain economic gains in particular sectors or policies, even when such environments are not ideal from Western points of view.

4. The quality of statistics or national income analysis, and even of models, is far less germane to development strategy, policy thrusts or institutional change than Myrdal argues.

5. Recent vital accomplishments in the area of policies and reoriented country plans and programs constitute institutional changes of significance not dealt with or acknowledged by Myrdal.

6. Economic incentives and individual- and private-sector motivations play a larger role than Myrdal has credited to them.

7. The agricultural revolution in Asia is evidence of a far more dynamic and hopeful sector than the subsistence-custom-village-bound farm community Myrdal describes.

8. Myrdal's view that education is one of the most serious drags on development has long been widely accepted, but that innovative breakthrough essential to meet the mass need has been lacking.

The strongest theme throughout the three volumes is that institution-changing and manpower galvanizing ("Investment in Man") are the neglected elements in Western approaches. The suggestion is not remote from real aid-donor concerns. For example, the AID mission in Pakistan reports that "our AID program should increase its emphasis in the general area of human resource development," but is not clear how to go about it. The chief of Pakistan's Water and Power Development Authority cites as his most critical problem "(a) the lack of trained personnel at all levels, and (b) the need for reorganization and decentralization to improve administration." The East Pakistan Industrial Development Corporation complains of "inadequate management" in promoting private-sector investment. Another report says that "Nepal's greatest, single lack is trained manpower" and that "the Government of Nepal's goodwill towards development has been sometimes frustrated by its own administrative ineptness." Similar references abound in reports from other AID Asian missions.

With all this, Myrdal's criticisms of Western approaches seem overplayed and suffer from an absence of familiarity and relevance to actual policies, programs and practices promulgated by Western aid donors, particularly in the last several years. What is stimulating about these volumes despite the overstatements is that there is grist for everyone's thinking, whether agreeing or not, including and especially for activists in aid missions around the world who could benefit from the accumulated wisdom and detail. What follows is an inside reaction to Myrdal's treatment of these and other issues which are of relevance to many aid donors.

Western Economists and the Development Process

Economists have preempted the field of development since World War II, Myrdal complains, and their approaches have been wrong. Myrdal has long espoused the economist's cause. One thinks of Wilde: "Each man kills the thing he loves, by each let this be heard." He makes a plea for approaching economic development more as an interdisciplinary effort than an economic problem or one of any particular discipline. This line of argument culminates in the statement, "Rarely, if ever, has the development of economics by its own force blazed the way to new perspectives."

Even if true, the statement is not very helpful. It is undoubtedly true that rarely has any one force blazed the way; it has always taken a combination of circumstances and thought processes and approaches which often combine several fields. On the other hand, the case could be made that it is simply not true. Many of the new perspectives that have been generated, expounded, or projected into practice in the last twenty years were basically economic in concept. The capital-output ratio as an alternative, if imperfect, parameter for estimating capital input requirements; the dynamic role of capital and technological change; the experiment with planning; the role of the market in marshaling incentives; the catalytic agents inherent in the concepts of absorptive capacity, spread effects, unbalanced growth, underemployed labor, utilization of capacity, liberalization of trade, decontrol of price and trade practices; the agricultural revolution in incentives and inputs — all these reverberate within an economic context and have surely offered new insights into the development process.

Meanwhile, concepts in political science, anthropology, sociology, and the other disciplines seem to have offered less by comparison of an effective operational nature over this period. There have been books in these areas, but they have not helped to provide pragmatic programs or policy directions. This has been so not because the economists did not read or would not listen, but because of the difficulty of translating analyses or treatises emanating from those fields into meaningful lines of action.

Myrdal thinks that the economist develops his arguments, theories, and recommendations for change out of the surrounding political stimuli. Smith, Malthus, Ricardo, Marshall, Marx, Keynes — all were aware of their political environment, Myrdal argues, and based their prescriptions for action out of and within the framework of those environments. Yet, there are variations. India has chosen a democratic system with strongly socialistic preferences in its rhetoric and its planning. Given this framework over a twenty-year period, it has nevertheless been largely in economic rather than in political relationships that change in India has been wrought. The political framework has not changed much, but the economic scene and economic policy approaches have varied considerably.

Myrdal sees the Western economists as victims of their own prejudices and environments. He thinks the theories they have applied to less-developed countries are based on Western theories and training; and this cannot be done without distorting the whole development process from its natural channels. He is also highly critical of the aggregate national income data and concepts that Western economists apply to the less-developed countries. These make sense in the Western world, he would argue, but not in the less-developed countries where statistics are too poor to be regarded seriously. He is highly critical of all the attempts Western economists have made to develop models using what he would regard as almost totally spurious data sources and compilations. He argues that Western economic prescriptions for development in Asia cannot work because the institutional framework is so radically different, and these institutions do not change in response to economic models or mechanical policies.

The economist would reply that his task is to observe, record, and analyze the facts for meaningful relationships and indications of trends and policy implications. Whether this is done by Indian or Western economists is largely a matter of the competence required to do the job effectively. To argue that it should not be done or that data thus gathered should not be used as benchmarks by which to measure change seems unreasonable and wrong. If criticism is to be made of Western economists, it should be made on the basis of the inherent correctness or effectiveness of policies they recommend or urge upon the indigenous governments, given the limitations of what facts can be gathered. When World Bank and other economists favored Indian devaluation in June 1966, was this a correct economic policy or not? Is it correct to attempt a freeing up of Indian markets by reducing price and other administrative controls and establishing financial incentives to stimulate economic activity? Do such recommendations stimulate the economy or do they not? Are the fiscal, monetary, and trade liberalization policies that Western economists recommend the right ones for the respective countries or are they not? Whether such recommendations come from Western, indigenous, or any other economists would seem to be irrelevant.

Myrdal's complaint that Western economists are too optimistic and therefore unscientific in dealing with the growth prospects of the underdeveloped countries is oddly querulous. He offers no scientific or scholarly support for these allegations nor substitute means or methods for obtaining better statistics or guidelines. There is a great deal of rather pompous assertion in many portions of these volumes which is largely unencumbered by scientific proof of any kind. What we do often get in return is an undertone of Swedish pessimism ambivalently corrected from time to time with hopeful prophecies and the mollifying condescension that "we make no claim to infallibility in the substantive content of our generalizations." However (and other reviewers of these volumes have missed the glimmers of hope), the gloom and determinism does occasionally fade, and Myrdal will bring himself to say that "history is not taken to be determined but within the power of man to shape it. And the drama thus conceived is not necessarily tragic."

There is a significant unawareness in these volumes of many of the institutional changes and policy directions which have been promoted in recent years in some of the Asian countries. The whole current approach to agricultural development in the Asian countries constitutes an institutional breakthrough. The shift in the Planning Commission in India away from heavy industry-oriented development toward priority emphasis on agriculture is an institutional change. Changes calling for more emphasis on private-sector development, improving incentives by allowing prices to rise, or offering support prices for farm commodities, as distinct from the previous practice of administered pricing for the consumer's sake, constitute revisions in the institutional framework. India, Pakistan, and other Asian countries have drastically reversed traditional attitudes and even codes and laws to promote widespread family-planning programs.

Myrdal's ambivalence is even more pronounced when, despite his very lengthy lecture on the damage done by the economic biases in Western approaches, he concludes by characterizing these volumes as "essentially a study of major economic problems in South Asia." In fact, his chapters on political, cultural, and other influences classify this as an interdisciplinary work. He also adds in a significant afterthought "that the work lacks historical depth due to practical limitations of time, research facilities and technical competence," a rationalization he chose not to concede Western economists seeking facts who suffered similar constraints.

The Value Premises Chosen

Myrdal elaborates at length on the difficulties involved in determining what value systems or premises prevail in the Asian milieu, how strongly felt they are, and then he establishes a value system by which he judges the effectiveness of approaches to Asian development. The value system is summarized in his "modernization ideals," which he believes essential for achieving economic progress. Briefly summarized these include rationality as distinct from superstition, class, or tradition; development and planning for development; rising productivity and level of living; social and economic equalization; improved institutions and attitudes (efficiency, diligence, orderliness, punctuality, frugality, honesty, self-reliance, rationality, and decisiveness); national system of government, courts, administration; national independence; political democracy, nationally and at the grass roots; and social discipline.

An underlying weakness in all Asian life, he contends, is a general reluctance to enforce obligations on people. Compulsion is rejected in all walks of life, and this he regards as a real deterrent to the whole development process. Unless and until these modernization ideals are widely accepted in the Asian countries, the march of progress will be slowed. Myrdal argues, too, that only by using indigenous language in all of the planning documents prepared with foreign technical help will development succeed.

As with many other criticisms about western approaches to Asian development, there is some mistaking of the superficial for the substance. As with statistics, language is perhaps less a vital matter than the quality of the ideas, the correctness of the assessment of what is needed, and the sensibility of the methods for meeting targets set by a good plan, given the data limitations. Knowledge of and expressions in the local language are to be preferred but are not always essential to promulgating good plans or policies. If these work, the results will have far greater influence than compulsory edicts or wider dissemination of what the plans or policies are.

Religion and Progress

The criticism against some of the cultural or religious inhibitions which thwart the implementation of development techniques is justified. In Myrdal's words "by characterizing popular religion as a force of inertia and irrationality that sanctifies the whole system of life and work, attitudes and institutions, we are in fact stressing an important aspect of underdevelopment, namely, the resistance of that system to planned or induced changes along the lines of the modernization ideals." The question of significance is perhaps whether religion is always antithetical to development. It will always be a force to contend with; our job is to devise approaches that accommodate the religious mores while optimizing the forces of progress. Is it possible to deal with a religious framework and at the same time make a dynamic contribution to development? Perhaps part of our problem is in defining "development." If the United States is regarded as the most developed (affluent) society in the world but is fraught with negative human forces and conflict, what constructive force can be introduced to prevent advancing societies from winding up with this social schizophrenia? Myrdal provides few clues.

Religious taboos undoubtedly interfere with Indian development in a number of ways, but Myrdal suggests that there is ample room for constructive approaches where religion need not conflict or hamper progress. He elaborates numerous influences of religious beliefs in southern Asia which contribute to his modernization ideals. This would be an area for other than the economist to explore. In passing, it may be said that Western development planners work in many areas to help the development process without focusing on religious obstacles. By producing competent and relevant planning in India, for example, and by devising effective economic policies to be pursued by the government — monetary and fiscal reforms, decontrol of price and other administrative bottlenecks, the consolidation of food zones, the wide range of pragmatic problems to be addressed in technical assistance — in all these areas the development planner can work to achieve significant improvement without necessarily having to insist upon abandonment of long-standing religious affiliations. Myrdal does argue subsequently that poverty generates stultifying attitudes more significantly than does religion.

Western Input and Time

On numerous occasions he argues that "people in this region are not inherently different from people elsewhere." Indian commercial talents are to be found competing successfully in many parts of the world in testimony to this fact. Then, as one makes his way through the flood of ideas, a peculiar inconsistency seems to emerge: Myrdal recognizes that the modernization ideals came from the Western influence through education and colonialism, yet he regards the Western approaches as being out of touch with the Asian environment. Western approaches could be improved, but from all that is developed following what may be legitimate criticisms, the thought lingers that in fact Western ideas have provided the catalysts of change and progress in Asia. Myrdal overlooks the fact that the most vital characteristic of the Western approach is its drive for innovational change and vigorous and efficient competitive enterprise, and that is what he would insist Asia needs.

Part of the difficulty in drawing clear lines is that Asia's problems result partly from the telescoping of events in a short time span — events which took several hundred years to evolve in Europe. The result is confusion, chaotic dovetailing and interaction of changes which keep the assimilation process in turmoil. Myrdal makes a good case that technological change and modernization cannot take place in the underdeveloped countries in the same gradual manner in which they evolved in the advanced countries. Such change, he asserts, is largely induced as a shock from outside and the nature of the population and resource relationships today, especially as the cultural lags have a drag effect, is such that change must be brought about far more rapidly and, therefore, with more stress and upheaval. Introducing more-rapid change while maintaining proper social and political balance is the hat trick for the economic planner of today.

Economic Realities

Population and Progress

Myrdal sounds the usual alarms about world population growth, but balances it with other insights and relationships typically overlooked these days. He points out that the population density of all of southern Asia is roughly that of Europe, excluding the Soviet Union, but is four times that of the United States. Nevertheless, he stresses that "the first thing to note is that contrary to what is often assumed, the man/land ratio in South Asia is not strikingly high in comparison with that in other parts of the world." It is even less repeated that the share of forests exceeds 60 percent in most of Southeast Asia, although it is less than 30 percent in India; much of Ceylon is still under jungle coverage. Quoting Myrdal, "the outer islands of Indonesia have hardly begun to be opened up and in Burma, Thailand and Malaya, not to mention Laos, there are vast stretches of cultivable, but uncultivated land." He points out that one-third of the population in India is concentrated on 6 percent of the land and that "vast areas continue to be almost uninhabited." He adds the point that in some regions where irrigation has not progressed, vast areas are not productive during the drought years, which means that irrigation could increase output as it fills in the troughs caused by drought-year devastation. In this sense irrigation could create new land over time. There is nowhere an assessment of alternative costs in these investments.

There is little evidence, Myrdal says, in quoting Benjamin Higgins, that the level of technology in Asia was markedly below that of Europe in the sixteenth century — in transportation, modes of manufacture, and agriculture. Even up to the eighteenth century, Indian goods could compete in world markets. What happened between then and modern times? He believes it was the rigid social stratification and the lack of rationalization that held such southern Asian countries back while Europe had its industrial revolution and shot ahead. As a consequence, economic incentive became submerged and inhibited beneath a heavy overlay of custom and noneconomic values.

There is a contradictory note to these developmental drawbacks in the behavior of Indian farmers who have shifted for economic reasons to growing nonfood crops because of the higher value yields. The shift simply reflects their responsiveness to price incentives. The cultural drag notwithstanding. Myrdal might have made more of the fact that modernization ideals have a way of getting through to businessmen anywhere when the price is right and net economic gain is at the end of the road.

National Output and Structure of the Economy

Myrdal makes the case that income per capita figures are inadequate measures of welfare because of remittances in payment of non-resident foreign factors. These constitute a leakage which is not taken into account in the statistics because unavailable. This is less so for India than places like Malaya where foreign-owned plantations predominate. Here again Myrdal overplays the role of statistics in the development process. Such figures are but references in planning and have little to do with the substantive issues and programs devised to promote economic development. Planners use national account figures and rates of change as guides but not as substitutes for basic programs and policies which constitute the operational foundations for real change.

Labor Utilization

Myrdal complains that Western concepts of unemployment and underemployment are totally unadaptable to southern Asia, where intentional idleness, intermittent work, and labor inefficiency are endemic. The potential labor force, therefore, is much greater than Western underemployment concepts would have it. Assuming that it is, the capacity for growth may be greater than we thought, but we derive little use from the assertion; the task is just somewhat bigger than we thought.

Moreover, "the bulk of South Asia's indigenous agriculturalists have only peripheral contact with the market economy": the primary objective of agriculture in southern Asia is meeting subsistence requirements rather than selling crops to make a profit. He also claims that it is demands inherent in tenant payment rates to landowners and moneylenders rather than prices which set the amounts of crops made available for the markets. Were it not for what share-croppers owed to owners and moneylenders, only half of the produce would reach the market because more would be consumed on the farms. The farmers themselves are concerned only about subsistence or better subsistence. In other words, it is the moneylender and landowner who turned over crops to market, not the farmer themselves. However, the landowners are not interested in expanding outputs for trade activity too remote from their own immediate needs and practices. All of this underplays recent trends in the growing significance of the rural sector in absorbing labor and in the market as a source of income for eager kulaks.

Myrdal stresses again and again the reluctance of the well educated to do any kind of manual or less than white-collar or government work. They will not go to the rural areas to teach, work, or help in other ways to develop the masses. As a consequence, there are a rising number of unemployed also among the educated, for the government cannot absorb all of them, and the content of education does not suit them for opportunities in industry.

Investment in Man

This section of the book echoes a common line of argument to which foreign-aid donors should give critical attention because it is so prevalent. According to Myrdal, "while most of the planning in the other underdeveloped regions and most of the economic literature on development continues to be based on the notion that physical investment is the engine of development, there are today an increasing number of economists who denounce that view and who regard development particularly in underdeveloped countries as primarily an education process." This theme is reiterated by others, and it is important enough in terms of the emphasis on foreign aid to quote other supporters of this view in the Myrdal volume.

According to Harry Gideonse, for example,

> much of the past discussion of economic growth — in developed as well as in underdeveloped countries — appears to be as obsolete as the abandoned and useful furniture in the attic of an old family homestead. Clearly a new concept of "capital" — and a new political economy — is in the process of formulation since the old concepts, which were limited to tangible property are now manifestly inadequate. The main shift in the present development is characterized by the tendency to think of the cause of economic growth as the capacity to create wealth rather than the creation of wealth itself. The direction of the change in thought is suggested by the question: Can we formulate a theory of human capital which accounts for economic growth in terms of changes in the quality of human beings? . . . . orthodox economic and fiscal opinion continues to ignore the drift of current development and the significance to public policy of the new insight which is emerging. We continue to build models of economic growth on strictly materialist assumptions which overlook the role of capital investment in human beings in our own experience. We disregard the role of the development of human skills and trained imagination in our achievements by presenting a picture of exclusive preoccupation with physical and material achievement.[1]

The same theme is stressed by Ted Schultz:

> When poor countries enter upon the process of developing a modern agriculture and industry, with some notable exceptions, they invest too little in human capital relative to what they invest in non-human capital; skills and knowledge useful in their economic endeavor are neglected as they concentrate on new plants and equipment. Thus, an imbalance arises and as a consequence they fail often by a wide margin to attain their optimum rate of economic growth.[2]

Other educationalists in development such as Frederick Harbison and Charles Myers give heavy emphasis to this view.[3] Myrdal quotes numerous others in support of this theme.

In another context related to Europe, the same theme is at the heart of Servan-Schreiber's book *The American Challenge* (one of

Europe's big sellers since World War II) in which he asserts that it is the quality of American education in its teaching of innovative and flexible thought processes with respect to industrial and commercial enterprise which results in a high degree of managerial skill and adaptability. Such education has helped American industry to make massive inroads into European markets. According to Servan-Schreiber, "wealth and power are no longer measures in material terms. They are not gifts of nature or chance like oil or gold or even population. Rather they are victories won by the human spirit: the ability to transform an idea into a reality through the industrial process; the talent for coordinating skills making rigid organizations susceptible to change." And, according to this source, "education is the driving force behind technological innovation. If Europe really wants to close the technological gap, it has to improve its education, both general and special, and both quantitatively and qualitatively. There is just no other way to get to the fundamental root of the problem." If true of Europe — the thought is inescapable — what of Asia? The theme is repeated many times: "Modern power is based on the capacity for innovation, which is research, and the capacity to transform inventions into finished products which is technology," and "the training, development, and exploitation of human intelligence — these are the real resources, and there are no others," and "the new frontiers of human creativity in every area lie in information systems and their utilization."[4] Harvey Leibenstein made similar arguments in the *American Economic Review* when he stressed that management and organizational improvements have much greater impact on development than they are given credit for.[5]

Myrdal gives great stress to this role of education as a key to economic progress in the underdeveloped countries, as it has been in the Western world and in Japan. He believes Western model builders and planners have neglected this approach. On the other hand, it is clear that Myrdal overlooks, or at least does not treat adequately, the large educational budgets in the less-developed countries. Foreign planners have assumed indigenous educational efforts while financing specific categories of education (agricultural, vocational, or teacher training, centers of excellence, curriculum revision) and concentrating more aid on other aspects of development which Western aid donors have felt long neglected. The investment of the less-developed countries in education has been substantial; whether it is enough, whether the foreign input should focus more on education, and whether it is the right kind of education seems to be more in question.

Myrdal may exaggerate the omissions of Western approaches in the area of manpower development, but he raises a question as to what degree of emphasis should be placed in this area. Is it possible to determine the lag effects of current inadequacies? As Myrdal indicates, promoting education will call for fairly significant institutional reforms of a legislative-administrative kind if the task is to be accomplished.

Irrespective of Western approaches to this problem, Myrdal devotes several hundred pages to describing what he regards as the inadequacies of the quantity and quality of education in the underdeveloped countries. Other points he makes are as follows:

1. Literacy levels in all Asian countries, he believes, are greatly exaggerated. He regards illiteracy as a critical problem which has been neglected.

2. Adult education should be undertaken on a grand scale, as lack of it is the chief deterrent to education at lower ages and grades. He believes that adult education could have an immediate impact on development, whereas an increase in primary school enrollment could have only a delayed effect. The detrimental effects of an illiterate home and village setting on the young and the consequent lag effect on the whole development process is profound. While countries may have a good performance record on enrollment in primary schools (at least on the books), enforcement of attendance, quality of education, orientation toward traditional subjects instead of toward the modernization ideals, lack of discipline, learning by rote and recitation, language confusion and multiplicity, poor teachers, lax attitudes — all these militate against economic development.

3. Myrdal quotes Article 29 of the Universal Declaration of Human Rights, which says, "Every one has the right to education. Education shall be free, at least in the elementary and fundamental stages. Elementary education shall be compulsory. Technical and professional education shall be made generally available and higher education shall be equally accessible to all on the basis of merit." He believes this to be very far from being applied in India and elsewhere in Asia. He also ties all of these inadequacies to the low priority given to the fields of both health and education as a result of the "overriding importance of physical investment" in the planning approaches, particularly in the Western concepts and models for development. The result is a lack of proper emphasis in all kinds of institutional building and formation of the most effective attitudes contributing to progress.

4. The result of such inadequacies is a severe shortage of capable people in every walk of life. The lack of emphasis in Western nations on promoting good health or its important impact on

raising the productivity of man and his income is all part of our misconceptions, he claims, of what is needed in Asia.

5. The social taboo against manual labor must be broken down and built into the regular education system.

6. Something must be done about increasing education at the upper levels. The educational pyramid — the sharp tapering off of the education at the upper ages — must be corrected. Weaknesses in university education — rote learning, exam cramming, poor teaching, unscientific orientation, and the low aspiration level of the students (desire only for a secure government job) must be corrected. In summarizing the deficiencies in Indian education, he quotes the world confederation of organizations of the teaching profession: Poorly trained, poorly paid, and overworked teachers; overcrowded classes with a shortened school day; a very thin curriculum that does not cover even the bare essentials of primary education; makeshift classrooms and school buildings; textbooks that are far from attractive and even those available only in insufficient quantities; and essential teacher aids that may be entirely absent in the classroom — this is education in its most diluted form, which in some cases may almost be as bad as no education at all. In summary, he believes that all that has happened in the expansion of education in Asia since economic development planning got underway has been a simple expansion of an archaic system — nothing more.

The criticism of Western model builders is equally vehement on their neglect of the health factor in development, especially malnutrition, diseases, and debilitation resulting from inadequate care. He points to the severe shortage of nurses and of doctors caused again in part by the fact that service of this kind has not been fully accepted by Hindus. He regards a shortage of people — particularly nurses and midwives in Asia, considering the abundance of people — as a little short of fantastic.

Throughout all of these chapters, Myrdal blames Western economists and planners for their grossly exaggerated figures and ratios showing advancement in educationd and health, where he thinks progress has in fact been virtually nil. The continuing duplication of archaic attitudes, methods, and training systems is no substitute for reform of the whole manpower training process.

There is ample opportunity in these areas for indigenous governments and aid donors to reexamine their approaches and attitudes, in terms of assessing effective inputs to create a more dynamic system of education for change. This is an appropriate time for renewed emphasis in this area as foreign-aid levels decline, as self-reliance is more widely sought as a matter of pride, and as domestic resources rather than foreign exchange constitute the major source of support for educational development.

Notes

1. "Economic Growth and Educational Development," quoted by Myrdal from *College and University,* Summer 1963.

2. "Investment in Human Capital in Poor Countries," Myrdal quoting from *Foreign Trade and Human Capital,* pp. 14 and 15.

3. *Education, Manpower and Economic Growth* (New York: McGraw Hill, 1964).

4. Series of quotes from J. J. Servan-Schreiber, *The American Challenge* (New York: Atheneum, 1968), pp. 45, 46, 81, 83, 276, 277.

5. "Allocative Efficiency Versus X-Efficiency," June 1966. Other labor-force, entrepreneurial, management, and technological training aspects are treated in R. Ward, "The Challenge in Developing Human Resources," *The Challenge of Development,* Ward, ed. (Chicago: Aldine, 1967).

Part 3
Planning Programs and Strategies

11 The Pragmatics of Big-Push Development

The Dilemma

Chapter 8 dealt with the disappointment currently felt toward the developing countries, while indicating that it was, in important respects, unfounded. The question which remains for the 1970's to resolve: How much speed may a development program anticipate in attempting to achieve its stated targets? Granted the impelling humanitarian and perhaps political need to aid the poorer nations, how rapidly do these countries have a right to expect their living standards to increase? Development enthusiasts have argued that the urgent need for uplifting the poorer nations demands bold, massive programs which must be carried out as expeditiously as possible. Achievement of the high growth rates thus implied also calls for high levels of investment. While expounding the bold view, have we considered sufficiently the practical obstacles encountered when investment levels increase sharply? Can this decade, in fact, force the development process toward more-rapid growth than in the past?

Four points are our concern in this chapter: (1) to restate the urgent need, humanitarian and otherwise, for carrying on the world-wide economic-development campaign; (2) to point out the practical problems which stand in the way of demands for too rapid a pace for progress and growth in the underdeveloped countries;[1] (3) to examine the role of public versus private enterprise in development programs; and (4), to draw useful conclusions and to uncover areas for research from the discussion.

Out of the numerous theories of economic development and the voluminous literature on the subject,[2] there are two ideas most commonly expounded from which certain problems emerge. One is that the underdeveloped countries are still caught in the conventional "vicious circle."[3] The other is that only a big push — a massive investment effort — can produce the takeoff toward self-sustaining growth. It is extremely difficult to initiate real progress in countries like India, Indonesia, or other densely populated areas, where, as soon as some material gains are made, population growth rapidly offsets the advantages of economic progress. The first impact of economic development often brings sanitation and modern medical practices to poverty-ridden areas. The result is an immediate and precipitous drop in the death rate. At the same time, a small measure of improved material welfare is sufficient to induce the family to increase its size. The combination of these two results outweighs the material progress brought on by a conscious development program. Thus, the rate of economic progress induced must be greater in the long run than the enhanced rate of population growth which results.

This situation raises a real question as to the adequacy of private capital flows, under any conceivable present or future circumstances, to effect the necessary rate of technological growth. It is doubtful that individual initiative, profit motivation, and drive for gain are sufficient by themselves, in Asia and Africa, to provide accelerated development of these areas. At the same time, the population explosion means that progress cannot await the gradual evolution of these "capitalistic" motivations. It follows from this hypothesis that economic development of the underdeveloped areas must be positively encouraged by national governments.[4]

In support of these views, one need only point to Japan, India, or Turkey, where historically economic development was given major emphasis through government encouragement. This is not to minimize the role of private foreign capital in the programs, such as those encouraged so effectively by the Export-Import Bank, the Bank for Reconstruction and Development (through the International-Finance Corporation), the investment guarantee programs of AID and other agencies. These devices for channeling private investment need to be greatly strengthened. Nevertheless, there is a certain paradox here: the Western powers are the leading private-enterprise economies in the world and seek to promote the private sector elsewhere. Yet, the patterns of economic development in many of the countries indicate considerable concentration of industrial output in public enterprises. Foreign-aid programs of recent years have stressed increased market-oriented decision-making, liberalization of trade, and decontrols to give private enterprise a freer hand to compete. Nevertheless, the governments of many underdeveloped countries are reluctant to abandon their ideological attachment to government direction of economic activity. State enterprises are common and their inefficiencies are protected by high tariff walls. Favored industries in the private sector are also protected by government regulations and access to licenses for imports and budgetary appropriations.

The reasons for this socialistic bias are not complex. Most economically backward countries need basic economic and social development before private enterprise can get started at all. Power stations, roads, railroads, communications systems, water facilities — all these must be provided to create the kind of atmosphere in which private enterprise best functions. Yet the creation of these basic utilities is not in itself a profitable venture. Lack of industry, urbanization, and mechanized travel and other inadequacies suggest insufficient aggregate demands to make public utilities of this kind profitable in many areas within developing countries. It follows that the initial impetus to development tends to come through government sponsorship. The difficulty, however, is that both the governments and peoples involved in development get used to centrally planned projects, government influence perpetuates them, and it becomes difficult to supplant this pattern when mining, manufacturing, or other industrial enterprises are initiated. There is also a lingering distrust of the private capitalist, a carryover of the colonial age. India has only recently initiated a new wave of nationalizations, including some of the private banks.

Given the humanitarian need, and indeed the economic need, for dynamic development programs, what is the cure for these two dilemmas: the vicious circle of low income, low investment, poverty, on the one hand, and, on the other, the incipient tendency to socialist or statist operations in less-developed countries striving to break out of the trap? The most frequently stated solution to the vicious-circle syndrome is that economic development programs must be extensive enough to produce takeoff. The rate of technological growth must be sufficient to generate a gross product growth sufficient to regenerate an adequate investment level to sustain the growth pattern.

Bold and imaginative solutions assume that domestic savings can be increased with vigorous domestic policies and that extensive foreign aid can provide the marginal input and catalyst to more-rapid growth. Instead of the approximately $1 billion of aid to India from Western and international donors, a big push might assure a $2 billion input, made up of program loans (to purchase imports of spare parts, equipment, and raw material for industry), project loans to build power units and other infrastructures or plants, and technical assistance in the form of training for Indians abroad or supporting Western technical advisors in India. The question arises; what are the difficulties involved in such a massive effort?

The Deterrents in Takeoff

The difficulties of an overambitious development program, however sympathetic one feels toward an extensive and dynamic approach, have become well known in the post–World War II world. It will clarify the issues to deal with them separately.

Imports

A dynamic increase in foreign-exchange availability suggests a large expansion in imports. An undeveloped economy without the industrial capacity to provide its own development equipment and know-how must import from the industrially advanced nations. Therefore, a sharp increase in investment from domestic resources will generate a need for more imports. From the very beginning, therefore, a development program poses a serious foreign-exchange problem for the undeveloped country. A sharp increase in foreign aid should help solve this problem, but experience has shown that absorptive capacity is also a constraint, so that a rapid increase in foreign-exchange availability tends to produce pipelines of unused assistance. Moreover, a flood of imports made available at low terms artificially underprices the cost of capital to the disadvantage of domestic production. Thus, a big push financed internally would generate import demand, which requires foreign exchange, either from export earning or foreign aid, while a big push financed from foreign aid can hamper internal production, promote excess industrial capacity as well as low-cost capital intensiveness artificially, and add to longer-range debt-service problems on the greatly increased loans, even if on low terms. Chapter 7 dealt with the seriousness of the debt-service issue for many developing countries.

Grants are still to be preferred over loans, as they will lessen the strain on foreign exchange over loans requiring hard-currency re-payment. Nevertheless, in either case the internal activity these external sources of funds generate will stimulate a high propensity to import as new programs and projects call for more equipment and parts.

Food Grants

Large-scale shipments of grains should relieve some countries by releasing the foreign exchange normally allocated to food imports. Yet, large-scale shipments of food-grains to Southeast Asia, for example, were severely criticized by local leaders because they upset the regional trading pattern. When India received $200–$400 millions worth of wheat from the United States, it would not buy as much rice from Burma or Thailand. Even domestic rice or wheat producers were adversely affected by the lower prices, since the imports relieved the pressure on prices in the domestic market. The incentive of farmers to buy fertilizers, new seed varieties, or pesticides were blunted by the low prices of their crops, produced by import of large volumes of wheat. Theodore Schulte of the University of Chicago has been particularly vehement in his criticism of U.S. Pl 480 policies.[5]

Domestic Inflation

Assuming U.S. grants of whatever equipment and know-how the undeveloped country needs, specific projects — whether a power station, a factory, a mining facility, or any other basic development — demand local labor and secondary needs, such as local food, housing, transportation, and supplies. Payment for much of this equipment and for the local labor would be in the national currency. The national government or those responsible for the development projects must provide this currency. The result of these substantial outlays is often inflationary. Turkey is a case in point, as it has in recent years experienced the benefits, the stresses, and the distortions of an overly ambitious development program. The impact of extensive development programs, promulgated in an atmosphere of impatient haste — and even when financed by foreign grants — almost inevitably generates serious inflationary pressures in the undeveloped country. Domestic stabilization programs in these countries in recent years have helped to avert serious distortions, but central banking has not always been constrained.

Thus, a measure indulged in by undeveloped countries launched on bold and imaginative programs has been simply to create credit to finance investment. This policy is often forced upon political leaders by the difficulties of raising domestic taxes on an already impoverished people. It is easier to utilize the central bank for credit releases than to tell local political leaders that taxes are going to be raised. The taxes, in any case, could not be sufficient to finance an ambitious investment program. Liberalizing the money supply, however accomplished, obviously cannot make a development program easier for the backward country; it can only accelerate the inflationary spiral, resulting in further strictures on its export trade, not to mention the worsening or distortion of real incomes at home. Ambitious investment programs will continue to face supply lags in less-developed countries unless new ways are found in this decade to enlarge absorptive capacity.

Increased Exports

Another feature of a bold, new development program would be to expand the exports of the undeveloped country as much as possible. This would enable the country to purchase more of the goods it needs for its expansion program. Here, the difficulty is evident in part from the consequent inflation. As a result of the inflation in the underdeveloped country, internal costs rise and higher-priced exports cannot be sold in competitive world markets. Consequently, export earnings tend to decline just when the need for imports is rapidly increasing, a situation aggravating the foreign-exchange difficulties. Grants from foreign countries can at best be only a temporary fill-in to a development program. Once the development program gains momentum, however, the need for imports increases, while the feasibility of increased exports to pay for them diminishes in the face of inflationary prices of the undeveloped country's goods.

Devaluations should be able to remedy the problem, but these are difficult to promote. Governments on occasion fall as a result of untimely or unpopular devaluations. Yet, these are often the key long-term solution. At the same time, export promotion of goods from less-developed countries to the developed world gets snagged on trade restrictions which prohibit many markets to exporters from other countries.

Spreading Prosperity

It is sometimes contended that once an expansive development program is launched, with new factories and extractive industries in operation, the local prosperity it engenders spreads through the country and eventually brings about a more-or-less balanced economy. While there is some obvious truth to this claim, nearly all manufactured products and many agricultural ones are sold in highly competitive world markets. This means that the industries that are encouraged in the underdeveloped countries must be as efficient as those in the advanced countries if the newly developed country expects to develop the export trade upon which it depends for a rising standard of living. World prices of many products fluctuate considerably, a fact which makes dependence on them for a substantial portion of the national income an unsettling factor in development programs.

In any case, a spreading prosperity, however desirable for the developing country, adds to the inflationary tendencies by providing rapidly rising incomes for the domestic population unmatched by rapidly rising production of the kind of goods the local population wishes to buy. Supply rigidities are everywhere. Some dualistic economies manage with their few export lines, which finance the needs of the isolated sector only. These neglect potential economic import substitution for the remainder of the economy.

Another aspect of the balanced-economy problem is that often specific projects are undertaken which when completed cannot be supported by the rest of the economy. For example, with the use of U.S. funds and technical assistance, Afghanistan engaged in developing power facilities. Once constructed, however, the market for the project's output was not sufficient to pay for its upkeep. Nor was the country sufficiently provided with native technicians to maintain and promote the use of the project. When the United States had completed its contract obligations, it was up to the Afghan government to maintain the facility. As it turned out, the expenses of upkeep were too much for the Afghan economy to meet through taxes; relations with the United States, as a result, became strained over the matter. Thus, development projects do not themselves promote a general prosperity; they may provide the basis for it, but achieving balanced growth is a serious practical problem, aggravated by inflation, equipment shortages, balance-of-payments distortions, and institutional and cultural or motivational obstacles. Total planning is thus a vital requirement, but rigidities prevent headlong progress in all sectors. New approaches will need to be developed in this and in coming decades to overcome these bottlenecks.

Devaluation

Another device for alleviating the impact of inflation on exports is a devaluation of the domestic currency; this improves the terms of trade for countries trading with the undeveloped country, and export earnings usually increase as a result. However, devaluation may not get at the root of the problem but merely buy time. With a trend of rapidly rising prices, caused by a combination of the factors already examined, devaluation in a rapidly developing country tends to merge into the general inflation. In other words, domestic prices continue to rise until the advantage of devaluation — lower export prices — is lost.

Devaluations are also occasionally offset by counteractions by governments unwilling to accept the opposition of particular groups in their societies. When India devalued in June 1966, the advantages to exports were to some extent offset by export taxes, while prices on imports were kept from rising by special advantages to importers. Thus, a favorable impact on Indian exports resulting from the 1966 devaluation took several years to manifest itself (due in part to two successive years of drought, by which time the extent of the devaluation effect became difficult to identify). At the same time, in cases where high protective tariffs protect inefficient domestic industries, devaluations can only scratch the surface until the government of the devaluing underdeveloped country is willing to reduce the protection and expose its industries to competitively induced technological inefficiencies. Besides all this, devaluations are difficult to promote politically, because they hurt certain groups (importers, depositors) more than others. They are thus often postponed beyond their effective date and are inadequate when they do occur. More systematic devaluation procedures need to be developed in this decade.

Domestic Stability

In order to carry on a continuing development program in a backward country, there must be stability of the government and the monetary system. It is difficult to attract capital to a country whose government is shaky. Paradoxically enough, it often happens that governments are shaky precisely because of the inflation brought on by extensive development programs. A "bold, imaginative" approach to domestic development on the part of a progressive-minded government may therefore lead to serious political upheaval if appropriate guidance is not applied to a development thrust. A development program, once begun, is also very demanding of more and more funds. The facilities, once built, must be maintained, even while they may operate at heavy losses due to an insufficient market for their output. Foreign-loan obligations must be met;

the severely strained domestic budget, moreover, must not be too far out of balance if the country is to remain solvent.

To provide domestic political and economic stability in the face of these problems is not an easy task and often governments fall in the attempt. Shaky governments, in turn, further exacerbate the difficulty, as foreign investors become wary of committing more capital to the country in question. Therefore, it becomes increasingly difficult for the undeveloped country to obtain loan extensions or new credits, short or long term, to finance import requirements.

Simultaneous Difficulties

These difficulties are not intended to be exhaustive.[6] They indicate the day-to-day practical complications incurred in a program of developing economically backward countries. What is more, all of these difficulties tend to occur simultaneously. One source of trouble is no sooner attacked than its remedy has stirred difficulties in other sectors. It is clear that we are faced with a dilemma. There is much enthusiastic support for taking impressive strides toward developing the needy areas of the world. Most will further agree that there should be no delay in our desire in this decade to help the less-fortunate peoples of the world. We are told that in order to defeat the insidious and potent compulsion of the vicious circle, development programs must be massive; small projects will not do and may even aggravate the evils of substandard living conditions by spurring population rates that exceed the ability of small improvements to offset them. This is one horn of the dilemma. The other is that massive development programs run headlong into the kind of practical difficulties briefly described here. They vary in complexity and combination from one undeveloped country to another; in every instance, they require a constant application of practicable economic criteria for solution. Basically, the problem seems to be one of timing: people want to get on with progress "in our time," but too much speed creates frustrating bottlenecks that check progress.

There is a strong tendency for economic-development programs in backward areas to promote nationalistic programs, and this despite the fact that most of the aid for development may come from Western private-enterprise economies. Herein lies a possible cure for the dilemma posed earlier. However ambitious developers are in promoting more-rapid economic development, the pace will of necessity be slow. Development of India, Turkey, or Africa will take a long time under the best of circumstances. Development is simply not a process which sees final results in a few years, nor even in ten or twenty years, as Western development demonstrates.

Role of Private Enterprise

From this point of view (which unfortunately seems neither bold or imaginative), it may well be argued that private enterprise should be a more prominent partner with national governments in development programs. That is to say, growth of the underdeveloped areas requires more private enterprise to balance the massive and rapidly expanding development programs carried out by national governments, programs which have led to the kind of practical problems we have been considering. Development sponsored by government planning tends to be too one-sided. On the other hand, encouragement of domestic private enterprise, using whatever local resources and talents are available to each region of an undeveloped country, might promote a broader pattern of income increases; these could establish in turn a broader production base on which rising incomes could feed.

There is, however, no question in the minds of most economists that economic development of underdeveloped areas can only be accomplished when a prominent role is given to the national governments concerned. In a word, economic development of undeveloped countries has (in the strict economic sense) a strong government policy bias. In its early stages, this is undoubtedly inevitable and perhaps desirable. It should, however, be no less desirable to balance this approach with a broad program of increased encouragement of private enterprise and the market system. This will inspire a more-natural development and will increase the share of the native populations in the development programs and at the same time promote more-balanced economic activity. Thus, the total amount of foreign capital directed to assisting the undeveloped areas need not be less than it has been — it should, indeed, increase — but it might be better directed to the goal of promoting the production and consumption of goods the local populations may take part in an increased share in producing and consuming.

Nearly every undeveloped country engaged in the battle for economic progress is confronted with these problems. There are some countries, India and Turkey, for example, which have in recent years exhibited all of them in rather clear relief. In 1958, Turkey received $359 million from the United States, West Germany, and the International Monetary Fund to help her out of her serious international deficit position, one brought on by an overzealous development program. To quote an authoritative source:

The Turkish authorities might be well advised in making use of their new breathing space (the $359 million) to give top priority to the strengthening of the country's basic payments position, relegating the fulfillment of their ambitious capital development plan to second place.[7]

Turkey's serious domestic inflation also raised another problem: foreign goods became cheaper than her own and this added to the impetus to import. Turkey's development program was said to be proceeding too rapidly:

Turkey should now take a close look at her development programme to see whether it will in fact take her through to external payments health before the latest aid programme runs out. If not, she should revise it to make sure that she does not have to pass the hat around again. For next time it may come back with much less in it.[8]

It is clear that the suggestion to revise Turkey's program meant that her development aims had to be more modest, particularly in sectors which developed too rapidly relative to the remainder of the economy. In accepting the $359 million in aid in 1958, Turkey was expected "to balance the budget, eliminate deficits on state enterprises, restrict credit expansion and hold back on capital investment to really worthwhile projects."[9] Today, more than a decade later, Turkey is said to be approaching self-sustaining growth, indicating that although balance-of-payments problems will not disappear (do they ever?), many of the basic hard lessons of fiscal responsibility and restraint are supposed to have been learned. Yet, at the beginning of this new decade, Turkey is again in the midst of financial crisis due to an overambitious investment program. A 1970 report stated the case as follows:

Turkey's present economic crisis is the cumulative result of maintaining a high rate of investment — some 20 percent of the GNP — and an annual GNP growth rate of around 6.5 percent since the inception of the first 5 year plan in 1963. Real resources have been over-strained to the point where shortage of money is more acute and the balance of payments problem more serious than at any time since the mid 1950's. Prices are reckoned to have risen by 8 percent in the past year and the trend remains upwards.[10]

Unless supply rigidities can be broken, a big push on investment intensifies the bidding for scarce resources, including imports, raises the cost structure for export industries and, hence, their prices, in turn weakening the market for Turkish goods in the world economy. By devaluing her currency in August 1970, Turkey promoted a resurgence of foreign-exchange earning and bank depositing of workers remittances earned abroad which had previously leaked off into black-market dealing.

There has never been any question about the need for an expeditious economic development of Africa, Asia, and the Middle East. And there has been no lack of enthusiasm for vigorous, dynamic, and generous programs of development. The purpose of this chapter has been to recall that the humanitarian need for economic progress in the uncommitted, underdeveloped world must take into account the severe practical difficulties involved in the most legitimate economic-development program. Native populations of many less-developed countries should not delude themselves into expecting miraculous cures for their ancient economic ills. The gap between their world and ours will not narrow in absolute terms in this generation, however massive the intended effort. Even so, growth in absolute terms can be impressive enough to satisfy the growth expectations of the people in developing countries.

Conclusions

To set up an all-inclusive program that would avoid the difficulties we have been examining would provide a brilliant and widely heralded finish to this chapter. Would that this were possible. In fact, such a program probably does not exist anywhere. Certain conclusions, however, are implied from our survey, which may be of relevance to our continued efforts in this new development decade.

Economic development of economically backward areas should not be one-sided. Single-minded development of, for example, power stations, mines, or rails is not enough. There should be a generous but long-range program for developing many productive enterprises so that output may match rising incomes, thus avoiding severe inflationary spirals.[11] This means selecting localized projects in numerous areas, training local labor, and providing incentives which are understandable within the particular culture.

With somewhat less emphasis on large-scale government projects and more on widespread local projects (no diminishing of funds expenditure implied), there would be less tendency for imports of equipment to rise so rapidly, thus causing balance-of-payments difficulties. The value of equipment needed might be no less in the development of local projects, but it is suggested that the importation of this kind of equipment will take place over a longer period.

The development of more local projects suggests an increasing role for private enterprise in the development programs, one which will act as a balance to the current concentration on government-controlled (and owned) development enterprises.

While economic development is one of the world's great needs and problems, it should be recognized that countries, like individuals and families, can live beyond their particular means. To desire a higher standard of living is a legitimate moral as well as economic aspiration for anyone or any people. But to desire and expect a doubling or tripling of one's standard in a few short years is legitimate only for those living at a starvation level. This principle is to some degree equally applicable to undeveloped countries. It is difficult for the present generation to say that their development efforts are for the next generation, but the evidence inclines to indicate that much of it is.

Technological progress has a slow incubation period, but once it has gained headway, the changes and innovative improvements come in swarms. Only a century ago the average man knew nothing of airplanes, cars, movies, electricity, electronics, synthetic products, aluminum products, dynamite, fountain pens, zippers, typewriters, chemical by-products, computers, radios, television, refrigerators, and an endess list of other items. Two centuries ago there were no railroads, steamships, mechanized farming, pencils, matches, canned goods, soda, and an infinite number of other items now so commonplace. In other words, it took since the beginning of time until relatively quite recently to begin the modern technological revolution. The process of building up to the current stage took literally thousands of years. We should not despair if the underdeveloped countries, still grappling with illiteracy and cultural blocks, must take another quarter century to achieve technological maturity.

What this summary suggests, finally, is that while the impelling need for economic development of the undeveloped regions often inspires extraordinary proposals and generosity in programs undertaken, the bulldozer technique may plough up more genuine trouble than it removes, at least in the short run. We need to recognize the enormous practical and policy difficulties involved and to be equally bold and imaginative about solving them in this new development decade.

There are a few simple formulas which can determine how much investment can be undertaken in an underdeveloped economy. P. N. Rosenstein-Rodan has offered a measure of absorptive capacity, but his cannot account for the effect of changed policies or new methods for changing or breaking down cultural bottlenecks.[12] This essay has dealt only with the practical obstacles encountered as the measure of absorptive capacity undergoes continuous testing during the development effort of the 1970's.

Notes

1. According to Staley and others, there are about 70 underdeveloped countries, 25 in an intermediate stage, and 14 highly developed. Nearly all of Africa and Asia (except the Union of South Africa and Japan) are in

dire need of development; much of South America and Central America, and Albania, Greece, Bulgaria, Rumania, and Yugoslavia in Europe. See Eugene Staley, *The Future of Underdeveloped Countries,* rev. ed. (New York: Harper, 1961) and P. Samuelson, *Economics,* 7th ed. (New York: McGraw Hill, 1967), p. 738.

2. Egbert DeVries, "A Review of Literature on Development Theory, 1957–1967" lists about 70 books which he judged to "give a fair insight into modern thought on economic development" *(International Development Review,* tenth anniversary issue, March 1968, pp. 50–51). Even this list is far from exhaustive. The wide range of knowledge and skills brought to bear in this area is also reflected in Ward, ed. *The Challenge of Development* (Chicago: Aldine, 1967). Gunnar Myrdal's *Asian Drama,* 3 vols. (New York: Pantheon, 1968) is a meaty compendium on Asian problems.

3. See Myrdal, *Rich Lands and Poor* (New York: Harper and Row, 1957).

4. Competent elaboration of these arguments is in Edward S. Mason, *Economic Planning in Underdeveloped Areas* (New York: Fordham University Press, 1958).

5. T. Schultz, *Economic Crisis in World Agriculture* (Ann Arbor: University of Michigan Press, 1965); "Production Opportunities in Asian Agriculture," in Hinrichs, Ward, Morss, eds. *Fiscal Incentives to Promote Agriculture* (in press).

6. The issue of income distribution is also a complex one. It is the educated elite who are able to manage investment successfully. They therefore reap its rewards and become even more wealthy. If you overtax them you dampen growth.

7. "Turkey's 'Sick' Economy," *The Financial Times* (London), 6 August 1958, p. 3.

8. Ibid.

9. *The Economist,* 9 August 1958, p. 481.

10. "Financial Problems Still Unsolved," *The Financial Times* (London), 18 May 1970, p. 26.

11. The Turkish wholesale price index, 1955–1959, went as follows: 119; 142; 164; 189; 219 (4 months). 1953 = 100. Monetary stabilization is vital to Turkey if it is to achieve self-reliance in the early 1970's.

12. The author has applied a formula devised by Rosenstein-Rodan to the Jordan economy for determining the capital inflow absorptive capacity. While such mechanistic formulas have inevitable shortcomings in practical application, some notion is conveyed of the difficult but necessary task of seeking new fields for development to enable a country to reach the capital-output ratio required to attain adequate growth in GNP and employment opportunities. The formula follows:

$$I = (cg - m) \, y + 7 \, y_1 \left(m - \frac{s}{y_1} \right)$$

Where:

I = capital inflow required

c = capital-output ratio

m = marginal rate of savings

y = GNP during the development period

y_1 = GNP in the initial year

s_1 = average savings rate $\left(\dfrac{s}{y} \right)$

g = growth rate of GNP (related to absorption capacity)
7 = Jordan seven-year program period (1963–1970)
Using Jordan data and the following assumptions for Jordan:

c = 3 to 1

m = 8 percent, the estimated average savings as percent of GNP of the past five years.

y = 1963 estimated GNP, projected at 6 percent per year to 1970, then summed (JD 1,295,000,000).

y_1 = GNP estimated for 1963, the initial year of the seven-year program of the JDB (131 million dinars, or $367 million)

s = $\frac{s}{y}$ 10 percent (total government and private savings as percent of GNP, estimated for 1963).

g = growth rate of absorptive capacity assumed to be same as growth of GNP, or 6 percent per annum.

Solving:

$$I = (\frac{3}{I} \times \frac{6}{100} - .08) \; 1295 \text{ million} + 7(131 \text{ million}) \; (.09 - .10)$$

$$I = JD \; 120.3 \text{ million} (\$337 \text{ million})$$

The capital-output ratio of 3 to 1 suggests that about $550 million of new capital formation will be required to generate a real GNP growth of 6 percent, while given the private and government savings ratios of recent years, the above calculated absorptive capacity for investment is about $340 million. There is therefore a question as to whether the capital investment can sustain the required level well into the future. This requires constant pursuit of new areas of potential development and investment. The formula is less important than the principle: maximum effective growth calls for development investment at the maximum absorptive capacity of the country, and such growth will probably produce self-sustaining growth sooner at less cost than investment at below this level would produce. A development effort should work on this approach rather than on arbitrary plans to reduce foreign aid without seeking to boost aid from alternative (domestic or external) sources. In view of the fact that Jordan's level of absorptive capacity was in the past below what was required to generate an adequate capital-ouput ratio to achieve growth in GNP of 6 percent, aid-giving agencies have the task of expanding capital absorptive capacity by seeking new development investment outlets. Cf. Rosenstein-Rodan, "Determining the Need for and Planning the Use of External Resources," in Ward, ed., *Challenge of Development,* pp. 93 ff.)

12　A Strategy for Developing Countries in the New Decade

How can developing countries improve on their opportunities to increase the flow of foreign aid in this skeptical decade? It has in the past been seldom seen, but most admired by donors to developing countries, that a residual requirement for aid reflected a genuine self-help commitment by the recipient country. This has become increasingly evident as foreign-aid fatigue has set in in recent years. Moreover, outside planners are unwelcome and their own recommendations unheeded when they call for a firm commitment of the recipient country's own resources. Nevertheless, a genuine and realistic self-help strategy is not only in the best interest of the developing country's own long-range development, but it enhances rather than detracts from the ability of the less-developed country to obtain foreign assistance. Nothing puts off donors so firmly as a five-year or annual plan strategy which is built up inductively from a long list of unrealistic and remote projects and expenditures in various sectors of the economy or government, which cannot be met from domestic resources, and which therefore imply a major foreign-aid commitment to keep the economy moving forward. A project list is no substitute for planning good policy, leading to a framework for optimum domestic commitment to development, in turn leading logically to a residual which donors might seriously consider meeting.

Nor is a litany of exaggerated claims as to what has in fact been achieved or what will be achieved the appropriate answer. Anything less than optimum domestic commitment to a plan by the developing country produces distrust, a groping for the real gaps and requirements, and ultimately a negotiated foreign-aid commitment in which neither side finds confidence and satisfaction. The strategy of building up an artificial case for $100 million in aid in the hope that a level of $60 million can be gained in the bargaining process is an outmoded, ineffective, and unsophisticated approach for arousing and maintaining foreign donor interest in a developing country. What is more, the atmosphere of unreality will also tend to discourage foreign private investors, whose chief discouragement to begin with is often uncertainty, to which the unreal strategy for seeking foreign assistance only contributes added skepticism.

If these preliminaries can be accepted, what kind of strategy would be most realistic and effective in the 1970's? The approach I have often helped formulate in developing economies may offer some suggestions. The data below were collected in Afghanistan as working tools for the planning process. A five-year plan strategy would require strong self-help overtones, and this is conveyed in the rising domestic mobilization of resources. Such a statement would have been drafted by the chief planners and perhaps reviewed by the prime minister. Ideally, the message, with supporting "proof" as shown in the tables, would be developed in the manner described below.

New Directions in Afghanistan's Third Five-Year Plan

Afghanistan's Third Five-Year Plan proposes challenging and hopeful new directions in the country's drive for more-rapid growth. The new policies described in the plan to promote a better investment climate for enterprise, a more-systematic approach to raising revenues while allowing for some rise in living standards, continued emphasis on a self-sufficient agriculture, promotion of smaller-scale industry, an improved performance on exports, and an effort to stimulate incentives and the business talents of the Afghan people provide, we believe, a framework within which Afghanistan can seek to achieve an enhanced tempo of progress toward eventual self-sustaining growth.

While sector growth rates can only be estimated and must be

backed by specific project detail, this pattern of growth forms the basis of what could develop and realistically be achieved in the course of the Third Five-Year Plan. Afghanistan is still an under-developed country, where statistics are far from accurate. Therefore, there is much to be said for beginning with what are known to be deficient sectors and focusing efforts in such areas. It is clear that agriculture requires improvement, that industry and the private-investment climate need to be promoted, that educational levels are grossly inadequate, that administrative and managerial and labor skills are far from being sufficient to provide the needed inputs to sustain a rapid rate of progress. Afghanistan must obviously take advantage of what resources it has and at the same time seek to enlarge its capacities for growth.

Nevertheless, despite the paucity of proven data, there is an advantage to providing a framework for progress which will contain the basic assumptions and thrusts of the directions in which the Afghans expect the economy and its policies and programs to go. The data provided here are designed to present such a framework to show what impact our dedication and effort to a well-conceived plan can produce. At the same time, reference can be made to specific chapters dealing with individual-sector programs and with budget and trade policies. Afghan officials are fully aware that unless the policies, programs, and efforts discussed in this plan are vigorously pursued, the salutary growth expectations indicated in these tables will not materialize, which in turn will disrupt expectations throughout the plan period. It will not do simply to describe what the Afghan government would like to do; it must strive with its utmost to achieve what can realistically — and perhaps in a few instances a little idealistically — be achieved in a five-year plan.

The Increased Commitment of Afghanistan's Resources

As a part of this framework of Afghanistan's new development drive, the country's officials and people should strive to carry the maximum share of the investment effort. To this end, as will be indicated in the numerical projections, the policies designed to commit Afghan resources from the public budget, from private investment sources, and from a hoped for improvement in the balance-of-payments performance are vital to the plan and constitute ambitious, but not unattainable, targets for the public and private sectors to meet.

At the same time, the commitment of Afghanistan's laws, institutions, and resources to development can only prove effective if adequate foreign exchange is provided, privately and by foreign aid, to support the projects and programs upon which the taxation, investment, and other policies in the plan depend. It bears repeating that this plan should seek to maximize the commitment of Afghanistan's scarce resources to the new directions and the quickening tempo of development the government of Afghanistan is anxious to create. This self-help effort is an essential foundation for development in every independent nation. With this dedication by the government and people of Afghanistan, foreign assistance is sought only to fill the gap between the total investment needed to generate an optimum growth rate and the public and private resources the Afghans themselves can bring to bear in the crucial drive toward self-reliance. It is within this context and framework that this summary of the plan strategy discusses some of the quantitative results the government should hope to achieve from the Third Five-Year Plan.

The Impact on GNP and Sector Growth

The Afghan planners should expect the policies and programs in the individual sectors to produce a GNP growth of about 4.2 percent a year as compared to the growth rate in the Second Five-Year Plan of about 3.2 percent a year. This is not as high a growth as attained by some developing countries, but this plan will necessarily be preoccupied to a considerable extent with the parallel task of building the administrative, manpower, and technical foundations for what could be a genuine takeoff in the Fourth Five-Year Plan period. These activities are less directly income-producing than other activities, but they are essential to Afghanistan at this still fairly early stage of its development. This effort, nevertheless, will be intermingled and complementary to the programs proposed for the individual sectors.

Agriculture constitutes well over half of the GNP of the country, although it is expected that this share will decline as other sectors such as manufacturing or commerce advance more rapidly (Table 12.1). The share for agriculture at the end of the Second Plan was 60.6 percent; the share should decline (as it does in nearly all developing countries) to about 56.7 percent by the end of the Third Plan (Table 12.2). The agricultural programs outlined in the chapter on agriculture, many of them already well underway, should produce a growth rate of 3.2 percent a year as compared to the rate of about 2 percent during the Second Plan period.

Commerce and banking as a service sector should continue to

Table 12.1: Afghan Third Five-Year Plan Gains in GNP by Industrial Origin*

(Constant 1967 prices, millions afghanis)

	1963 (Actual)	1967 (Budget)	1968	1972	Growth p.a. Second Plan	Growth p.a. Third Plan
GNP	53,774	61,175	63,430	77,890	3.3	5.2
Per capita	3,734	3,872	3,915	4,400	.9	2.8
Agriculture	31,594	33,681	34,315	40,495	1.6	4.2
Commerce, banking	6,709	8,273	9,047	12,000	5.2	7.2
Handicrafts	6,205	6,813	6,913	8,198	2.3	4.3
Manufacturing	1,845	2,513	2,943	4,821	8.0	13.0
Construction	1,215	1,423	1,543	2,114	4.0	8.0
Transport, communications	1,159	1,456	1,583	2,161	5.8	8.0
Mining	237	317	354	520	7.5	10.0
Electric power	339	400	457	717	4.1	12.0
All other domestic	255	270	275	364	1.3	7.4
Net foreign balance	4,216	6,029	6,000	6,500	9.0	2.1
GNP Breakdown						
Consumption (including TC)	45,612	50,174	51,916	62,220	2.4	4.4
Ordinary budget	1,595	2,759	2,995	4,717	12.0	12.0
Private	43,843	46,540	48,221	56,503	1.6	3.9
Total investment	3,946	4,972	5,514	9,170	5.9	13.3
Public development budget	1,446	1,860	2,280	3,700	6.5	13.0
Locally financed	1,395	1,720	1,750	3,400	5.3	18.0
Foreign financed	51	140	150	100	—	—
Private	2,500	3,112	3,234	5,470	5.5	14.0
Net foreign balance	4,216	6,029	6,000	6,500	9.2	2.0
Population (millions)	14.4	15.8	16.2	17.7	2.3	2.3

* Based on Ministry of Planning data and estimates.

197

Table 12.2: Changes in Sector Proportions as Percent of GNP
(1963, 1967, 1972)

	1963	1967	1972
Agriculture	63.1	60.6	56.7
Commerce, banking	13.9	14.8	15.2
Handicrafts	11.1	11.5	10.9
Manufacturing	3.6	4.5	6.4
Construction	2.3	2.3	2.5
Transport, communications	1.8	1.8	1.9
Mining (including gas)	0.4	0.5	0.6
Electric power	0.6	0.9	1.3
All other domestic	2.5	2.5	2.6
Net foreign balance	0.7	0.6	1.9

grow at a more-rapid rate than GNP, thus increasing its share in GNP from 14.8 percent in 1967 to 15.2 percent in 1970, even though the pace of change in this area is expected to level off relative to growth in the Second Plan period. Many of the new enterprises in this field were established during the Second Plan period, and more will be created during the Third Plan at only a very slight reduction in the rate of growth — still a very healthy 4.6 percent a year. It is hoped that a new Industrial Development Bank (a reorganized and revitalized Agricultural Credit Bank), a new liberal investment law, and the overall improvement in the investment climate will help to maintain this rate of advance in this, the country's second most important economic sector.

Given the stage of Afghanistan's development, there should be some decline in the share of handicrafts in total GNP as sectors indicative of a more-sophisticated economy begin to grow more rapidly. It will still be the third most important field of activity for the people, and it will continue to grow at a more-rapid rate of income in this area may indicate a shift of people in this traditional line of work to other fields, such as manufacturing, commerce, or other services.

The new plan has established some fairly ambitious targets, policies, and programs affecting manufacturing, especially smaller-scale activity. It is important for Afghanistan to develop, wherever it is economic to do so, suitable manufacturing enterprises and especially to promote the flow of private investment into manufacturing. If the appropriate policies and programs succeed, there should be a continuation and even a slight increase of a high growth rate in the manufacturing sector, even though the rate in the Second Plan was based on a low 1963 base. A new investment law has already been passed by the government. Establishment of the Industrial Development Bank and an Industrial Advisory Service should provide a logical complement designed to encourage and foster private investment. A credit system will be formulated which will enable new enterprises of demonstrable potential to borrow at conventional, rather than high black-market, rates.

There should be continued expansion of the relatively small mining industry, helped considerably by explorations and marketing of new mineral finds during the later years of the Third Plan period.

As all of these sectors move forward in the direction and at the overall rates anticipated, the demand for transport, communications, electric power, and other services should expand. Programs in these areas are designed to meet these infrastructural needs of the economy and are relatively modest compared to the major emphasis in the plan.

The Impact on Consumption and Investment

The overall rate of consumption should not increase in the Third Plan because of the greater allocation of total resources to investment. The overall rate of increase in consumption in the Second Plan was 3.2 percent. An approximation of this rate should continue in the Third Plan. However, some restraint has been introduced in the government's ordinary budget over its substantial annual growth in the last plan. This will not be an easy task with the pressures for higher salaries, not unrelated to improved training of personnel; growing operational expenditures related to development; and expanded government services. There will undoubtedly be some slippage in the rate of 6.3 percent a year that has been projected. The Afghan government should be determined to maximize the flow of Afghanistan's revenues into development, believing that this in the long run will hasten growth and provide the shortest route toward higher wages for all of the people, including government personnel.

At the same time, some growth of consumption over the Second Plan and over the population growth should be allowed on the ground that a commitment to development cannot postpone some steady improvement in basic consumption levels among the people. It should, in fact, help to justify in their minds the costs of the development effort represented by new taxes imposed and revenues called for as a result of other revenue-raising policies established.

Table 12.3: Afghan Third Five-Year Plan Gains in Domestic Resources for Development[1]

(million afghanis)

	1963 (Actual)	1967 (Budget)	1968	1972	Growth p.a. 2nd Plan	Growth p.a. 3rd Plan	Total 2nd Plan	Total 3rd Plan
1. Revenues (domestic)	2,120	3,950	4,105	5,645			15,763	24,165
Yields from new taxes	—	—	375	700			—	2,576
2. Total revenues	2,120	3,950	4,480	6,345	17.5	10.0	15,763	26,741
Ordinary expenditures	1,595	2,759	2,995	4,076				5,051
Foreign debt service	216	304	639	1,106				17,574
3. Total current expenditures	1,811	3,063	3,634	5,182	14.0	9.0	12,753	9,167
Current surplus	309	887	846	1,163			3,010	3,000
Foreign commodity aid	112	1,000	600	600			2,865	7,118
4. Net revenue available for development	421	1,887	1,446	1,763			5,875	2,250
New resources	—	—	350	550			—	700
Deficit spending	1,024	— 37	100	180			2,730	10,068
5. Total Afghan resources for development	1,446	1,850	1,896	2,493	6.2	7.0	8,605	12,000
6. Foreign project aid	3,406	3,160	3,100	2,500			15,329	22,068
7. Total public-sector development expenditures	4,842	5,010	4,996	4,993			23,934	21,385
8. Total private-sector investment[2]	2,500	3,112	3,234	5,470	5.5	14.0	13,969	
Total development investment from Afghan sources (5 + 8)	3,946	4,962	5,130	8,463	5.8	13.4	22,574	31,953

1. Based on Ministry of Planning data and estimates.

2. These growth expectations for private investment are high for Afghanistan, but here is a case where ambitious targets, vigorously pursued, will appeal mightily to Western market-oriented donors and reflect commitment by the government to attain these levels. Given the yields from new agricultural technology (miracle seeds, fertilizer), agriculture could readily increase its investment levels greatly.

Impact on Afghanistan's Commitment

Afghanistan's commitment to development should perhaps be most effectively reflected in the desire to increase the government's development budget and in anticipation of a rising proportion of total investment. The estimates and proportions are subject to some margins of error, but the government should prefer to see private investment increase at a rate of over 8 percent a year rather than at the rate of 2 percent a year as in the past. With total government and private consumption leveling off, a doubling of the annual growth in total investment would give the economy the infusion of new capital and effort sufficient to produce the GNP annual growth rate of 4.2 percent and a rise in per capita income of about 2 percent a year. In the aggregate and in the sector components of the economy, these expectations seem both reasonable and attainable. In order to stress the importance attached to the Afghanistan resource commitment to this plan, Table 12.3 shows some of the favorable consequences to be brought about over the next five years. Total resources committed to the Third Plan should double over those of the Second Plan. Total Afghanistan private investment should rise from 36.5 in the Second Plan to 43.6 billion afghanis (50 afghanis = $1.) in the Third Plan. It should be expected, however, that some proportion of this investment would be from foreign sources. Thus, total investment from public and private Afghan sources would rise from about 41 billion afghanis to about 52.6 billion afghanis, an increase overall of 28 percent over the plan period.

Impact on Budget Trends

Total domestic revenues have been increasing at a high annual rate in the past and new taxes and improved administrative procedures should sustain a growth rate of about 11 percent a year through the plan period. Even though this rate is less than the past growth performance, the absolute increase over the period is larger than in the Second Plan, which started from a relatively low base.

At the same time, the anticipated growth in the ordinary budget has been reduced, as mentioned earlier, from 14.6 percent a year to 6.3 percent, producing, in combinations with revenue growth, a current surplus of about 2 billion afghanis by 1972. There will be some new resources coming into existence, new mineral finds and other resources, for which there has been allowed a level of 358 million afghanis by 1972 (Table 12.3, line 3). Deficit spending (line

Table 12.4: Gains in Afghanistan Global Balance of Payments from
Third Five-Year Plan Performance
(million afghanis)

	1963	1966	1967	1972	Growth p.a. Second Plan	Growth p.a. Third Plan
Receipts						
Exports	4,418	5,200	6,100	8,500	4.0	8.6
Travel	—	105	158	375		
Earnings from embassies	750	563	565	665		
Other receipts	150	160	165	180		
Total Afghan earnings (rising)	5,318	6,028	6,988	9,720	3.1	8.5
Payments						
Imports (commercial)	4,455	4,800	5,023	6,000	1.9	4.5
Foreign debt service	216	304	974	1,146		
Afghan embassy outlays	75	113	120	128		
Investment income	150	165	325	563		
Travel	50	285	300	375		
Other payments	25	40	43	60		
Total Afghan outlays	4,971	5,707	6,785	8,272	3.4	5.0
Net balance (growing receipts)	347	321	203	1,448		
Foreign assistance (declining)						
Project-aid absorption	3,406	3,160	3,100	2,500 (low estimate)		
Commodity imports	112	1,000	600	500		
Total	3,518	4,160	3,700	3,000		
Foreign-exchange need (plan level)			4,600	4,600 (high estimate)		
Minus project absorption,			—3,100	—2,500		
and commodity aid			— 600	— 500		
and Afghan Performance Factor*			— 203	—1,448		
Difference between plan level and low estimate			697	152		
(to allow for fallout of plan elements)						

*Net foreign-exchange balance which reflects successful export promotion and some restraint on nondevelopment
oriented imports.

4) has been reduced over the level of 1963 in line with efforts to check inflation. However, 180 million afghanis is undoubtedly a lower level than it need be, and this source could be expanded moderately as an effective input into development should the need arise. Combining the current surplus anticipated by 1972 with returns from new resources and deficit spending produces a contribution to development from the Afghanistan budget of over double its level in 1963. The budget performance in the Third Plan therefore doubles the contribution the budget made from Afghanistan resources to the Second Plan.

Impact on the Balance of Payments

At the same time, total foreign resources for the plan should reach a minimum of 16.3 million afghanis. This, however, represents a decline in the level of aid in 1967, 1968, and 1972, which may be inadequate if all the elements of the plan are as ready for serious analysis as is planned for them. The lower level of foreign assistance indicated in Table 12.2, therefore, based on a conservative assessment of the country's ability to absorb project and program activity. If this level does in fact prove to be low and if policies and programs measure up to aims, the suggestion (reflected in Table 12.4) that some flexibility be allowed which would enable Afghanistan to tap additional sources of foreign assistance as and when required by plan performance is warranted. The size of the gap in foreign-exchange requirements will also depend upon the balance-of-payments experience. Afghanistan's needs for assistance are, in essence, conditioned upon the country's own optimum input and performance, as it should be.

Afghanistan can and should continue its efforts to identify principal export commodities, such as karakul, fruit, carpets, cotton, and wool and promote increases in these (Table 12.5) as a direct means of increasing its own foreign-exchange earnings. New products should be added wherever economically feasible in order to maximize these export earnings. The principal foreign-exchange earners would be cultivated as indicated in the plan (and in Table 12.5), while nonessential imports, both consumer and durable investors goods of low priority, would be checked. The resultant improvement in the balance of payments is reflected in Table 12.4, where it is expected that by the end of the Third Plan a favorable current balance of about 1.5 billion afghanis could be provided toward foreign-exchange needs. Gradual but steady progress in the balance-of-payments performance is a vital necessity if the country is to stand eventually on its own resources.

Table 12.5: Gains in Exports, Second and Third Plans Compared
(million afghanis)

	1963	1967	1968	1972	Growth p.a. Second Plan	Growth p.a. Third Plan
Karakul	1,148	1,035	1,140	1,246	— 1.0	2.4
Cotton	623	1,110	667	1,350	15.4	5.0†
Dried fruits	655	1,044	1,118	1,395	12.2	6.0
Carpets and rugs	640	675	664	750	1.6	6.1
Wool	450	525	589	590	3.9	0
Fresh fruits	164	320	340	501	1.7	10.0
Oil seeds	98	103	300	310	.6	.6
Raw skins	81	154	162	216	17.2	7.4
Casings	57	137	140	237	25.0	14.0
Medicinal herbs	14	94	94	94	—	—
Copper	—	—	496	783	—	12.0
Sheep skins	22	23	23	23	—	—
Ores	—	—	—	58	—	—
Others	39	99	135	306	26.0	22.1
Total exports	3,991	5,319	5,868	7,859	7.3	7.6
Possible added results*				751		
Total exports with optimum growth			5,868	8,500		9.5

*From special incentive measures and policies to promote exports.

†Assumed over 1967 level.

Impact of a Successful Plan

Should the balance-of-payments expectations materialize, Afghanistan should expect its foreign-exchange needs from foreign aid to be reduced to the extent that net current earnings increase. On the other hand, if the best expectations are realized and if some of the programs and policies bring early results, this could call for a greater foreign-exchange commitment as these projects and programs move ahead more rapidly than planned. Therefore, it would be preferable to have a growing commitment and the country's own performance in this plan tied to a flexible concept of foreign assistance, where an attempt is made to determine the full absorptive capacity of the country, commit against that capacity the maximum level of Afghanistan's resources, and then count on an adequate level of foreign assistance to make up the difference. In this way, the country could hope for a genuine opportunity to get the highest possible growth rate of GNP and hasten the day when the country could muster sufficient resources, including foreign exchange, to finance its own growth process. A strong drive over the next few years with adequate assistance could mean less foreign assistance is the long run and, from Afghanistan's point of view, an earlier target date for self-sustaining growth.

The Afghan government should realize that there is risk in suggesting a range rather than an absolute level which may be needed over the next five years. The risk is that the lower level will be taken as the more realistic one. Nevertheless, to attempt to project a hard and fast level of foreign exchange required — in fact to adhere rigidly to any series of projections — is unrealistic. With the present quality of the statistics, it is not possible to make precise forecasts, particularly over a five-year period. This is why there has been added to the plan an important chapter on plan implementation. It will provide an annual opportunity to recommend, as the basis of current status and progress, the logical and practical steps to be taken in each sector, partial sector, or specific policy or program area in the year immediately ahead.

Where resources are required to further the policies and programs which will optimize progress, the Afghans should consult, when and where possible, its own resources to further these policies and programs. However, having committed its maximum resource effort, Afghanistan's shortest route to success in achieving the growth target is to count on foreign assistance to fill what should be a declining gap between the total investment requirement associated with the growth target and the country's own resources.

The impact of a successful plan would be reflected not only in the eventual reduction of foreign concessionary aid but just as significantly in the growing independence of agriculture and industry. Success in the agricultural program will reduce dependence upon food imports. Success in industry and manufacturing, including economic import substitution, will release foreign exchange for essential development imports.

In this and other ways, all of the elements of the plan, as quantified in the tables, are interrelated. Success in partial planning at the project or policy level will produce success at the aggregate level, as incomes and tax yields rise to feed the government's budget requirements. As revenues rise, the development investment budget can in turn expand. Moreover, as the level of activity rises in the economy, policies designed to encourage private investment will bear fruit, and as in every growing economy, successful private investment will feed upon itself and, through enlarging markets and whetted incentives, will call forth a larger commitment of domestic savings to investment in enterprises in many different sectors.

Simultaneously, sensible monetary and fiscal measures such as Afghanistan has successfully pursued recently with respect to reduction of deficit financing will contain inflation and prevent further erosion in trade lines where there is an advantageous relationship between internal and external prices. This will help the export drive, while scrutiny of imports, together with appropriate import substitute enterprise, will check foreign-exchange outlays for imports. The net gain in exchange then becomes available for imports required for agriculture, manufacturing, and other essential sector activities.

A final desideratum for the Third Five-Year Plan is to maintain a continual process of reassessment of progress, digressions, bottlenecks, or new directions and requirements. This should not be left entirely to the formulating of annual implementation programs. Once these specifics are formulated, the planning and operating ministries will monitor progress on various aspects of the overall plan and its implementation of specific projects, policies, and programs.

Finally, and most significantly of all, the government of Afghanistan should be fully aware that its currency is overvalued and that other trade policies pursued have restricted exports and the flow of imports. Consequently, in presenting the Third Five-Year Plan, the government should announce a devaluation of the currency, to make its exports more competitive in world markets, and it should combine this significant self-help measure with legislative investment which will place 75 percent of imports on a liberalized list. This will promote private enterprise and market-oriented incentives which should play a larger role in the development process.

With the self-help commitment indicated above and in the tables and with the two major policy steps just announced, donors who have an interest in assisting Afghanistan toward self-sustainment in a reasonable time span will be more willing to contribute to the residual foreign-exchange requirement which follows from this maximum self-help commitment by the people and government of Afghanistan.

The emphasis in the above strategy for Afghanistan is on new directions and suggests self-help policy reform as a framework for the new five-year plan. It poses desirable growth targets which rational indigenous or foreign planners can logically accept. It states clearly that appropriate domestic policies must provide the bulk of the necessary resources and set realistic performance targets. The development budget, private investment, new tax measures, an export push with rising strength shown in the balance of payments — all these reflect an apparent willingness of Afghanistan's people and government to act on its own system to produce growth patterns. This strategy also includes one or two bold new policies, difficult to take, but very significant in impact, which would appeal to donors. These are lines of argument and planning too seldom encountered in my experience, and yet they would appeal greatly in logic to planners and other officials in potential donor countries, even if such donors are unable to meet all of the developing country's requirement for aid.

13　Identifying the Priority Catalysts: A Country Case

In order to grasp the economic significance of the current upheaval in the Middle East as it bears on the development process, it is essential to know the elements of progress, or lack of it, that preceded the war of 1967 between Israel and her Arab neighbors. This paper focuses on the country of Jordan, where the writer lived for two years prior to that war and which he has revisited since. Lessons learned from this case relate in many ways to the Middle East area as a whole.

The June 1967 war interrupted a short, but impressively rapid, economic development performance by a country that had been regarded a decade earlier as little more than a distress case. A brief review of the elements which describe the growth of Jordan in the recent past will help in understanding the future potential.[1]

The Structure of Jordan's Economic Growth, 1954–1966

The nonagricultural sectors whose aggregate value added tripled from 1954 to 1966 accounted for about 82 percent of the increase of Jordan's GDP over that period. Agriculture, whose value added doubled, accounted for the remaining 18 percent. As a result, nonagricultural value added came to represent 82 percent of gross domestic product in 1966, up from about 73 percent in 1954. The increase in nonagricultural activity was undoubtedly spurred by the large inflow of foreign aid and by the rapid growth in tourism and remittance earnings from abroad, which helped provide the finance for the imports required for nonagricultural activity.

Within manufacturing, the subsectors, namely food processing, textiles, petroleum refining, chemicals and products, nonmetallic minerals, and basic metals contributed nearly 70 percent of the total value added from 1957 to 1967 in mining manufacturing.[2] Mining and quarrying alone contributed only 15 percent, all other manufacturers another 15 percent. The relative growth in sector activity is also seen in Table 13.1.

Table 13.1: Growth Rates of Major Sectors, Jordan

Sector	Percent Per Year Annual Growth 1954–1966	Value Added as Percent of GNP 1954	Value Added as Percent of GNP 1966
Construction	16.6	2.6	5.0
Factor income from abroad	14.4	5.2	8.2
Manufacturing	12.2		
Mining, quarrying	11.2	6.9	10.5
Electricity, water	11.2		
Services	10.4	7.3	7.5
Ownership of dwellings	10.0	6.1	6.0
Transport	9.6	8.1	7.8
Trade, banking	9.4	18.8	17.1
Livestock	8.5	7.8	6.3
Public administration and defense	8.3	14.7	11.9
Crops and forestry	4.6	15.6	8.4
(Indirect Taxes)	15.0	6.9	11.3
		100.0	100.0

These growth rates can be misleading in that some sectors are small in absolute terms relative to the total GNP. Construction, for example, is the smallest sector by value added, representing less than 3 percent of GDP in 1954, but grew rapidly on this low base to over 6 percent of GDP by 1966. The ubiquitous evidence of industrial, commercial, and government building activity over the past decade impresses even the casual visitor. This activity, in turn, generates and spurs activity in many supply-related enterprises, while the employment creates pervasive effects throughout the economy. Net travel (tourism) earnings grew from $2.6 million in 1959 to $19.7 million in 1966, gross travel from $8 million to $31.5 million, and remittances from $12.9 to $29.6 million.[3] The major lines responsible for the growth of manufactures have already been mentioned. In mining the major growth element was the impressive increase of phosphate mining from a little over 200,000 metric tons in the middle 1950's to over 1 million tons in 1967.[4] On the supply side this has been due partly to the development of new deposits at Al Hasa, and on the demand side to expansion of exports to Yugoslavia, India, Japan, Italy, Pakistan, Turkey, and Czechoslovakia.[5] A potash plant at the south end of the Dead Sea has been in the planning stage, but its progress was interrupted by the war and by postwar unrest. Estimates of quarrying activity are not available, but Jordan's marble products are of good quality and have been effectively developed for the tourist industry and to some degree for export. Marble, granite, porphyry, basalt, and other stone exports were valued at nearly $1 million before the war with Israel in June 1967. The growth rates in electricity, water, services, ownership of dwellings, transport, trade, and banking are correlated with the general growth of activity reflected in the 8–10 percent average annual growth of GNP. The petroleum refinery, which began production in October 1960, is the largest single industrial unit in Jordan, with value added of $6 million in 1966. Construction, mining and quarrying, and food manufacturing had value added to $26 million, $7 million, and $6.5 million, respectively, in 1966. The 1967 levels were not substantially different.[6]

Crop output in Jordan — particularly wheat and barley — fluctuates sharply with the rainfall. For example, when average rainfall was about 42 millimeters in the 1959/60 season, Jordan's wheat crop was 43,600 tons. When rainfall reached 100 millimeters in the 1961/62 season, wheat output was over 138,000 tons, then dropped to 76,000 tons in 1961/62, when rainfall had dropped to about 64 millimeters, then rose again to 278,000 tons when rainfall exceeded 140 millimeters in 1964/65.[7] In 1965, wheat represented 50 percent of the value added by crops and forestry. Crops that are irrigated (tomatoes, other vegetables, and fruits) are less affected by rainfall fluctuations and these have grown in importance since 1954 with the development of the East Ghor Canal and other irrigation works.[8] The irrigated output has undoubtedly helped to reduce the effect of the drastic fluctuations in wheat output. The output values in Tables 13.2–5 have been smoothed to eliminate seasonal effects of rainfall.[9] Grains and legumes, which are almost totally unirrigated, have had negligible growth, as compared with the doubling and

Table 13.2: Industrial Origin of GDP and GNP*
(JD millions)†

		1954	1955	1956	1957	1958	1959	1960	1961	1962	1963	1964	1965	1966
1	Agriculture	13.5	11.4	17.0	14.7	15.3	17.09	18.85	18.75	22.42	23.08	24.12	26.77	27.18
2	VA in crops and forestry	9.0	9.4	9.6	10.1	10.7	12.12	13.48	14.48	14.70	15.12	15.60	15.71	15.51
3	Crops and forestry output	10.4	10.5	11.2	11.7	12.3	13.74	15.18	16.72	16.92	17.26	18.01	18.16	18.00
4	Intermediate costs	1.4	1.1	1.6	1.6	1.6	1.62	1.70	2.24	2.22	2.14	2.41	2.45	2.49
5	VA in livestock	4.5	2.0	7.4	4.6	4.6	4.97	5.37	4.27	7.72	7.96	8.52	11.06	11.67
6	Livestock output	5.1	2.9	8.3	5.2	5.8	5.86	6.20	5.05	8.69	9.11	9.83	13.22	14.19
7	Intermediate costs	.6	.9	.9	.6	1.2	.89	.83	.78	.97	1.15	1.31	2.16	2.52
8	Non-agriculture	37.3	40.5	46.3	53.6	61.2	70.09	74.82	85.57	87.72	95.58	101.38	116.84	122.09
9	Mining, manufacturing and electricity	4.0	4.8	5.8	6.2	6.8	6.89	7.58	9.50	8.80	11.55	13.56	17.90	19.53
10	Construction	1.5	1.9	2.1	2.4	3.0	4.66	4.50	4.50	6.15	6.12	5.45	7.87	9.28
11	Transport	4.7	5.9	7.2	8.8	9.8	10.70	11.12	12.64	12.53	12.77	12.03	12.60	14.42
12	Trade and banking	10.9	10.9	12.3	14.1	16.9	18.81	20.44	25.55	25.09	27.78	29.52	33.54	31.69
13	Ownership of dwellings	3.5	3.5	4.4	4.7	5.0	6.30	7.13	8.01	8.58	9.38	9.93	10.69	11.20
14	Public administration and defense	8.5	9.0	10.7	12.4	14.5	14.95	15.79	16.74	17.06	17.61	19.70	21.41	22.03
15	Services	4.2	4.5	3.8	3.8	5.2	7.78	8.26	8.63	9.51	10.37	11.19	12.83	13.94
16	GDP at factor cost	50.8	51.9	63.3	68.3	76.5	87.18	93.67	104.32	110.14	118.66	125.50	143.61	149.27
17	Indirect taxes	4.0	4.9	5.6	6.2	7.0	8.36	8.86	9.27	10.28	11.39	13.43	16.66	20.89
18	GDP at market prices	54.8	56.8	68.9	74.5	83.5	95.54	102.53	113.59	120.42	130.05	138.93	160.27	170.16
19	Factor income from abroad	3.0	5.2	4.8	6.1	4.5	5.60	7.39	7.00	11.93	8.56	11.67	12.93	15.15
20	GNP at market prices	57.8	62.0	73.7	80.6	88.0	101.14	109.92	120.59	132.35	138.61	150.60	173.20	185.31

Sources: Michael Mazur, unpublished Ph. D. dissertation material, M. I. T., Cambridge, Spring 1969, derived from R. S. Porter, Economic Trends in Jordan 1954–1959 (Beirut, 1961), mimeographed. Jordan Department of Statistics, The National Accounts 1959–1966, (Aman, 1967). The differences in data are due to smoothing of agriculture data in this table.

*All figures are in current prices except for Row 3, the major components of which are in 1964 prices.
†1 Jordan Dinar=$2.80.

tripling of output in vegetables, fruits, vines, and olives, a significant portion of which is irrigated.

The future growth potential in ouput of both dry-land and irrigated crops is substantial.[10] Another study in this project estimates improved practices and varieties could increase wheat production more than threefold, barley by double its present level, lentils and other legumes fivefold, and fruits and vegetables by at least 50 percent.[11] The average value yield per acre from fruits and vegetables is already several times as large as the yields from grains. AID,[12] UN teams,[13] and other donors continue to assist Jordan in the improvement and further development of both dry land and irrigated cropping in Jordan.

Economy After the 1967 War

Following the war with Israel in June 1967, Jordan lost, at least for the time being, the west bank which had generated about 40 percent of Jordan's GNP,[14] nearly all of its tourist earnings,[15] and substantial foreign-exchange earnings from remittances and agricultural exports. Nevertheless, the west bank had been a net balance-

Table 13.3: Annual Growth Rates by Sectors*

		1954/55– 1965/66	1954/55– 1959/60	1959/60– 1965/66
1	Agriculture	7 %	7.5%	7 %
2	VA in crops and forestry	5	7	3.5
3	Crops and forestry output	5	6.5	4
4	Intermediate costs	6.5	6	7
5	VA in livestock	12	10	14
6	Livestock output	11.5	8.5	15
7	Intermediate costs	11	3	18
8	Non-agriculture	11	13	9
9	Mining; manufacturing and electricity	14	10.5	17
10	Construction	16	22	11
11	Transport	9	15.5	3.5
12	Trade and banking	10.5	12.5	9
13	Ownership of dwellings	11	14	8.5
14	Public administration and defense	8.5	12	6
15	Services	11	13	9
16	GDP at factor cost	10	12	8.5
17	Indirect taxes	14	14	14
18	GDP at market prices	10.5	12	9
19	Factor income from abroad	12	10	14
20	GNP at market prices	10.5	12	9

Source: Same as Table 13.2.

*All growth rates are annual rates annually compounded.

Table 13.4: Adjusted Value of Output in Crops and Forestry
(JD millions)*

		1954	1955	1956	1957	1958	1959	1960	1961	1962	1963	1964	1965	1966
1	Grains and legumes	4.728	4.763	4.807	4.855	4.906	4.965	5.026	5.011	5.000	4.985	4.975	4.964	4.955
2	Wheat	2.964	3.047	3.133	3.222	3.311	3.405	4.501	3.502	3.502	3.502	3.503	3.503	3.504
3	Barley	.655	.662	.670	.679	.687	.696	.704	.679	.656	.633	.610	.588	.568
4	Others	1.109	1.054	1.004	.954	.908	.864	.821	.830	.842	.850	.862	.873	.883
5	Vegetables	2.364	2.514	2.596	2.969	3.510	4.572	4.892	6.809	6.912	7.016	7.477	7.350	6.610
6	Tomatoes	.693	.750	.751	.881	1.048	1.502	2.111	2.768	2.871	2.877	3.315	3.122	2.499
7	Cucumbers, melons and watermelons	.847	.965	1.098	1.251	1.424	1.622	1.847	1.846	1.846	1.845	1.844	1.844	1.843
8	Others	.824	.799	.747	.837	1.033	1.448	1.934	2.195	2.258	2.294	2.318	2.384	2.268
9	Fruits, vines and olives	2.521	2.456	2.784	2.852	3.229	3.428	3.873	4.150	4.417	4.728	4.869	5.084	5.443
10	Grapes	.663	.672	.756	.879	1.035	1.224	1.452	1.504	1.470	1.405	1.329	1.251	1.178
11	Olives	1.177	1.052	1.244	1.148	1.317	1.245	1.399	1.419	1.573	1.612	1.771	1.828	2.012
12	Citrus	.010	.015	.022	.030	.046	.086	.106	.243	.318	.577	.552	.699	.851
13	Other fruits	.617	.717	.762	.795	.831	.873	.916	.984	1.056	1.134	1.217	1.306	1.402
14	Construction on farms (labor)	.280	.280	.280	.260	.180	.100	.080	.160	.140	.290	.150	.220	.540
15	Tobacco	.160	.170	.420	.420	.270	.360	.110	.390	.290	.100	.150	.400	.310
16	Forest products	.320	.270	.270	.300	.200	.310	.200	.200	.160	.140	.130	.140	.140
17	Total	10.373	10.453	11.157	11.656	12.295	13.735	15.181	16.720	16.919	17.259	18.011	18.158	17.998

Source: Same as Table 13.1.
*1 J D=U.S. $2.80

of-payments deficit area, although not to the same extent or proportion as the economy as a whole. Therefore, Jordan's balance of payments was relatively worsened as a result of the loss of the west bank.[16] The deficit was more than covered, however, by large grants from the Arab oil states.[17] Economic activity on both the east and west banks declined sharply following the war, with the Arab banks on the west bank closing down. There is some flow of trade from east to west bank, but recession set in on both banks following the war. Activity on both banks has gradually resumed as the necessity to carry on became evident, but investment decisions are understandably cautious and moderate. Uncertainty is the deterrent to full resumption of activity in the sectors discussed above. Agriculture in the Jordan Valley has been disrupted by intermittent hostilities across the Jordan River border between the occupied west bank and the east bank. The East Ghor Canal has been bombed on occasion in reprisal raids.[18] On the other hand, exports of agricultural and other commodities do not seem to have been seriously affected by the split-up of the country.[19] Imports[20] have declined sharply, however, reflecting the cautious spending outlook within the country in the face of the uncertainty.[21] A sector breakdown of activity in the postwar period is not available, but it would undoubtedly reflect a depressed economic situation on each bank. The 1967 GNP for the two banks combined, therefore, would be lower

Table 13.5: Annual Growth Rates of Value of Output in Crops and Forestry*

		1954/55-1965/66	1954/55-1959/60	1959/60-1965/66
1	Grains and legumes	0 %	1 %	0 %
2	Wheat	1.5	3	0.5
3	Barley	−1	1	−3
4	Others	−2	−5	1
5	Vegetables	10	16.5	5
6	Tomatoes	13	20	8
7	Cucumbers, melons and watermelons	6.5	14	1
8	Others	11	16	5.5
9	Fruits, vines and olives	7	8	6
10	Grapes	5.5	15	−0.5
11	Olives	5	3.5	6.5
12	Citrus	45.5	50	42
13	Other fruits	6	5	7
14	Construction on farms (labor)	5	−20	27
15	Tobacco	7	7	7
16	Forest products	−7	−3	−9.5
17	Total	5	7	4

Source: Same as Table 13.1.

*All growth rates are annual rates annually compounded.

than that for 1966 when the country was united, although preliminary reports[22] show it higher.[23] The unemployment situation on the east bank is severely aggravated by the addition of at least 200,000[24] displaced persons from the west bank, who fled during the June 1967 war.[25] Thus, if special postwar grants in aid are excluded and the refugee burden is added, the east bank economy is far from viable. The east bank is able to function well only because of the contributions made to Jordan by the oil-rich Arab countries of over $100 million a year.[26]

Such, in brief, is the context within which further development in Jordan must take place. Once a political holding operation, Jordan, in little more than a decade became decidedly hopeful about the prospects for eventual economic self-reliance. Should peace and cooperation prevail between Israel and the Arabs, the opportunities for continued rapid growth and consequent assimilation of the unemployed are numerous. The refugee problem created by the 1948 war had by no means disappeared prior to June 1967, but with Jordan's real GNP growing at an average rate of about 10 percent a year for at least a decade, refugees were finding ways to supplement their welfare income or rations or to leave their camps altogether for better jobs and housing. In some instances, the country's rapid growth reached into the refugee camps and was slowly transforming them into suburbs of larger cities or into separate town entities.

All of these growth characteristics have been blunted by the June 1967 war and its aftermath. The task of whatever peace settlement develops will be to reconstruct and refurbish the development momentum that prevailed prior to the war. Resumption of Jordan's recent past growth would soon follow a genuine political settlement in the area, though eventually a somewhat slower growth rate could be expected. Without a political or de facto settlement, both the political and economic outlook for a truncated Jordan would seem problematic at best.

Epilogue to the Future

The prospects for Jordan's future, economically, under various assumptions, range from optimistic (a generally favorable political settlement) to pessimistic (no Middle East political settlement) and a lower-level equilibrium trap economically for the east bank.

The projections to 1980 presented in Table 13.6 assume a general Middle East political settlement in which (1) the west bank is returned to Jordan in the early 1970's, (2) Jordan will still receive a share of the income generated from Jerusalem's unique tourist attractions, and (3) more freedom of tourist traffic and trade will be permitted between Jordan and Israel. Under these assumptions Jordan would be able to resume the high rate of growth it experienced in the last decade.[27] The projections assume resumption or expansion of investment in developing accommodations and measures for attracting tourists to the area; promoting optimum development of vocational and higher educational programs that upgrade the quality of labor, thereby contributing to Jordan's manpower needs as the economy progresses; broadening employment opportunities for Jordanians in Jordan or abroad; and supporting projects designed to increase earning and employment from agriculture and mineral resources, such as water[28] and land development from manufacturing, and from export of potash and phosphate.[29] A provision in the projection is also made for the possibility of Israel's granting Jordan free access to a Mediterranean port.

Even before new programs and efforts are launched, Jordan could improve the effectiveness of present policies and programs with modst financial investment. With improved fiscal management in the Jordan government, resources available for development could be increased. Better enforcement of tax laws and reform of the tax structure to extend coverage and reduce waste, inefficient employment practices and outlays for the military — all these could make substantial resources available to the government of Jordan for development. A program for promoting exports and checking the importation of luxuries and semiluxuries would also improve the chances for long-term balance-of-payments equilibrium.

Table 13.6: Jordan's GNP, Actual and Projected

	Actual				Projected			
	1954	1959	1966	Percent Growth Per Year 1954-1966	Percent Growth to 1975	1975	Percent Growth to 1980	1980
GNP (current prices)a $ millions	161.8	277.6	532.4	10.6	6.5c	937.0	8.5	1405.5
Population b	1410	1636	1954	3.0	2.7	2491	3.0	2890
GNP per capita ($)	115	170	272	7.6	3.8	376	5.0	486

a For 1954, R. S. Porter, Economic Trends in Jordan, 1954-1959, Middle East Development Division, Beirut, July 1961 (mimeographed). For 1959-1966: Government of Jordan, The National Accounts, 1959-1967, updated. The two series are not precisely comparable, but the statistical discrepancies have been adjusted to eliminate nearly all of the discontinuities. These figures differ from GNP data presented in Tables 1-4 due to smoothing in earlier tables of agriculture data and adjustment of indirect taxes. The official U.S. data on Jordan's GNP can be taken as the real GNP. (AID, Statistics and Reports Division, Economic Data Book.)
b No estimates of the 1954 or 1959 population are official, since the first census was not taken until 1961. The 3 percent growth per year rate is the 1961-1966 rate projected back to 1959 and 1954. Some reduction in growth is expected to result from emigration from the region as a result of the conflict with Israel. The rate is presumed to increase again as peace prevails.
c A lower growth is assumed to account for the years in which the country will have been divided and hence depressed between 1966 and 1975. A settlement and return of the west bank is assumed with an arrangement with respect to Jerusalem to enable Jordan to share in its revenues.

Jordan's farmers could increase the productivity of lands already under irrigation by planting more than one crop a year. Agriculturalists in Jordan believe that with such an effort, output of vegetables could increase at least by 50–60 percent in five or seven years. As indicated earlier, programs now under way in improving methods of growing wheat in Jordan through summer fallowing, fertilizer use, weed control, and improved seed varieties could triple wheat output.

By way of recommending a specific priority ordering of invest-

Table 13.7: Ratio of Annual Earnings to Annual Cost of Selected Alternative Investments in Jordan[a]

	Annual Gross Revenue ($ 000)	Annual Capital and Operation and Maintenance Costs ($ 000)	Ratio of Annual Revenue to Annual Cost, Capital and Operation and Maintenance (Col 1 ÷ Col 2)
1. Tourism [c]			
A. Medium estimated revenue, capital costs 10%, 40 Years Life	354,000	50,000	7.0
B. Medium revenue, capital costs 12%, 30 Years Life	354,000	54,000	6.6
C. Low estimated revenue estimate, capital costs at 12%, 50 Years Life	148,000	36,000	4.1
2. Illustrative returns (due to education) from employment per 100 men:			
A. In Kuwait			
Cost @ 10%, 30 Yrs	400[d]	168.0[e]	
Repercussions factor 2	800[f]		4.8
B. In Jordan			
Cost @ 10%, 30 Yrs	200	168.0	
Repercussions factor 2	400[f]		2.4
3. Ranking water, mineral returns [g]			
A. Ghor Safi (E Bk) 1,250	1,250	450	2.8
B. Jordan River (Both Bks)	4,000	1,504	2.7
C. Wadi Wala (E Bk)	3,500	1,400	2.5
D. Groundwater (E Bk)	1,750	725	2.4
E. Groundwater (W Bk)	1,500	651	2.3
F. Groundwater (East Highlands)	15,500	6,820	2.3
G. Phosphate [h]	10,400	5,200	2.0
H. Yarmouk River (E Bk)	29,500	14,750	2.0
I. Wadi Mujib (E Bk)	2,500	1,350	1.9
J. Zerka River (E Bk)	4,500	2,646	1.7
K. Potash	16,500	10,500	1.6
L. Small Wadis (E Bk)	5,000	3,900	1.3
M. Local supplies (W Bk)	2,500	1,950	1.3
N. (Desalting Jordan Water Per Acre, High Yields)	500	515 (per acre)	.9
O. (Desalting, Low Yields)	300	515 (per acre)	.6

ment potential, the table below indicates that investment in tourism, education, water-cum-agriculture development and in minerals would produce the best prospects for high returns to Jordan's economic growth in a peaceful Middle East. It is, in fact, very likely that with full cooperation in the area, these priorities basically would provide the most promising impetus to prosperity for all of the Middle East countries in that most longed for consummation — a postsettlement era.

aThese are rough estimates based on the incomplete data available, but they seem to coincide with what one would conceptualize about these alternatives. The rate of return on Jordan hotels, for example, is about 20 percent and on education leading to a Kuwaiti job about 18 percent. The returns on water investments are bound to be less than these rates. Adding the necessary refinements to these data (particularly production costs) will change some of the magnitudes and ranking of particular projects, but we would not expect these schematic arrangements of the sector priorities to change.

bOperating costs (production costs) other than for operation and maintenance of capital.

cSource: Battelle Memorial Institute, The O & M costs represent an average spread over different types of facilities as well as a pro rata proportion of the commodity returns on retail outlets which benefit from tourist trade. The facilities other than hotels are restaurants, roads, publicity agencies, airport maintenance, travel agencies, tourist police, shops, etc. The Battelle Memorial Institute *Report on Jordan Tourism* calculated that for every $28 spent per day per tourist, $16–$20 represented the cost per day of all the facilities needed to accommodate each tourist. The cost is assumed to be $18 per tourist per day. This produces a ratio of revenue per tourist per day over cost per tourist per day of 1.6 to 1. However, difficulties in applying production costs to all of these alternatives have led this writer to omit them, dealing only with capital and O & M costs. On this basis, if it is assumed that tourist facility production costs average out at approximately 50 percent of gross revenues (a level indicated by some sources), this would reduce costs per tourist per day by about $14, leaving a ratio of revenues to capital and O & M cost per tourist per day of 7.0 to 1. The Battelle Report made three estimates of the level of anticipated tourist expenditures which can be achieved ultimately (1986) by Jordan. These range from $502 million a year to $148 million a year, with a median (and Battelle's preferred) estimate of $354 million. If it is assumed that Battelle's preferred estimate of tourist earnings and if the 7 to 1 ratio is applied, the annual capital and O & M costs would be about $50 million, of which about one-half would represent the carrying costs of the capital investment (the opportunity cost of capital in Jordan is, no doubt, at least 10 percent and is spread over the life of the facility, assumed to be forty years). The total investment necessary to accommodate this assumed level of tourist earnings is expected by the Battelle Report to total $235 million. Using a rate of 12 percent over thirty years on the opportunity cost of capital instead of 10 percent over forty years would produce a ratio of annual revenue to annual cost of about 6.6 to 1 (1.B. in the table).

Even assuming that for the total investment of $235 million, one could expect only the minimum tourist spending indicated in the Battelle Report and a 12 percent cost of capital over 50 years, with O & M double the annual carrying cost of capital, the ratio of annual revenue over annual cost over the estimate life of the facilities would be higher than on any of the water projects (1.C. in the table). (Data from Battelle Memorial Institute, "Jordan Airports Feasibility Study," July 1967, especially IX-15, 16, 17.) This is another way of saying that the 20 percent estimated return on investment in, for example, Jordan hotels, and the 18 percent return on education of Jordanians leading to a job in Kuwait which returns remittances cannot be matched by investments in water development. This does not suggest that investment in water projects must not proceed but that a better appreciation of their alternative costs is useful.

dSalary per hundred men. With a total four-year cost per men of $16,000 the Kuwait salary produces an 18 percent gross rate of return (an increase in income of $3,000 over an income in Jordan without a college degree but with secondary schooling, assuming an average of rising income to be expected over the period to $4,000 a year in Jordan), as compared with the 10–11 percent calculated for education in the United States (Theodore W. Schultz, *The Economic Value of Education* [New York: Columbia University Press, 1963], quoted in J. W. Hanson and C. S. Brembeck, eds., *Education and the Development of Nations* [New York: Holt, Rinehart and Winston, 1966], p. 135. Also a rate referred to by Frederick Harbison and Charles Meyers, *Education, Manpower and Economic Growth,* [New York: McGraw Hill, p. 9]. Considering the fact that Kuwait's per capita income is roughly equivalent to the U.S. per capita and that the scarcity effects on teacher demand, costs of education, income forgone, and real purchasing power are commensurately adjusted, this rate of return is not surprising. These calculations ignore other costs incidental to obtaining and maintaining a job outside the country (travel, higher relative living costs, etc.), just as other alternatives in this list ignore some other costs. This ranking requires refinement but is suggestive of the probable priority ordering of investment alternatives.

eCost per year over thirty-year working life. Assumes a cost of $4,000 a year for each of 100 Jordanians, including income forgone each year for four years while getting a BA degree, total cost of $1,600,000 @ 10 percent for thirty years. A study undertaken by AID's Education Division (Bureau for Near East, South Asia), November 1967, supported these estimates. The program there for developing the potential in Jordan education assumes an investment of $72 million. The annual cost of this input @ 10 percent for thirty years would be about $7 million. To get a 5 to 1 ratio on gross Kuwaiti earnings per year would take about 8,750 Jordanians. The 1961 census estimated that over 60,000 Jordanians were working abroad. By now this figure is probably higher, conceivably by 12 percent or more. If this figure is 75,000, the 8,750 required to meet the earnings level to produce the 5 to 1 ratio would represent roughly a 12 percent increase in workers abroad earning an income at the Kuwaiti level (not necessarily in Kuwait). Thus, a 20 percent increase in Jordanian workers abroad is not beyond reach by 1975. Not all Jordanians need to go abroad to produce a return on the investment of $72 million in Jordanian educational infrastructure, but it would take more Jordanians working in Jordan to produce the same yield, as their marginal productivity is lower than when they go abroad to work. One could assume that although not all the income earned abroad is returned to Jordan, the advantages that accrue to Jordan by reducing unemployment and by a higher net gain in receiving a more scarce form of currency (foreign exchange) make up for the portion of his income the Jordanian worker spends abroad. These are conjectures at this point, but point to direct orientation of education investment toward end results that can produce higher returns.

[f]It is common knowledge that education has contributed significantly to economic growth. The increase in physical capital per worker accounts for "only a rather small percentage of the increased output per man" (Richard T. Gill, *Economic Development: Past and Present* [Englewood Cliffs, N.J.: Prentice Hall, 1963], p. 74). Technological change contributes significantly more. This is to a large degree the contribution of education. Schultz (see note d) referred to studies that attribute 21 percent of U.S. growth between 1929 and 1957 to education. This "repercussions factor" is the term this writer has used to reflect the multiplier or secondary effects of education on the Jordan economy. There is no way to attribute this effect precisely to individual incomes, but the effect is certainly there and is probably no less than twice the initial income effect. The factor of 2 applied to the Kuwaiti income also reflects the relative importance of foreign exchange to Jordan. The education a teacher receives also has a higher secondary effect because of the number of students influenced over the period we are dealing with, whereas an engineer, for example, may affect only his particular enterprise. An estimate of the return to Jordan's education investment over the past decade has yet to be made, but the budget allocated about $100 million to the Education Ministry and private investment must add considerably to this.

[g]Generally, these numbers give ground water development preference over deep well or dam construction.

[h]This oversimplifies by using one-half the investment of $103 million called for in the potash plant (AID Potash Loan Paper, 24 May 1967), since phosphate operations are already functioning. Present plans call for a 2 million ton output, but both marketing and transportation constraints remain to be worked out (the desert road is inadequate to handle 2 million tons).

[i]According to AID reports, a desalination plant would produce 118 million cubic meters of water a year covering 39,000 acres (2.45 acre feet per acre) at a cost of 17 cents per cubic meter, or $20 million. This is equivalent to $515 an acre for the capital and O & M cost of the water alone. Set against a $500 per acre yield which might be assumed for Jordan higher value crops, this would still produce a negative return of $15 per acre, excluding production costs. If one assumes production costs of 20 percent of the gross revenue per acre (a ratio regarded as appropriate for Jordan in a number of studies), this would add another $100 per acre in costs. This would make the total loss about $115 per acre. This estimate of the negative return on desalination, arrived at independently with tentative estimates of costs and yields, compares with estimates of the subsidy an Israeli desalting plant would require made by other experts, although both Israeli yields and at least the O & M costs would probably be higher. A $615 O & M and production costs per acre, set against a $500 per acre gross earnings, produces a gross loss on the 39,000 acres presumed to be irrigated by the plant of about $4.5 million. One report referred to a $52 million subsidy required for the plant, which at 10 percent over the life of the plant (say fifty years) is about $4.9 million, or if at 8 percent, thirty years is $4.6 million. Obviously, at $300 per acre gross yield, the losses would be larger by 7.8 million.

Notes

1. For a brief economic history of Jordan with emphasis on the pre-1967 period, see Nasser Aruri, "Jordan: Economic Growth and Dislocation," *The Arab World,* 15 (July–August 1969), pp. 3-7. Also see The International Bank for Reconstruction and Development, *The Economic Development of Jordan* (Baltimore: Johns Hopkins Press, 1957).

The student of Jordan's economy will find the following to be valuable tools: U. N. Statistical Office, Department of Economic and Social Affairs, *Yearbook of National Accounts Statistics, 1968,* vol. II, *International Tables* (New York: United Nations, 1969), E.70.XVII.3 containing information re population, manpower, agriculture, industrial production, mining, energy, internal and external trade, communications, consumption, international capital flow, etc.; *The Middle East and North A¡rica, 1969–70* (London: Europa Publications, Ltd., 1969, pp. 387–397 containing an economic survey of Jordan as well as statistical charts on major aspects of the Jordanian economy up to 1967/68 (e.g. population, agriculture, industry, finance, transport, etc.). Also see Reader Bullard, ed., *The Middle East; A Political and Economic Survey,* 3rd ed. (London: Oxford University Press, issued under the auspices of the Royal Institute of International Affairs, 1958).

2. Government of Jordan (GOJ), Department of Statistics, *The National Accounts,* 1959–1967, p. 34.

3. GOJ, *National Accounts,* p. 19.

4. AID Statistics and Reports Division, *Economic Data Book,* January 1969.

5. GOJ, Department of Statistics, *External Trade Statistics,* 1965.

6. GOJ, Department of Statistics, *The National Accounts,* 1959–1967.

7. Richard J. Ward, "Focus in Jordan Agriculture," *Land Economics,* May 1966.

8. This is developed by Richard J. Ward and George Soussou, *Priorities in Jordan Agriculture,* U.S. Operations Mission in Jordan (USOM/Jordan), November 1961.

9. Because of this smoothing, these tables produce aggregates somewhat different from later tables, which do not have smoothed data.

10. For a background assessment of the Jordanian agriculture situation in the early 1960's and growth potential, see A. M. Goichon, "La Terre et L'Evolution Sociale en Jordanie," *Orient* [Paris], 6e année (2e trimestre, 1962), pp. 25–74.

11. Marion Clawson, Hans Landsberg, Lyle T. Alexander, *The Agricultural Potential of the Middle East* (unpublished), January 1969.

12. USAID commitments to Jordan for the 1969 fiscal year totaled $1.491 million, all of it in technical cooperation and development grants; *The Foreign Assistance Program, Annual Report to the Congress for Fiscal Year 1969* (Washington, D. C.: U.S. Government Printing Office, 1969), p. 51.

13. For example, a UN special fund agreed to make available to Jordan some $540,000 for the second stage of an agricultural marketing project; *Middle East Economic Digest (MEED)* [London], 13 (28 November 1969), p. 1477. Also see *Argus of Arab Economy; Economic Review of the Arab World* (a publication of the Bureau of Lebanese and Arab Documentation, Beirut) 3 (December 1969), p. 13.

14. Also see "Post-war Economic Difficulties in Jordan," *MEED,* 14 (22 May 1970), p. 609.

15. Tourists from Western Europe and the U.S. decreased from about

205,000 in 1966 to less than 22,000 in 1969 and tourism revenue declined from JD 11.5 million ($32.2 million) to JD 5 million ($14 million); cf. ibid.

16. An article entitled "Is Jordan's Economy Dependent on the West Bank," *Israel Economist,* 23 (October–November, 1967), pp. 225–226 suggested that the east bank's balance-of-payments position is better off because the west bank normally ran a deficit of about $10 million. The loss of the west bank, therefore, it argued, would save the east bank this additional burden. This is a misleading assessment. In the past, Jordan has been running an annual deficit with the world of about $50–$60 million. Thus, if foreign capital inflow were allocated on a per capita basis, the west bank should have been running at least a $25 million deficit. In this sense, it might be argued that the west bank was contributing $15 million a year to the east bank. In short, the west bank was the more nearly viable part of Jordan. The simplistic assumption that divesting itself of the west bank with a deficit will improve the east-bank economy overlooks the effects of the benefits of the larger volume of economic activity the united economy of Jordan generated for both banks. While the west bank may more than be compensated in new activity with Israel, the east bank will not benefit, except to some extent indirectly, from west bank/Israel economic intercourse. For discussion and conflicting views on this issue, see E. Kanovsky, "The Economic Aftermath of the Six-Day War, Part II," *The Middle East Journal,* 22 (Summer, 1968), pp. 278–296 and criticism of the east-bank viability concept propounded by Kanovsky by Richard J. Ward in the same journal (Summer, 1969), pp. 285 ff.

17. Immediately after the June 1967 war, Jordan received approximately $55 million in emergency grants from other Arab countries. At the September 1967 Arab summit conference at Khartoum, Libya, Saudi Arabia, and Kuwait promised Jordan $40 million annually "as long as the effects of the aggression last." Jordan also received lesser amounts of aid from Western donors; U.S. Department of Commerce, "Jordan Continues Revival," *International Commerce,* 75 (11 August 1969), p. 22. This article assesses Jordan's economic situation as of August 1969.

18. See, for example, Tad Szulc, "Israelis Damage Key Jordan Canal in Reprisal Raid," *The New York Times,* 11 August 1969, pp. 1, 4; 24 August 1969, p. 19; 29 September 1969, p. 6; *Le Figaro,* 13 April 1970, p. 10. By 20 May 1970, the East Ghor Canal was operating again after having been damaged by Israeli military actions on 1 January 1970; *MEED,* 14 (29 May 1970), p. 645.

19. AID *Economic Data Book,* July 1968, shows commodity exports at the 1966 level on nine months of 1968 data and phosphate exports also keeping up with the 1966 level. The estimates are presumed to deal with both east and west banks.

20. For Jordanian import-export trade from 1966 through 1968, see *MEED,* 13 (26 December 1969), p. 1590.

21. For Jordanian expenditures in 1969, see ibid., 14 (22 May 1970), p. 610.

22. Ibid., 13 (7 March 1969), p. 317, citing GOJ Department of Statistics, *The National Accounts, 1954–1967.*

23. According to a later (May 1970) report in *MEED,* "the provisional 1969 GNP figure — which includes certain sectors of the West Bank — suggest that the 1967 figure [JD 206 million, ($776.8 million)] has again been achieved"; however "the East Bank is not expected to surpass

the 1967 per caput figure until 1971 or 1972 because of the increase in its population" ("Post-war Economic Difficulties in Jordan"). What prosperity there has been in Jordan since 1967 is "most observers agree . . . largely superficial, based not on solid economic infrastructure, but on an artificially high level of consumer spending. This trend, they say, can at best lead to the sort of service-oriented economy on which Lebanese prosperity is so carefully balanced; at worst to massive inflation and ultimately a collapse of the economy" (ibid).

24. In 1967, *The Economist* [London] also reported approximately 200,000 refugees in Jordan. See "Refugees, A Matter of Form," *The Economist,* 224 (5 August 1967), p. 481. Later reports reflect that since 1967 there has been an "influx of some 300,000 new refugees [in Jordan], increasing the East Bank population by at least 15 per cent" ("Post-war economic difficulties in Jordan," p. 609).

25. See Richard J. Ward, "The Long Run Employment Prospects for Middle East Labor," *The Middle East Journal,* 24 (Spring, 1970), pp. 148–150. Also consult International Labour Office [Geneva], *Year Book of Labour Statistics, 1969,* 29th issue (Geneva, International Labour Office [n.d.]) which contains statistical tables regarding total and economically active population, employment and unemployment hours of work, labor productivity, wages, consumer prices, exchange rates, etc. in various countries including Jordan.

26. In addition to annual contributions originally agreed upon at the 1967 Khartoum summit conference, Jordan also received in October 1969, $4.2 million as a first installment of a $15 million loan from Saudi Arabia for highway development *(MEED,* 13 [31 October 1969], p. 1357). On 3 March 1970, Amman announced the signing of an agreement with the Kuwait Fund for Arab Economic Development (KFAED) for a JD 3 million ($8.4 million) for the development of Jordan's phosphate industry *(MEED,* 16 [20 March 1970], p. 349). One should also take into consideration the fact that members of resistance organizations, Saudi Arabian troops and Iraqi troops have spent approximately JD 7 million ($19.6 million), JD 2 million ($5.6 million) and JD 5.5 million ($15.4 million) respectively in Jordan; cf. "Post-War Economic Difficulties in Jordan."

For other economic assistance to Jordan, i.e., aid from the World Bank for the construction of a 15-mile road between Amman and Zerka and for educational projects, see *MEED,* 14 (15 May 1970), p. 588. Also see ibid. (6 February 1970), p. 163 for a report on an Amman-Bonn agreement under which Bonn will make capital aid worth about DM 25 million ($16.8 million) available to Jordan. Also see *Argus of Arab Economy;* 3 (May 1967), p. 7. For technical assistance provided by Pakistan International Airlines (PIA) to the Royal Jordanian Airlines (Alia), see *MEED,* 14 (15 May 1970), p. 588. For a U.S. wheat loan to Jordan, see *Argus of Arab Economy;* 3 (June 1969), p. 6.

27. There are differences of view on whether Jordan experienced any inflation in the decade prior to the June 1967 war. AID, Statistics and Reports official assumption has been that there was virtually no inflation, while Oded Remba, in "Why Jordan Can Survive," *The New Middle East,* no. 6 (March 1969), p. 28, reported price changes of about 1 to 1.5 percent a year. The real growth of Jordan's GNP could, therefore, be assumed to be between 8–10 percent per annum in the decade prior to 1967. We have adopted the AID position that there was no inflation.

28. For a review of the Jordan River problem prior to the Six-Day War, see Samir N. Saliba, *The Jordan River Dispute* (The Hague: Martinus

Nijhoff, 1968); Friedrich J. Berber, *Rivers in International Law,* R. K. Batstove, trans. (New York: Oceana for the Institute of World Affairs, 1959); James B. Hays, *TVA on the Jordan; Proposals for Irrigation and Hydro-Electric Development in Palestine* (Washington, D. C., Public Affairs Press, 1948); Walter Clay Lowdermilk, *Palestine* (London: Victor Gollancz, 1944); Charles T. Main, Inc., *The Unified Development of the Water Resources of the Jordan Valley* (Prepared at the request of the United Nations under the direction of the Tennessee Valley Authority, Boston: 1953); Georgiana G. Stevens, *The Jordan River Valley, International Conciliation,* no. 506, 1956; Joseph L. Dees, "Jordan's East Ghor Canal Project," *Middle East Journal,* 13 (Autumn, 1959), pp. 357–371; M. C. Ionides, "The Disputed Waters of Jordan," *Middle East Journal,* 7 (Spring, 1953), pp. 153–164. Also examine Fred J. Khouri, *The Arab-Israeli Dilemma* (New York: Syracuse University Press, 1968), pp. 225–229, et passim.

29. The most immediately available source of new revenue is phosphates — resources of which are thought to be almost unlimited. Production at present is running at some one million tons a year, virtually all of which is for export. Plans under consideration foresee an expansion of production to some 1.5 million tons a year, giving a yearly revenue of about JD 6 million ($16.8 million).

14 Increasing Aid Without Foreign Aid

The need of foreign aid for less-developed countries, irrespective of the origin of such assistance, will undoubtedly increase in the years ahead. Even with the best of expectations about self-help the foreign-exchange requirements for all underdeveloped regions will rise. Estimates put the actual annual gap in 1970 at about $12 billion.[1] Increasing the contributions of all developed countries will help to fill this gap in the future, although the U.S. participation may in fact decline. The pressure for increasing the U.S. contribution through multilateral channels will, nevertheless, undoubtedly increase over the next decade. We need to be considering more urgently what other means might be tapped to facilitate the flow of assistance to the underdeveloped countries.

Reduction of Trade Barriers

To help meet the foreign exchange gap, increased efforts will have to be made in this decade to increase specific exports from underdeveloped countries to the developed countries through reduction of trade barriers of various kinds now in effect against the imports from less-developed countries. The suggestion has often been made, but little has been done on specific commodities, despite the fact that by far the largest potential market for exports from less-developed countries is the industrial countries, which now effectively cancel out comparative advantages less-developed countries might derive from innovative processes based on low labor cost. One economist has suggested that "the economic future of underdeveloped countries is in significant measure dependent upon the future commercial policies of developed countries, especially the United States, the United Kingdom, and Western Europe."[2]

A recent *Fortune* summary of a study underway concluded as follows:

> Exports from the developing world now make up only a tiny fraction of total world trade in manufactured goods. In 1967, for example, the developing countries accounted for about two-thirds of the world's population, but less than 5 percent of its exports of manufacturers. In 1968, by a U.N. estimate, manufactured exports from the developing countries rose by a robust 15 percent, but export penetration of rich-country markets remains small even for those products in which the developing world would seem to have a cost advantage. Eighteen of the most industrialized countries together imported nearly $3.8 billion of processed food in 1968, but less than 20 percent of these imports came from the developing countries. For wood products, textiles, and leather goods and footwear, the figures were 14.2 percent, 14.6 percent, and 15 percent. These numbers argue a strong potential for expansion. They also argue that the rich countries can afford to open their doors wider.[3]

Commodity trade barriers set up in various developed countries against the goods of the less-developed countries were estimated to reduce export earnings in a recent year by at least $4.5 billion on primary goods and an undetermined amount on manufactures.[4] Harry Johnson estimated the loss as follows:

Table 14.1: Effects of Developed-Country Trade Barriers on
Primary Export Earnings of Less-Developed Countries
($ million)

Agricultural protectionism	2,000
Sugar protection	500
European duties on coffee, cocoa, bananas	125
U.S. quotas on lead, zinc	45
U.S. quotas on petroleum	1,100
U.S. surplus disposal	685
Total loss	$4,455

Table 14.1 omits certain processed agricultural goods and manufactured goods. Protectionism against manufactured exports from the less-developed countries is denying them legitimate foreign-

exchange earnings as well. In 1962, the total value of manufactures imported by developed countries from underdeveloped countries was $1.6 billion of which $400 million came from Hong Kong; $370 million from India; $100 million from Israel and Mexico; $110 million from Iran and the Philippines; and $130 million total from Pakistan, Taiwan, Argentina, and Brazil. Recent data indicate that these ten countries accounted for three-quarters of the total imports from the underdeveloped countries and no other country accounted for $5 million or more. The principal product classes discriminated against were clothing, textile fabrics other than cotton, cotton fabrics, pearls, and precious and semiprecious stones. These accounted for two-fifths of the total. Exports of processed foodstuffs from less-developed to developed countries had a value of $329 million.[5]

Successive Kennedy rounds of tariff reductions have tended to hide the fact that these barriers against products which are of special significance to the export earning capacity of the less-developed countries have still not been eliminated. The gains from such reductions would not solve the foreign-exchange problems of the underdeveloped countries, but it would be a considerable help. The long-run effects on multilateral trade could be highly significant.

Tables 14.2–4 show the effective rates of protection in the developed countries against selective commodities and commodity groups exported from the underdeveloped countries in the primary, processing, and manufacturing categories.[6] In addition to these barriers, there is a long list of nontariff barriers in the developed countries against the trade of the less-developed countries:[7]

Foreign-Trade Policies
    licensing requirements
    quota restrictions
    negotiated export limitations
    foreign-exchange restrictions
    state trading
    procurement policies favoring domestic products
    antidumping and similar regulations
    subsidies to exports
Administrative Practices
    classification of goods for customs purposes
    documentary, marking, and packaging requirements
    incomplete or delayed publication of customs information
Internal Economic Policies Affecting Imports
    internal taxes for revenue purposes
    taxes applied to imports to compensate for indirect taxes borne
      by comparable domestic goods

pricing policies and price-control regulations
restrictions on advertising of goods
Internal Health and Safety Regulations Affecting Imports
sanitary regulations
technical specification requirements
regulations applied for national security reasons

Table 14.2: Estimated Effective Rates of Protection* of Value
Added in Industrial Products of Special Interest to Developing
Countries in Four Major Markets, 1962

Item	United States	United Kingdom	Common Market	Japan
Thread and yarn	31.8%	27.9%	3.6%	1.4%
Textile fabrics	50.6	42.2	44.4	48.8
Hosiery	48.7	49.7	41.3	60.8
Clothing	35.9	40.5	25.1	42.4
Other textile articles	22.7	42.4	38.8	13.0
Shoes	25.3	36.2	33.0	45.1
Wood products including furniture	26.4	25.5	28.6	33.9
Leather	25.7	34.3	18.3	59.0
Leather goods other than shoes	24.5	26.4	24.3	33.6
Rubber goods	16.1	43.9	33.6	23.6
Plastic articles	27.0	30.1	30.0	35.5
Synthetic materials	33.5	17.1	17.6	32.1
Other chemical materials	26.6	39.2	20.5	22.6
Chemical products	19.5	19.8	16.0	28.8
Ingots and other primary steel forms	106.7	98.9	28.9	58.9
Metal manufactures	28.5	35.9	25.6	27.7
Non-electrical machinery	16.1	21.2	12.2	21.4
Electrical machinery	18.1	30.0	21.5	25.3
Bicycles and motorcycles	26.1	39.2	39.7	45.0
Precision instruments	32.2	44.2	24.2	38.5
Sports goods; toys, jewelry, etc	41.8	35.6	26.6	31.2

Source: B. Balassa, "Tariff Protection in Industrial Countries: An Evaluation," *Journal of Political Economy,* Table 1. The selection of items from
Balassa's table is based inter alia on the text and tables of an interim report
of the UNCTAD Secretariat, *Measures for Expansion of Markets in Developed Countries for the Exports of Manufactures and Semi-Manufactures
of Developing Countries* (UNCTAD, E. Conf 46/PC/20, 6 May 1963).

Note to Table 14.2

The traditional theory of tariffs assumes that only final consumption
goods are protected and that they are produced entirely with original factors of production. Recent revisions and refinements, however, recognize that
a tariff on a good used in a productive process is equivalent to a tax on

the output of that process, and therefore there is the consequent necessity of distinguishing sharply between the structure of tariff rates on commodities entering international trade and the structure of rates of protection accorded by the tariff structure to the specific processes or stages of production that make up the productive system. The latter are commonly referred to as rates of protection of value added, or implicit or effective rates of protection. The effective rate of protection afforded a particular industry by the tariff structure can be defined as the maximum protection by which the value added per unit of output by primary resources employed in the domestic industry can exceed the value that they would add if all imports entered free of duty. For example, an apparently low tariff rate on a processed agricultural product, when combined with duty free entry of the raw product, may entail a very severe barrier to importation of the product in processed form. This compares the price of the processed good in the developed country on which the tariff is imposed, with the price of the processed good if it were processed by the underdeveloped country using its own raw materials and imported without a tariff. Tariffs should also be conceived of as protecting the use of domestic labor, and the effective rate of protection should also be measured on the basis of the part of value added that consists of labor costs. (The definitions here are more or less paraphrased from the Bavesi article cited in Source for Table 14.3.)

Impact on the United States

The U.S. balance-of-payments concern implied in the above, which militates against promoting further imports into the United States from the less-developed countries, could be offset by the counter-argument that such imports could reduce the underdeveloped countries' aid requirements from the United States. In other words, an argument could be made for a rising effective aid level which would include both the aid inputs and the increased earnings component by the less-developed countries derived from rising exports to the developed countries. Data on such imports are available and trends can be traced country by country and year by year. Identifying increases in earnings from selective commodities exported could achieve gains in this area without great fanfare and would be consistent with U.S. policies and GATT initiatives. It would also serve to address the issue of the growing foreign-exchange gap of the underdeveloped countries on a more economic and businesslike basis than do aid negotiations which often include broader, more complex, and more ambivalent political considerations. Nor would reductions in trade barriers by the developed countries affect adversely, in any significant way, various sectors within the U.S. economy. Such effects, in fact, are often greatly exaggerated. Economists are generally agreed on this point. To quote Ellsworth; "The facts indicate that not even the complete abolition of the U.S. tariff would cause serious injury to more than a small segment of

Table 14.3: Nominal Tariff Rates and Effective Rates of Protection of Value Added and of Value Added by Labor (%), United States, 1958–1960, for Industrial Products* of Special Interest to Developing Countries

Description	SIC No.	Description	Nominal Tariff Rate	Effective Rates of Protection Value Added-Total	Value Added by Labor
Bicycles	3751	Motorcycles, bicycles and parts	17.5	34.3	67.4
Cutlery	3421	Cutlery	35.4	50.8	417.6
	3423	Edge Tools	19.1	27.3	67.4
Electric motors	3621	Motors and generators	13.0	16.1	29.9
Electric fans	3634	Electric housewares and fans	16.0	23.2	78.8
Glass and glassware	3211	Float glass	14.9	19.1	46.2
	3221	Glass containers	23.9	37.5	126.7
	3229	Pressed and blown glass, n.e.c.	15.0	18.7	40.3
	3231	Products of purchased glass	32.1	51.2	300.0
Internal combustion engines	3519	Internal combustion engines	10.0	13.1	26.4
Iron and steel, semi processed goods	3321	Gray iron foundries	8.0	9.7	15.6
	3322	Malleable iron foundries	18.2	29.4	40.5
	3312	Blast furnaces and steel mills	6.1	8.5	17.5
	3315	Steel wire drawing	10.0	8.7	16.7
	3323	Steel foundries	9.0	11.4	18.3
	3391	Iron and steel forgings	13.1	27.3	45.1
	3461	Metal stampings	16.0	25.7	49.7
Leather footwear	3131	Footwear cut stock	11.0	14.9	27.9
	3141	Footwear, except rubber	12.4	14.4	26.1
	3142	House slippers	16.2	30.2	59.7
Leather goods	3151	Leather gloves	33.3	68.6	195.2
	3161	Luggage	20.0	30.4	69.8
	3171	Handbags and purses	20.8	34.1	70.5
	3199	Leather goods, n.e.c.	12.0	15.3	30.6
Linoleum	3982	Hard surface floor coverings	14.0	19.2	55.7
Machine tools	3541	Metal-cutting machine tools	15.3	19.8	30.2
	3542	Metal-forming machine tools	14.5	20.1	28.6
	3544	Special dies and tools	26.7	35.8	62.1
	3545	Machine tool accessories	26.7	36.6	70.0

	3548	Metalworking machinery, n.e.c.	15.3	21.9	48.3
Metal manufactures	3341	Secondary non ferrous metals	7.0	23.7	59.4
	3351	Copper rolling and drawing	8.8	7.5	16.2
	3352	Aluminum rolling and drawing	10.5	22.2	56.0
	3356	Rolling and drawing, n.e.c.	16.7	32.7	83.3
	3357	Nonferrous wire drawing, etc.	14.3	21.2	50.6
	3362	Brass, bronze copper castings	10.0	12.8	21.5
Plywood	2432	Veneer and plywood plants	16.8	37.9	80.4
Pulp, paper paperboard	2611	Pulp mills	0.0	—2.2	—5.6
	2621	Paper mills, excl. building	0.3	—6.9	—13.4
	2631	Paperboard mills	9.0	14.9	51.4
	2646	Pressed and molded pulp goods	9.5	11.8	32.8
	2649	Paper and board products, n.e.c.	4.4	7.6	18.1
	2661	Building paper and board mills	7.8	6.9	15.5
Radio receivers	3651	Radio and TV receiving sets	12.5	20.2	51.9
Rubber manufactures	3011	Tires and inner tubes	8.9	7.7	40.3
	3021	Rubber footwear	15.8	19.7	40.3
Rugs and carpets	2271	Woven carpets and rugs	20.1	17.8	35.3
	2272	Tufted carpets and rugs	20.1	28.3	195.4
	2279	Carpets and rugs, n.e.c.	20.4	33.2	85.0
Sewing machines	3636	Sewing machines	10.9	13.3	17.7
Soap	2841	Soap and other detergents	8.6	9.9	73.7
Steel furniture	2514	Metal household furniture	17.8	30.0	67.3
	2522	Metal office furniture	18.0	25.3	69.0
	2531	Public building furniture	18.0	28.5	56.6
Wooden furniture	2511	Wood furniture, not upholstered	14.3	21.6	39.6
	2512	Wood furniture, upholstered	14.3	14.7	27.3
	2521	Wood office furniture	18.0	27.7	54.8

Source: The underlying tables computed by G. Bavesi for his article "The U.S. Tariff Structure: Estimates of Effective Rates of Protection of U.S. Industries and Industrial

Labor," *Review of Economics and Statistics,* May 1966. The estimated effective rates of protection used are the lower of Bavesi's two alternative sets of estimates.

*The selection of products is based on the list of semimanufactures and manufactures of importance in the export trade of developing countries examined by GATT, Committee III, printed as Appendix II to *Measures for the Expansion of Markets of the Developed Countries for Exports of Manufactures and Semi-Manufactures of Developing Countries,* UNCTAD E/Conf. 46/6, 14 February 1964. Unfortunately, some important items in the list could not be matched with Bavesi's estimates.

American industry. The great bulk of our industry, agriculture, and mining would be relatively unaffected by tariff suspension."[8]

This argument is given added authority by a study in process by I. M. D. Little, Maurice Scott, and Tibor Scitovsky, in which it is emphasized that import liberalization policies do not cause serious unemployment. These authors point out that if exports from the developing countries to the O. E. C. D. countries continue to increase at the 1953–1965 rate, the increase over the next few years would amount to about $300 million annually. The effect of this volume of import on the twenty-two developed countries involved would be negligible. In fact, these economists show that if that volume were to triple to $900 million a year (an unlikely high estimate) the impact on employment in the developed world would be marginal. The authors divide the $900 million increase among the O. E. C. D. countries in proportion to their imports from developed countries as of 1965, producing an increase of $387 million in imports to the United States, of which $122 million would be textiles, eliminating about 11,400 jobs of 1.1 percent of those employed in the industry. Imports of clothing would increase by $75 million, displacing 8,900 workers or 0.8 percent of the textile labor force. It is pointed out that these would be the two most seriously affected markets, "but in each the displacement of labor would be less than the number of employees who voluntarily leave their jobs in a normal year."[9]

Further, the authors point out that even this fails to account for the beneficial impact on U.S. sales to the less-developed world when exports from less-developed countries are sold for dollars. The dollars earned buy U.S. goods, and these countries in turn buy from the United States. Thus, the net effect on employment would indeed be small, even in the short run, while in the long run, beneficial adjustments to lower cost imports, added to normal growth in various markets, would increase employment and probably some exports and possibly lead to reductions in discrimination against our imports abroad.

Once the United States assumes leadership in an effort of this kind it can seek to persuade other developed countries to follow its

Table 14.4: Nominal and Effective Protection of Processing of Agricultural Products, United States and European Economic Community

| Processing industry | U.S. | | E.E.C | |
	nominal (%)	effective (%)	nominal (%)	effective (%)
Coconut oil (refined)	5.7	57.5	15.0	150.0
Jute fabrics	3.1	5.3	23.0	39.6
Cigarettes	47.2	89.0	n.a.	n.a.
Hard fiber manufactures (cordage)	15.1	38.0	n.a.	n.a.

Source: H. Johnson, *U.S. Economic Policy* p. 46; see note 4 to this chapter.

lead, thereby opening a very substantial potential for increasing the foreign-exchange earnings of underdeveloped countries in European and other markets. This, too, could ease the pressure for more direct-aid contributions.

Identifying Commodities for U.S. Barrier Reduction

The practical recommendation that follows from this is that in subsequent GATT negotiations more effort could be placed on reducing developed-country barriers on selective commodities exported from the underdeveloped countries. The effort would involve examination of such exports currently reaching the U.S. market (or if the effort is broadened, other developed-country markets), ascertaining the barriers restricting entry, and seeking sufficient influence in the negotiating procedure to bring about reduction of the barriers. This would include similar action on the nontariff barriers listed earlier. A request from a Pakistan mission on this matter is a practical case in point.[10] To be consistent in promoting liberalization, the Pakistan instance may suggest ways of pursuing some liberalization of our own which would be to the benefit of both the United States and Pakistan. Other items may be selected for similar action in other countries. The selective approach allows for flexibility in the extent to which the effort might be carried forward in an initial round.

Elimination of duties on manufactured goods would lead to the following relative increases in imports of manufactured goods: Japan, 46.2 percent; United States, 43.6 percent; United Kingdom, 38.2 percent; European, 33.6 percent; and Sweden, 17.4 percent.[11] If the elasticity of supply in the United States is assumed to be one-half higher than in other countries, as might be reasonable, the relative increase in U.S. imports would be 56.6 percent.

The crowning argument in favor of pressing forward with this vital problem area in the 1970's is that it is the only way the less-developed countries of the world can win the struggle for ultimate balance-of-payments viability. It is also very likely the only way the affluent countries of the West can ever hope to be relieved of more politically volatile foreign-aid programs. Some progress has been made on this problem in the last decade, and recognition of the need is far more widely understood now than it was only a few years ago. Yet protectionist sentiment is on the rise in Europe and the United States and is still common to many other countries, notably Japan.[12]

The coming decade will therefore see this issue coming to the crossroads, when risks must be taken in order to promote the most rational road to balanced international economic growth between the affluent and less-developed worlds — broader acceptance of a free inflow of goods into the markets of the developed countries.

Notes

1. John Pincus, *Economic Aid and International Cost Sharing* (Baltimore: Johns Hopkins Press, 1965).

2. Delbert Snider, *International Economics* (Homewood, Ill.: Irwin, 1963), p. 548; and Alfred Maizels, *Growth and Trade* (Cambridge: Cambridge University Press, 1970).

3. "The Poor Countries Turn from Buy Less to Sell More," *Fortune,* April 1970.

4. Harry Johnson, *U.S. Economic Policy Towards the Less Developed Countries,* unpublished MS, Washington D.C., 1965; and *New Trade Strategy for the World Economy* (Toronto; University of Toronto Press, 1969).

5. Johnson, p. 51. The data refers to 1961.

6. These are all from Johnson's work.

7. Quoted in Johnson from UNCTAD E. Conf. 46/6, *Measures for the Expansion of Markets of the Developed Countries for Exports of Manufactures and Semi-Manufactures of Developing Countries.*

8. P. T. Ellsworth, *The International Economy* (Macmillan, 1958), p. 455.

9. The report of Little, Scott, and Scitovsky is summarized in the April *Fortune* article; additional arguments are presented in W. P. Travis, "The Effective Rate of Protection and the Question of Labor Protection in the United States," *The Journal of Political Economy,* May–June 1968, and in comment on this paper by Stephen E. Guisinger and Daniel M. Schydlowsky, in Harvard University Development Advisory Service Development Report No. 126, February 1969.

10. East Pakistan has expressed the disappointment of the authorities in the unwillingness of the United States to reduce restrictions against Pakistan textiles (U.S. Embassy message, 26 August 1966), even while we are pressing them to liberalize their own trade regime.

11. H. Johnson, quoting from Bela Balassa, "Tariff Protection in Industrial Countries: An Evaluation," *Journal of Political Economy.*

12. This was elaborated by John E. Field, "United States Investment Abroad — New Challenges for Management and Labor," U.S. Department of Commerce 58th Annual Meeting, panel 27 April 1970, Washington, D.C.

15   Commodity Trade or Technical Aid: Changing Aid Emphasis

Several studies made recently (Leibenstein, Harberger, and others) suggest that the effectiveness of some of the devices the United States has been striving to apply in its foreign-aid effort in the past may have only a fractional influence on development, while increased efforts to promote better organization, better management, improved skills, better methods, and innovative research could account for much more in the process. The validity of these studies should be tested in less-developed countries in this decade to determine whether U.S. efforts and negotiating and bargaining power could be focused on higher-yield policies. Coupled with the widely discussed disappointment with the development process in recent years, whether justified or not, it might be useful to consider these findings.[1]

Each one of the conclusions drawn from these studies may have implications for the emphasis still placed on trade liberalization, promoting reduced restrictions internally and across borders, promoting private versus government subsidized industry, and possibly on the proper proportions of program or project loan and technical assistance.[2] Some of the conclusions and questions raised may be enlightening for the new direction aid is expected to take in the 1970's.

The Welfare Impact on GNP of Reduced Trade Restrictions

The United States devotes much negotiating effort and leverage to promoting reduction of restrictions to trade. While the Leibenstein-Harberger studies ostensibly stress restrictions which affect price rather than quantities (their "allocative efficiencies"), the conclusions suggest that commitment of effort and negotiating leverage would produce greater economic gains elsewhere than on reducing trade restrictions, however desirable they may be. At the same time, the rather broad claims that are made for liberalization aimed at eliminating quantitative restrictions may escape the indictment of recent studies, but continued efforts at assurance should be supported by detailed analyses and measures of the real effects of liberalization. Reducing restrictions to trade is desirable in any case, but are the attempts to achieve liberalized trade regimes worth the cost in terms of the alternative uses of foreign assistance? For example, what would half of the close to $400 million program loan to India in a recent year have produced if it had been invested in modern educational facilities, technology adaptation, or means of improving the managerial or technological efficiency of export industries?

It is often indicated in the economic literature that economic trade has never been a crucial determinant in the history of the development of large nations. Where it represents a small percentage of the GNP, it is the internal economy that requires the bulk of the development effort. Obviously, this is an oversimplification and external-trade policy does affect the internal economy. Nevertheless, while foreign aid is inevitably balance-of-payments oriented, in its current form it tends to enhance the propensity to import. It seeks to mobilize unused industrial capacity by providing foreign exchange for imports otherwise unavailable to the country's industrialists. This form of assistance is coupled with policies to promote further liberalization of imports and devaluations to improve selectivity of priority imports. However, would not the entrepreneur who has sufficient motivation to invest in imports also be willing to invest in some alternative if the imports are not available? Would he not seek to utilize local factors either to produce a substitute for the imports he cannot obtain or by creating the internal demand for the factor to provide incentives for some manufacturer to begin producing it at home? Is there not the danger that the availability of more expensive imports will create built-in high-cost productive processes, when less expensive labor techniques might have been applied indigenously to provide the inputs at lower cost? In other words, is not the efficiency, technological skill, and innovation of the entrepreneur and his enterprise more important than simply the availability of imports? These are questions which have not been adequately addressed in our development efforts. These questions have particular relevance if an industry is also shielded from competition by high protective tariffs. In this case, the imports only serve to perpetuate inefficiency and noncompetitive production. This lowers the standard of living for the indigenous population and postpones the ability of the country to enter competitive world markets.

There is no doubt that liberalization policies and decontrol of administrative trading procedures stimulate enterprise and competition among producers and manufacturers internally. It is, however, necessary to examine tariff structures behind which these enterprises operate, as well as the alternative indigenous means that might have been used to provide manufacturers with factors they needed rather than imports. Technical assistance which focuses on improving more directly the research, innovative, and efficiency skills of those in indigenous industry is an area which has been neglected in foreign assistance to the less developed in favor of providing imports in the hope that these together with decontrols will create a market-oriented environment capable of fostering efficiency through response to incentives.

GNP and Monopolistic Enterprise

The welfare loss to the GNP resulting from monopolistic enterprise, including heavily subsidized government enterprises, "is of trivial significance."[3] This point suggests that expenditure of negotiating effort to reduce, for example, the role or the inefficiency of the State Economic Enterprises (SEE's) in Turkey or of government enterprises anywhere will have but a small effect on the GNP. This does not mean that it would not be desirable procedurally and for other reasons to reduce SEE inefficiency and to foster private-enterprise competition for the SEE's. All it could mean is that we should not expect much of an impact on the GNP to result from reducing such government enterprise inefficiencies or from eliminating such enterprises in favor of putting them under private ownership and operation, with less of the monopolistic appendages (subsidies, market controls of various kinds, etc.).

However, insisting on private-enterprise operations or more freedom of entry into various industries as a condition of a foreign-aid loan may produce important political and ideological gains, even though they do not affect the GNP much one way or the other. The value which is attached to the ideological gain, therefore, should be weighed against the economic gains in other areas which might be won and which at the same time might be even more effective in promoting the private sector (Leibenstein's "X-efficiencies," that is, technical advice to existing private enterprises, educating future managers and innovators, etc.).

GNP and Capital Inputs

It is said that only a small proportion of the increase in GNP is accounted for by inputs of capital.[4] Quality of management, plant layout, reorganization, materials handling, waste controls, work methods, psychological factors, and incentive payments — additional X-efficiencies — have far greater impact on output.

The point here is that investment in physical capital (plant, equipment, tools, etc., per worker) and labor has accounted for only from 20 to 50 percent of the growth in advanced countries, while residual components like technological change, education of the labor force, and other myriad qualitative X-efficiencies made up from 50 to 80 percent of the growth in GNP.[5] The physical resources or imports made available through project or program loans may have less impact on the growth of less-developed countries than the impact of the motivational incentives, training of labor, and management experience which use of the resources generates. This suggests the importance of determining not only what foreign-aid loans do for physical output and industrial capacity but what we might expect them to do for training of labor, improving management of all resources, stimulating innovation, improving methods and conditions of work, and eliminating waste. For example, "in one of the ILO Missions to Pakistan an improvement in labor relations in a textile mill in Lyallpur resulted in a productivity increase of 30 percent. Nothing else has changed except that labor turnover was reduced by one-fifth."[6] Other studies show that psychological factors which affect worker morale have affected productivity from 7 to 18 percent. Broadly applied, can such gains be matched with the resources made available to the less-developed countries as a material inputs to industrial capacity? Far too little attention has been applied to this area.

Consulting Services

Consulting advice to management on enterprise operations, improved personnel relations, better marketing, budgeting, and accounting have increased productivity by 53 percent.[7] Technological change (a function of research and innovative management) and dissemination of knowledge have a greater impact on growth than improved allocative efficiencies.

Many of these potentially high-yield steps can be uncovered and organized for action with the help of technical advice or consultation. According to J. Johnston, one-quarter of the annual increase in national income is accounted for by consulting services.[8] Should a condition of loans include more consulting services of various suitable kinds to existing industry (not necessarily only to those created by project loans)? Program loans affect total output only marginally. In other words, assume program-loan commodities and spare parts increase the level of the Indian GNP in one year by 5 percent. Does this contribute adequately to improving Leibenstein's X-efficiencies of the other 95 percent, where a small gain would add considerably more than a large gain on the smaller segment our loans affect? This is not an easy area to investigate, but it has thus far been neglected.

The Effects of Population Reduction

That population reductions which can be anticipated over the next decade will not have a dramatic influence on development is somewhat relative, but it is indicated in some studies that the Indian population growth rate may be reduced from 2.5 (it may be slightly higher) to 1.6 percent a year with wider application of current family-planning programs over the next decade. However, this does not account for the reduction in the death rate that is likely to take place over the same period due to better and possibly cheaper medical applications for maternity and infant care and for other deficiencies. A more realistic reduction over the next decade may therefore be from 2.5 percent a year to 2 percent. This reduction would take place gradually over the period, so that the effective reduction would be between 2.5 percent and 2 percent. If we project the increase of India's population of 500 million at 2.5 percent a year and at 2 percent, the resulting "saving" on the number of people by 1975 would be 33 million; the 1985 saving on a lower growth rate would be considerably higher but less, perhaps, than we tend to think.

Table 15.1: Indian Population 1965, 1975, and 1985

	1965 (million)	1975 (million)	Percent Annual Growth Rate	1985 (million)	Percent Annual Growth Rate
	500	643	2.5	826	2.5
	500	610	2.0	708	1.5
Family-planning saving		33		118	

What do the figures in Table 15.1 imply? They imply that the impact of the family-planning drive will probably not be very noticeable over the next five years and will not be dramatic, in an overall economic sense, even over the next ten years. These growth rates have taken into account the effect of family-planning programs only on the birthrate. The reduction in the death rate over this period may eliminate part of the advantage of the programs, although predicting how much is difficult. If we assume that the actual population saving by 1975 resulting from a combination of reduced birth and death rates will be 25 million and that wheat intake per person in India is 180 kilograms, the total wheat saving would reach about 4.5 million tons by 1975, some if not all of which will be made up of domestic increases in output in India. This is not an unimportant result for ten years of attention, and there are other gains associated with this result, but it obviously can only be one of the many variables that must be pushed in the development of India. How much of our negotiating time and effort should be spared from other potential growth factors where the input-output yields are more dramatic? Self-help efforts in this area may not be the most advantageous trade-off we can get for foreign assistance. It is clear now that food will not be the problem; the quality of capital investment will be our chief concern in the years ahead.

Human Capital

"The rewards given by the market to engineers, technically trained managers, agronomists, and other technicians themselves justify the investment in their training at a rate of real return which compares favorably with the best returns on investment in physical capital equipment."[9] This is an old theme supported in studies by Harbison, Schultz, Harberger, Lewis, and others. It stresses again the importance of the direct development of human capital as compared to providing material resources. The example is often given of the recovery of Europe. Marshall Plan aid represented only a few percentage points of Europe's GNP, while the indigenous contribution of built-in trained labor and technological and managerial skill made up the major contribution. In agriculture, Schultz has indicated a social yield of 35 percent a year from agricultural education.[10] Underdeveloped countries' policies which foster an acceleration of applied knowledge to efficient use of resources would presumably generate high yields. To some extent liberalization policies which help expand production and facilitate more ease of entry by individuals into enterprises where training automatically takes place addresses this problem, but the stress is indirect. The impact may be less than the time and leverage expended warrant in getting such policies implemented over other human-development policies and better practices worth promoting.

Capital Inflows

If Asian incomes are to grow by 2.5 to 3.5 percent per capita annually the annual capital inflow will have to increase by at least several billions net of debt service.[11] The United Nations estimated the import gap of the less-developed countries in 1970 to be $12 billion, while $5 billion seems to be the most commonly used level of additional aid required if per capita income growth is to reach 2.5 to 3 percent a year. The chances of the U.S. contribution to aid increasing are probably not good, while the level from other donors may rise some but not as much as may be needed. Self-help will be called upon to make its contribution, but constraints upon exports (against manufacturers, primary goods and on other potentials) are expected to check foreign-exchange earnings.[12] Should PL 480 shipments be shifted to Title IV dollar-repayable terms, the addition to debt service in five years could be $50 million in India alone. This would only add to the aid requirement, although not significantly, provided export earnings or aid from other donors continue to grow. The stiffening of terms for aid and the decline in aid in recent years will, therefore, intensify problems in less-developed countries, widen the growth gaps, and postpone advances for a still longer time.

Financing Imports

Barring striking changes in aid policies, future import increases will have to be financed primarily by exports. Private foreign investment as a source of capital will not contribute significantly, and import substitution tends to be counteracted by contributing to the propensity to import.[13] If U.S. aid is not likely to increase, because of internal pressures, while non-U.S. sources may increase some but not much, less-developed countries will have to look to exports for their growing import needs. The gap of from, say, $3 to $8 billion levels by the end of five years will have to be met by a concerted drive to generate export earnings. Alternatively, growth plans will have to be modified, which in turn would add to the widening gap between less-developed and advanced countries. According to data collected by Pincus, the chances of increasing primary or manufactured goods exports from the underdeveloped countries are very limited unless they and the developed countries institute some sharp policy changes.

The less-developed countries' share in world exports has been declining for some time. While Pakistan and Turkey have shown improvement in export performance, the rapid growth in demand for imports has increased the deficit in the overall balance for Pakistan, and workers' remittances have helped to ease Turkey's tight reserve situation. Indian exports showed little advance in the last decade. These trends reflect the situation for all less-developed countries, whose exports grew by about $2 billion between 1956 and 1966, while their imports grew by $6 billion.

The presumption should be that as these nations develop, foreign aid will make up less and less of the trade gap and export earnings will make up more and more. The demand for imports will remain high in developing countries, but if nonprivate capital aid is to be phased out eventually in the process, adequate emphasis should be applied to the means of financing the imports from the underdeveloped countries' own earnings. U.S. aid has tended to contribute significantly to the propensity to import in aid-recipient countries. Mason makes the point that "the hidden development effort [in India] has been seriously handicapped by the installation of more capacity than could effectively be supplied with commodity imports."[14] To the extent that such capacity is not purposefully export-oriented, the foreign-exchange gap could continue to widen with growing pressure for more foreign assistance, resulting also in higher levels of debt service.

Private investment as a source of foreign capital will be limited by discouraging rates of return in the underdeveloped countries. In 1956, private investment (net) represented 3 percent of their total exchange receipts; in 1966 it represented only 2.2 percent. The efforts to encourage private investment abroad through investment guarantees, tax incentives, and other promotional safeguards will not be sufficient to overcome poor profit expectations as compared to alternative uses of capital. In any case, the impact on the total economy of the less-developed countries is marginal. In this case, more effort spent on export-promotion activities or on getting the developed countries to lower barriers to imports from underdeveloped countries may have more impact on growth of the latter than all the efforts expended to increase the flow of private investment, however desirable it may be.

Export promotion is also tied to the growing debt-service problem. Long ago, arguments were made against the day of reckoning for borrowers that they should focus on investing in exportable industries; invest in industry of high capital turnover (therefore, not capital intensive infrastructure); and avoid investing indigenous savings in home-consumption industries where the propensity to import is high.[15] This does not mean that aid funds need be specifically oriented to these ends, but it may mean that we should strongly urge the less-developed countries to orient their resources, whatever their origin, in these directions.[16]

To generate adequate growth rates per capita for developing countries it may be that the combined aid to them will have to address all of the elements in the development equation to produce success. Yet, foreign-aid emphasis could conceivably focus on elements which will produce bigger yields. Policies designed to add resources (by financing imports) or to reallocate resources (reduce restrictions, promote private investment) and necessary, but policies designed to orient U.S. aid or to affect the human variable more directly in order to improve the use or manipulation, in a technological sense, of the resources the less-developed countries already have may produce considerably higher growth yields in the years to come.[17]

Notes

1. For example, UN publication No. E/4191 and No. 65.I.26, *The United Nations Development Decade at Mid-Point (Appraisal by the Secretary General)*, 1965.

2. Harvey Leibenstein, "Allocative Efficiency vs 'X Efficiency,' " *American Economic Review*, June 1966, quoting studies by Scitovsky and Wemelsfelder on the European Common Market, A. Singh on the Montevideo Treaty Countries of Latin America, and others.

3. This theme is supported by Arnold Harberger in "Using the Resources at Hand More Effectively," *American Economic Review*, Proceedings, May 1959. Leibenstein uses a case where 50 percent of the national income of an economy derives from industry run by government or which is heavily subsidized. The impact on the GNP of the misallocation of resources "is less than 2 percent" (Leibenstein, p. 396).

4. Studies in proof of this are many.

5. See, for example, Robert Solow, "Technical Change and the Aggre-

gate Production Function," *Review of Economics and Statistics,* 39, no. 3 (August 1957); Moses Abramowitz, "Resource and Output Trends in the United States Since 1870," National Bureau of Economic Research, Occasional Paper No. 52 (1956); Solomon Fabricant, "Basic Facts on Productivity Change," National Bureau of Economic Research, Occasional Paper No. 63 (1959); John W. Kendrick, *Productivity Trends in the United States* (Princeton; Princeton University Press, 1961); Edward F. Denison, *Sources of Economic Growth in the United States,* Committee for Economic Development, Supplementary Paper No. 13 (January 1962).

6. Leibenstein, p. 401.

7. It is estimated that one-quarter of the annual increase in national product is accounted for by consulting services (Leibenstein, p. 404, quoting J. Johnston, "The Productivity of Management Consultants," *Journal of Royal Statistical Society* (1963). The values of technical cooperation per capita in FY 1966 is illustrated as follows: Jordan $1.80; Afghanistan $.55; Nepal $.30; Turkey $.14; Iran $.09; Pakistan $.06; India $.02. The average for the groups as a whole would be $.56.

8. Quoted by Leibenstein, p. 404.

9. Harberger, p. 144.

10. T. Schultz, *The Economic Crises in World Agriculture* (1965), p. 68.

11. John Pincus, *Economic Aid and International Cost Sharing* (Baltimore: Johns Hopkins Press, 1965), p. 39.

12. Ibid. Pincus, Gill, Kuznets, Gerschenkron, and others remind us of the many disadvantages the late comers face in development as compared to the early comers. The concept of self-help is critical in development, but it should mean that the environment for certain incentives has been less easy to arouse in the less-developed countries than in the early phases of developing the present advanced countries.

13. Ibid., p. 6.

14. Edward Mason, "The Future of Foreign Economic Assistance," unpublished draft, 12 July 1966.

15. J. J. Polak, "Balance of Payments Problems of Countries Reconstructing with the Help of Foreign Loans," *Readings on International Trade* (AEA), 1949.

16. Obviously devaluations help, but income and price inelasticities for primary export commodities check the growth of such exports. New export channels must be opened up.

17. It will not suffice for India simply to accept the cast-off or obsolescent technology of Western advanced countries or even to use their technology. India will have to "leap over" or capitalize on the world's best current technology to break through to new ways (which may be peculiarly Japanese) of manufacturing, combining, meshing of materials, or selling, if it is to modernize and compete. Otherwise, by the time it has adopted the latest technique from another country it is already on the way to being outclassed by a lower-cost innovation from abroad.

16 A Health-Sector Concept of Regional Economic Development and Social Change

Defining the Problem

The appropriate role and thrust of public health projects in the formulation and implementation of social and economic development programs has long been a matter of controversy. This chapter describes some of the philosophy that has prevailed, describes a health-oriented development concept, and then indicates its interrelationships with the whole development process.

On the one hand, a majority of physicians and other health-sector professionals have contended that the availability of greater quantities of conventional health resources, especially when concentrated in "centers of excellence," will lead to wider adoption of improved levels of personal and public health. A minority of others, however,

*This chapter was conceived and jointly created by Dr. Robert Milch, Peat, Marwick, Mitchell & Co., former Special Assistant in the White House for Health and Life Sciences under President Johnson.

faced with mixed historical evidence eschew this "trickle down" theory and stress belief, rather, in a "bottleneck" theory.

In this concept, an organized broad-scale health effort could act as a catalyst to development by providing direct social, welfare, or employment benefits and create preconditions in social values and practices leading to limitations to family size. However, this effort is thwarted by barriers or bottlenecks, such as lack of trained personnel, commitment to build infrastructure, or willingness to initiate a variety of health-related projects which, in turn, frustrate the spread of employment opportunities, markets, and the growth of income. The result is that both the regional and national economy is denied health-generated growth potential, while the current static conditions simply support continuation of depressed levels of economic activity in the "low-income trap" syndrome.

On the other hand, during the 1960's if not before, many development specialists were disposed to maintain (1) that, at best, health projects or known and decisive forms of biomedical science and technology, even when well organized in relatively immobile and homogeneous or near-homogeneous populations, were only indifferently related to quantifiable levels, or indices, of public health; (2) that environmental conditions and still poorly understood interdisciplinary cultural and economic factors played a large (and possibly dominant) role in determining indices of health, quite apart from the quantity or quality of health resources and the degree of organization of health-care systems; and (3) that, at worst, rather than mobilizing idle and neglected resources, apparently successful health programs and activities simply aggravate already worrisome population burdens.

As a consequence, there has been little agreement in either poor, disadvantaged nations or poor, disadvantaged ghettos of otherwise advanced societies as to where health programs should be directed; how far they should be extended; what means they should employ; what costs and benefits can be expected; what other policy measures are required in deploying appropriately targeted "social health/ medicine" and "health science/technology" programs and services for the purpose of deliberately abating the recurring worldwide cycle of poverty and disease; and how health programs can be utilized to stem population growth.

The relatively low priority which has until only recently been generally accorded health programs in development projects can also be attributed to the prevailing philosophy of development fostered by the successes of the Marshall Plan in post–World War II Europe. The relatively close relationship then observed between capital formation (input) and aggregate output or economic growth led to a conclusion that physical investment was in fact the necessary and sufficient condition for, and the "engine" of, development. The Cobb-Douglas type of aggregate production function was considered the best index by which to measure progress or dynamic growth. It was only later recognized that such principles were not unqualifiedly applicable to non-Western settings and that physical investment in land, labor, and capital could not account for all of the observed increases in national product and income, even in highly developed, technologically advanced countries. Thus, a "residual factor," concerned principally with improvement in population quality ("investment in man"), came to be recognized as an important and perhaps crucial factor in development processes.[1]

For the most part, however, this widened concept of the capital-output model has dealt most extensively only with the role of education and levels of educational attainment. Yet, an entire array of other infrastructural factors, organizational, attitudinal, cultural, are known to have been operative in the case of successful development programs, and these have been seriously neglected in many, if not most, analytical or planning exercises. The health impact on this process has been one of the most neglected of these elements. The accumulated empirical and experimental evidence now demonstrates that the inherent physical and intellectual capacities of the labor force profoundly affect labor productivity; that these inherent capacities of labor will vary inversely with levels of protein-calorie malnutrition in prenatal and early postnatal stages; poverty, ignorance, and cultural traditions (that is, taboos and local customs) often adversely affect knowledge of nutrition even when adequate and appropriate food supplies are available (even on a free-distribution basis); and that by relating health to family welfare and longevity of offspring, family size reduction may be accepted.

The matter is further complicated by the fact that there has been no substantial body of theoretical or empirical knowledge which clearly links measurable health (and nutrition) inputs in a positive manner to measurable social or economic outputs.[2] In the rare instances where adequate and reliable statistics are available, the data come largely from advanced countries and some of the more-progressive poorer nations and, therefore, do not adequately reflect conditions in less-developed countries or regions, which are ostensibly the prime objects of technical assistance and loan projects. Where data are available for so many of the poor and the disadvantaged nations, which purport to measure levels of real income, capital growth, social welfare, health conditions, actual degrees of education, political balance, and other parameters of social and economic existence, they are frequently inaccurate or suspect.

The situation is also complicated in some traditional societies by a prevailing attitude and philosophical approach which equates an increase in population size with a linear expansion of the natural resource and power base of the society. Such a view considers an increase in population not only beneficial to the society but a necessary precondition for achieving security in old age in a maximum number of sons and a guarantee of security in numbers over real or imagined adversaries. Therefore, for a powerful mixture of often but not always commendable economic, political, social, cultural and religious reasons, only programs and activities at a microscopic (individual and family) level are generally supported by such societies. Macroscopic (national, regional, or community) policies and actions, which are typically governmental in funding and administration, are often viewed with skepticism and suspicion or are opposed outright. These more centrally promoted programs are directed toward what Robert McNamara of the World Bank has called "the basic problems of development — nutrition, employment, income distribution, and trade."[3] Lacking general public support and appeal, therefore, affirmative results of many microscopic programs, especially when pursued in isolation from related programs, are threatened with, if not automatically foredoomed to, frustrating inconsistency and ineffectiveness.

The Health-Nucleus Development Concept

The health-nucleus concept is assumed to be based on empirical grounds and posits the following:

1. Development is significantly an economic process which requires, above all, systematic application of management and entrepreneurship skills in many sectors of activity.

2. Successful management and entrepreneurship is, however, a function of a mix of indirect interdisciplinary influences which affect economic benefit-cost calculations.

3. Employment and economic trade activity are vital determining factors in regional and national economic growth and change.

4. The state of equilibrium in traditional or emerging societies is, in fact, metastable and not stable, and slight but deliberately and consciously focused programs and actions tied to a development strategy may initiate very large-scale "takeoff" processes.

5. Health-cum-employment-cum-trade activity constitute an inseparable and interdependent triad of sectoral programs and activities which can jointly serve this purpose of advantageously perturb-

ing a metastable economic equilibrium in the direction of dynamic economic productivity and growth.

6. Population-control programs can also more effectively be promoted within a regional general family health program than as separate birth-control programs. This also counters the positive influence of such health programs.

The health-nucleus concept also calls for the deliberate development of new communities within easy commuting (by foot or bicycle) distance of potential sources of new employment (preferably diversified and labor-intensive) which are partly induced by health-related activities but which lead to economic activity oriented toward both domestic and export markets. The strategy emphasizes a joint venture of comparatively modest governmental investments in the health sector (the construction of health support facilities, necessary roads, potable-water and sewage facilities, and housing units and the establishment of training programs) and substantially larger private investments in the business-jobs sector (the establishment and operation of construction operations, infrastructure building, manufacturing plants, and commercial support activity). Commercialized agricultural activity will also increase.

Finally, it assumes that both public and private investments will occur in close temporal proximity of one another for each region. Thus, each center will be able to support its own region, and accessibility to the center from all parts of the region should discourage agglomeration in the immediate vicinity of the center.

Health is considered in this context principally in terms of programs and activities which are geared to sustain with adequate housing and employment a higher minimum basic "quality of life" for individuals and families. The process, as described below, will generate not only better health, but employment. Moreover, the household units of employed individuals and their families will be supplied with potable-water and sanitary-drainage facilities, have a covered floor and roof (preferably with heating-cooling and gas or electric utilities), and have separate (however compact) kitchen, toilet, and living areas.

The organized system proposed for delivering health-care services is oriented to the prevention of illness and the maintenance of personal good health (health) rather than being primarily oriented towards the treatment of established illnesses (medical care). Programs and services would be housed in simple health-center units which require only minimal specialized equipment; are strictly limited, at least in the first instance, to a specified array of ambulatory-care "prevention and awareness" and emergency-care services; and are financed through a combination of government payments (general revenues and taxes) and payments by employees and their employers through regulated prepayment plans. Paraprofessional health workers, supervised or employed by planning ministries or ministries of health, assume primary responsibility for overseeing the continuing health and medical-care needs of employed individuals and their families; for providing family-planning, nutrition, health-education, and dental-hygiene services; for case-finding and immunizing against communicable diseases; for detecting chronic or preventable diseases and accidental and birth injuries; for rendering emergency medical-care services; and for referring and transporting patients to previously stipulated treatment centers for necessary medical care and hospitalization. The training of such cadres is in itself a development-oriented effort. No hospital beds or other special treatment facilities or equipment need be contemplated until such time as the prospective demand for such medical-care services warrants the relocation of physicians and the construction of on-site hospital and related ambulatory-care facilities.

In operational terms, it is expected that governmental sponsorship of health programs and services of the described type and of related preapprentice types of vocational training programs (in health care but also in construction) would serve as the initial "nucleation site" for the development program. Subsequent preplanned and scheduled support activity — housing, and employment opportunities — would then be developed in other sectors interfacing with health, as stimulated by the new process.

Developmental Tie-ins

Figure 16.1 presents a dynamic interface depiction of one specific health-impact factor — housing. "Messages" and pressures "go out" from the health unit or nucleus. The immediate concern of the "medicos" is the more direct and conventional health inputs of less-developed countries: potable water, nutrition, health, education, preventable-disease practices, and family-planning advice where life is threatened. These get first attention in the nucleus. Indirectly, these can have a powerful influence upon the productivity of male and female labor, but this is not in the minds of the medicos.

When the economist injects the development process into the health nucleus, a further awareness of the interrelationships with the world far beyond the health unit is generated. Miserable housing becomes an environmental bottleneck to what the medicos are trying to accomplish within the health unit. Thus, the housing sector must be pressed into action. The credit or loans and foreign ex-

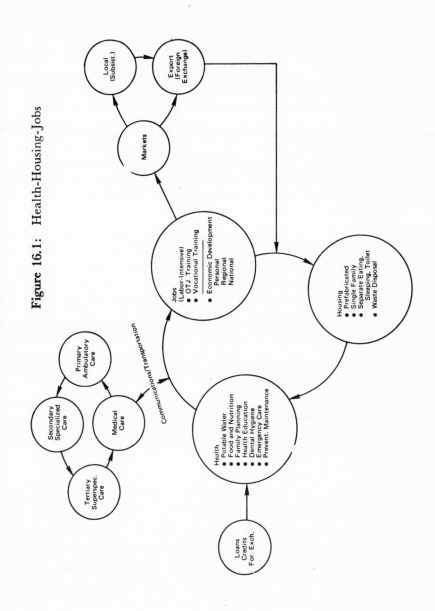

Figure 16.1: Health-Housing-Jobs

255

change needed must be allocated. Homes must be provided that at the very least have a neutral effect on the health of family members. This calls for low-cost construction of clean, more spacious quarters which include the minimum needs for sleeping and eating and provide other basic facilities free of disease-promoting features.

To function, the health center must be accessible to the specific region. Communications and transportation become a matter of concern and action so that full health services can be provided. Activating the housing, communications, and transportation sectors constitute but the beginning of a spreading process. To build houses, trained labor is needed. Both on-the-job (OTJ) and vocational training in the varied arts of housing construction get under way to feed the process. Labor must be located and transported to training and construction sites. Thus, the regions must be geographically accessible, and a sufficient number of regions should be developed to avoid agglomeration of populations at one particular center.

This cycle of health, financing, housing, and job training in itself initiates chain reactions extending to markets which must provide the inputs to the financing, training, and construction sequence. Rising activity from new jobs and supply ventures helps the local economy to begin reaching beyond the local subsistence features of the environment from which the region has emerged, to the more distant domestic or foreign community from which the region may purchase (import) products or to which it may sell products for domestic currency or foreign exchange. Improved health, training, and housing will in turn promote increased productivity and aggressiveness on the farm or in the fabricating shop, from which, in time, a surplus of products will flow in search of markets. On the contrary, the opposite situation in the absence of this catalytic activity is the chronic textbook low-income-trap syndrome, which fosters high disease and death rates, low productivity and subsistence production, and no market orientation domestically or internationally.

The fear that dynamic health programs will exacerbate the population problem may be warranted. However, the current population explosion developed in the absence of a total-health concept which included a family-welfare orientation. The concept elaborated here will include health-based family planning and education on the security benefits which derive from longevity, better living levels, education, and other preoccupations which divert focus from the need to acquire numerous offspring.

Figure 16.2 broadens the concept further to implicate numerous intersectoral activities. Beginning at the left of the figure, creating an effective health unit in itself will call for immediate inputs of training both construction and paramedical personnel and inputs

Figure 16.2: Bridging the Gaps

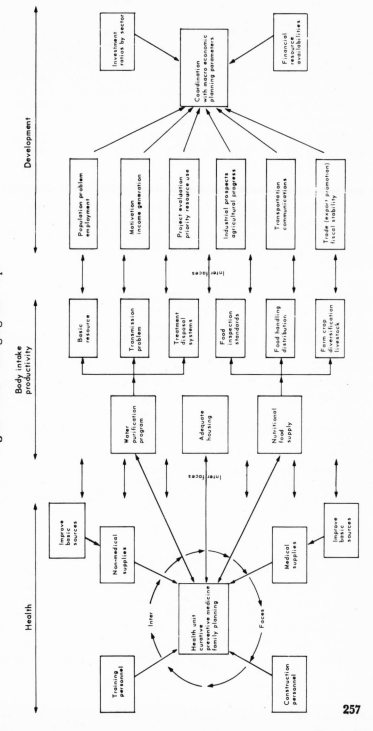

of medical and nonmedical supplies, which themselves must meet improved standards imposed by the new health awareness engendered by the concept. As soon as the unit cadres "feel their oats," they will begin to seek and demand improvements in the basic environmental factors causing the chronic high-disease–low-nutrition syndrome: potable-water sources, more-balanced food supplies, better housing, less unemployment or underemployment. These in turn lead to still more varied demands upon basic-resource inputs, geographic distribution (transmission) and treatment systems, food production, and handling and storage systems.

The cycle swings out to involve still broader concepts of growth. A core program of the health nucleus could well be a health-oriented family-planning program, which counters the positive impetus to population growth induced by improved health and lower death rates. The cycle of activities generates cells of new activity which begin to mop up the unemployed, reduce underemployment, and spur motivation for peripheral activity. The pressure for improved facilities and infrastructural support leads to more-formal project orientation, more-sophisticated agricultural planning, a greater domestic manufacturing effort (some import substitution derived), and better means of interconnecting all of these through more-efficient transportation and communication media.

The impetus for all of this activity from the health nucleus may seem exaggerated, yet it can be taken in part as the medico's view of the world as it inhibits and impinges on his effort to perfect and accomplish his role. Other specialists may construct a case for their view.

By traditionally viewing the developing world from the other end of this spectrum, the economist need find little difficulty in accommodating or adapting this exaggerated focus to his own macroeconomic or even priority-sector view of the world (the right side of Figure 16.2). He has developed his macroeconomic framework — the investment needs and benefit-cost criteria — which helps him identify priority sectors and projects. He knows the domestic resource constraints and foreign-exchange availabilities generated indigenously or loaned or granted from abroad. He has laid out the national accounts to determine the growth, capital-output ratios, domestic savings requirements, and gains that can reasonably be expected. It is as much his task to keep the health-nucleus cadre from overkill as it is to keep other sector emphases from making excessive demands on the limited goals and resources which pertain to the total process. He will examine the market, trade, balance-of-payments, and fiscal impacts and introduce guiding policies and strategies to both capitalize on the health-concept impetus and keep it within the flow and direction of macroplan goals. He will react to the impingement of progress induced by health programs upon other vital thrusts and force the programming into the properly coordinated interfacing with other sector or action-generating nuclei.

Initiating the Procedure

The pragmatic procedures for initiating or implementing the health catalysts to growth could proceed in two phases.

Phase I: Planning and Design

This phase should proceed in five steps, as follows:

1. Review with the planning organization and with local officials and health groups, including the ministry of health, existing plans and possible alternative regions for a proposed comprehensive regional health nucleus project.

2. Identify and specify on-site advantages, available resources, and the current status of planning for new industrial or agricultural development in each region, and select regions which are best adapted to the health-cum-development concept and best suited to perceived needs and opportunities of local regions.

3. Establish, quantify, and obtain consensus approval of goals to be achieved by the overall development program and of the subgoals to be achieved by each sector element of the program, such as health, housing, water facilities, and agricultural diversity.

4. Develop, revise as necessary, and obtain consensus approval of recommended and alternative objectives; design operational plans for accomplishing specific goals and subgoals in the health and housing sectors; and relate these to similar plans in the business-jobs and other sectors.

5. Develop estimates of cost and resource requirements and revenue and expense, cash-flow, income-statement and balance-sheet projections for establishing and operating the proposed health program and for constructing the required health, housing, or other facilities.

Phase II: Implementation, Monitoring, and Evaluation

The ultimate product of the proposed Phase I effort would be a detailed program for integrating economic and social development plans in a specific region in a particular country. During Phase II the planning organization and nationals of the country should be assisted in implementing recommended and approved program plans and in monitoring, evaluating, and revising, as necessary, operating results obtained under those approved plans.

Phase I would sort out the actual dimensions of the health-nucleus task involved and the problems which will be confronted in starting the process and in extending it beyond the immediate confines of the health unit itself. Phase II would postulate the plan for actually, physically carrying through the other sequential elements of the process as described in the previous pages.

The health nucleus concept is envisaged not as a panacea but as a device for mobilizing the specialist in a sector of activity which has until now played far less than its optimum role as a catalyst in the varied panoply of interdisciplinary parameters which help or hinder the ongoing processes of human developmental progress.

Notes

1. For example, Theodore Schultz, *The Economic Value of Education* (New York: Columbia University Press, 1963); J. W. Hamm and C. S. Brembeck, eds., *Education and the Development of Nations* (New York: Holt, Rinehart and Winston, 1966); and F. Harbison and Charles Meyers, *Education, Manpower and Economic Growth* (New York: McGraw Hill, 1964). These are but representative of a large body of research in this area.

2. The literature on the subject is sparse but growing. For example, John Bryant, *Health and the Developing World* (Ithaca: Cornell University Press, 1969); F. Vintinner et al., "Occupational Health, the Development of a New Public Health Discipline in Peru," in R. J. Ward, ed., *The Challenge of Development* (Chicago: Aldine, 1967); Jacques May and Donna Mc-Lellan, "Nutrition, Health, Development (Formula for Progress in Africa)," in *War on Hunger* (U.S. Agency for International Development publication), Washington, D.C., October 1970; James Banta, "Effecting Changes in Health Behavior in Developing Countries," ibid., August 1968; Eugene Campbell, "Development Indicators and Investment in Health and Education," ibid., June 1970; Frederick McJunkin and Arthur Holloway, "Global Community Water Supply Program," ibid., February 1969.

George Foster, *Traditional Cultures and the Impact of Technical Change,* New York, Harper & Row, 1962; Maurice King, *Medical Care in Developing Countries,* Chapter 1, Oxford University Press, New York; Gunnar Myrdal, *Asian Drama,* Vols. I-III, New York, Pantheon Press, 1968; Moshe Prywes, Michael Davies, "Proceedings of the Fourth Conference on Health Problems in Developing State," *Israel Journal of Medical Sciences,* Vol. 4, No. 3, May–June, 1968, Israel Medical Association, National Council for Research and Education; Hans Singer, "Obstacles to Economic Development," *International Development: Growth and Change,* McGraw-Hill, New York, 1964, pp. 55–64; James Banta, "Effecting Changes in Health Behavior in Developing Countries," *Archives of Environmental Health,*

Vol. 18, Feb. 1969; Walsh McDermott, "The Role of Biomedical Research in International Development," *Journal of Medical Education,* 39(7): 665–669, July, 1964.

3. Robert McNamara, Address to the United Nations Conference on Trade and Development, Santiago, Chile, April 1972.

17   The Possibilities for Fiscal Innovating in Development Policy

Introduction

Perusal of past issues of the *National Tax Journal* leads me to suggest that strategy-oriented tax policy for promoting more effective development in less-developed countries requires still more attention of the experts. Even when AID organized the Istanbul international seminar (November 1968) to promote agriculture development, the emphasis on the role of fiscal policy was ambivalent. Asia had just emerged from two successive years of devasting drought, and thoughts were still partially directed toward measures to relieve the pressures on farmers. Yet, even as the conference took place, unprecedented bumper crops and surpluses were occurring in Asia, and strategists were considering fiscal measures for tapping the precipitous rise in economic farm rents or quasi rents. Therefore, the

*Reprinted from Proceedings of the Sixty-second National Tax Conference, held at Boston, Mass., 29 September–3 October 1969.

multifaceted question posed was; Should farm productivity be taxed, subsidized, or both selectively?

The issue for foreign (or even indigenous) experts is further complicated by the hypersensitivity of the subject of taxation in less-developed countries. Defenses facing tax assaults on any hitherto unsurveyed citadel bristle with obstacles, but in the less-developed countries even the exploratory terrain around the subject is unfriendly. Subsidies are more likely to provide entrée as an incentive device, since the recipients have only cause to rejoice, while those who provide the wherewithal are ineffectually dispersed through the collective revenue system. The very simple procedural act of locating a site to hold a fiscal or tax seminar in less-developed countries is therefore discovered to be anything but routine, such being the apprehension and the power of groups or sectors who must worry about political controversy generated by newly proposed or theorized tax approaches. The very title of such conferences must therefore be broad and generalized to gain official acceptance, after which papers and discussions within the agenda may be quite blunt on theorizing or specifying who should or should not be taxed.

The papers and discussions presented at the Istanbul Conference are available elsewhere. My comments here as a development (rather than a tax) specialist derive from those papers and discussions and pertain to the lines of research which seemed most needed in light of recent developments concerning the role of the agricultural sector in the overall development process, both in the short and longer term.

There is no doubt that research has played a significant role in the current green revolution. Since Mendel's research began to open up the secrets hitherto locked in the tiny seed at the beginning of this century, remarkable things have happened. The results of hybridization and other innovative plant-breeding practices is plain for all, even for nonagriculturalists, to understand and to witness. Doublings and triplings of yields have actually occurred.

At the same time, both those "in the know" and those needing to know are wondering with Clifton Wharton; Is the green revolution a taxable cornucopia or a Pandora's box?[1] Despite the hopeful events of recent years in the incredible rise in the use of fertilizers, pesticides, the new miracle varieties, and other dynamic inputs previously denied farmers in less-developed countries for various reasons in the past, even the experts are wondering what potentially explosive problems — what dangerous ferment — stirs beneath the new abundance. Thus, while the Istanbul seminar dealt with many particular problems in given countries, as well as with general conceptual problems about price relationships and the role of fiscal policies in activating productive incentives, what needs considering now is the real significance of the agricultural transformation that appears to have taken place and what the role of fiscal policy in optimizing investment choices.

What does it mean for man's ability to feed rapidly-growing populations — not simply more stuff but better stuff — a more balanced, optimally nutritional diet? When do we stop pushing subsidized fertilizer for wheat or rice and start to push it for vegetables, fruits, and nuts? When do we stop price-incentivizing the grains and start goading for productivity in dairy or animal products? When do we quit gauging the mechanical time-and-spatial dimensions of food-grain self-sufficiency and face the need for a balanced posture toward productivity, management of optimum buffer stocks, the switch to alternative cropping, and the lateral (new think) leap to either tree or vine crops, livestock, nonfood land crops, or fortified foods leading to reduced farmland use and hence transfer of land outside the farm sector altogether? What mix of tax-subsidy-price policy will promote the appropriate allocation of human and natural resources?

As intimated by John Mellor, how do we phase price relationships between food and nonfood products so as not to prevent desired intercommodity shifts. As he said, "A price policy which attempted to hold old price relationships might prove extremely expensive in financial terms and would be counter-productive as well."[2]

These are questions which lead to research, and they certainly lead to implications for fiscal-policy measures. If grain surpluses are imminent (at least at old consumer prices) can we now give up the obsession with price support and subsidy and focus fiscal efforts on longer-term measures and programs of stabilization, increased effective demand by lower relative prices, and growth of farm income? In the inevitably evolving process of diversification, what mix of fiscal incentives can be devised for inducing not only the large commercial farmers who avidly applied the modern technology but the survival-conscious peasant farmers who didn't, to switch or phase over to new crops (even nonfood crops) or to livestock when only part of their lands are adequate to satisfy consumption?

There is, thus, a great deal of what might be called procedural research or surveying to be done at present to determine where we have come before we can determine where we are to go now. We know that fertilizer, pesticide, water, and even labor-versus-equipment-use are new to millions of farmers, but we are unsure to what extent these applications are being properly managed or are leading to new crises. We are also told, for example, that the new crop varieties are highly relished and greedily attacked by new mini-monsters or genotypes. Some argue that an ecological boomerang may be produced by the wide-spread use of chemical insecticides, which accelerate a process of natural selection among pests, producing this "super-race of strong, resistant individuals."[3] This means new resistant varieties must constantly be sought and new plant-protection services quickly and efficiently deployed. In turn, this calls for a commitment of budgetary resources by governments to expedite effective training programs, larger research and extension staffs, and other infrastructural utilities. This in turn calls for devising appropriate revenue sources, presumably based on the benefit principle, although some Asian economists at the conference expounded a sort of compensation principle, reflecting the view that agriculture has been the victim of centuries of exploitation, domestic and foreign.[4]

Most new high-yield varieties require irrigation and water control. Thus, installation of irrigation complexes will generate serious cost problems, which will be a researchable bottleneck.[5] It is said that the massive Mekong River irrigation scheme will cost about $2 billion over the next twenty years, "roughly 35% of the annual national income of the four countries involved."[6]

In view of the prospects for more of such projects and of many less ambitious but equally essential ones, how can the costs of new irrigation complexes be reduced? Must we use the costly old methods? Are there no cheap but sturdy and dependable ways to provide irrigation? If new systems can be devised, could lower maintenance costs and rates be anticipated? There is certainly cause to hope that there is. We once used to think that anything made of plastic or thin metals was junk. Now, we find plastic tubing, piping, and all manner of cams, transfer belts, and parts performing deadly serious tasks. Similarly, light metals, once considered frivolous, now form automobiles, motors, and much other functional equipment. Miraculously, these light materials, compounded with what appear to the uninitiated as chemical miracles, are often tougher than the best steel. Research is also badly needed to find ways to reduce the costs of irrigation complexes. Cheaper materials are probably only part of the answer. Perhaps depletion allowances against the current heavy costs of irrigation construction or tax credits tied to investment in research in this field could be an innovative fiscal contribution to this cause. If, however, the yet undiscovered optimum method is the bottleneck, the "trained incapacity" of our irrigation experts must be overcome by bold lateral thinking and innovation spurred by incentive-oriented policy and generated by dynamic research.

Then, there is a whole range of new problems in marketing and distribution needing research for answers. If eventually food-grain productivity doubles or triples in the massive subsistence farm sector, demand and income elasticities will not absorb all of the increase. The enormous flows of new output into the marketplaces of India or Pakistan can prove a disastrous loss unless new market outlets are sought and developed. Market research may be somewhat off the path of pure scientific research, but to the extent that it leads to rational preparation and gyroscoping of the impact of ad hoc policy and action programs, such research can signal the need to act well in advance to mollify potential trouble. The potential for export markets, regional or otherwise, must be examined in an overall worldwide context. The factors which are likely to bear on export earnings — foreign-exchange rates, internal inflation, stultifying export taxes or import bans on inputs needed to utilize agricultural exports — need assessment as to their cost to the afflicted countries and as to the best means of eliminating these influences.

Does correlation between education and willingness to adopt new technology offer a simple dynamic or guarantee to future growth in agriculture?[7] We think it is so, as Anthony Koo outlined in one of the Istanbul papers on Taiwan, but do not really know. If it is so, how does a country marshal the resources and the energy to step up the literacy rate? How can we get rural sectors which have abundant savings (as Bharat Dhital of Nepal, Rawat of India, and others demonstrated in their Istanbul Conference papers) to view education as an investment in their own future welfare rather than, as they tend often to do now, only as an essential current operating input to the sowing and reaping? For the multimillions of illiterate children of these underdeveloped rural regions, in a word, today's sowing and reaping of wheat may be tomorrow's weeping and gnashing of teeth. Clearly, this is a problem in both cultural and fiscal strategy. Given the gains witnessed in the agricultural upsurge, is there not some social obligation of the sector to invest a share of the boon in educating its rural youth? What budgetary ratio or formula would be acceptable ·to underdeveloped countries' governments in this regard?

These introductory remarks illumine but a small corner of the massive laboratory where research must be done. Nor did the Istanbul seminar itself deal, except by implication, with all of them. The impact of the green revolution was not the basic theme of the conference, but rather the ambivalent themes of how price supports for outputs or subsidies for inputs would best contribute to increasing agricultural productivity and what taxes or other changes should agriculture pay out of its new-found affluence so as to provide investment resources for the economy, including the agricultural sector. A number of papers dealt with particular cropping or incentive problems not necessarily addressing those basic themes, but in the fiscal implications they were all related. Ranis gave us a kaleidoscope of the place of agriculture as a sector in the development of nations, but we gave little attention in our clashes to the role of agriculture in the economy of the year 2000. Will agriculture continue to dominate the less-developed economies? Will the orthodox view of a declining agricultural sector — in contribution to GNP, in labor-force size, in occupational importance — prevail in the land of rice, bullock, and campesino, as it has in the land of race cars, appliances, and urban clusters? Not long ago the question would not even have been asked. It was assumed the answer was always yes. Now, we are beginning to question this view.

Fiscal or tax policy and therefore fiscal incentives have a function in this category of problems, and from all appearances the agricultural sector will also be a focus of analyses on the critical employment problem over time.[8]

Research Needs

The appropriate identifiers of research needs are nearly always researchers themselves in special or particular topics, for in preparing their own research, they naturally have covered the field of existing knowledge and have a visceral appreciation of the lacunae thereby encountered. Ideally, therefore, seminar managers should request research requirements from authors in the topical or thematic areas developed in their papers. Time and distance made this too awkward an effort to mount, and I have, instead, taken the liberty of going through the Istanbul conference papers to identify what seemed likely researchable problems or areas. For what undoubtedly contains as many omissions as inclusions (after all, I have not been asked what research has been done, but what research remains to be done), I nevertheless offer the following more specific suggestions for research, based on the conference papers. I take responsibility for the inclusions and apologize for the obvious finite, but not the infinite, researchable items not included.[9]

Research Needs in Pricing, Taxing, and Subsidizing Inputs or in Outputs

1. Whether or not farmers respond significantly to changes in price; the extent to which the existing agricultural resources are

allocated efficiently under conditions of traditional agriculture; closely related, the extent of surplus farm labor under these conditions; the farm price-effects in the receiving country of PL 480 imports. (Schultz — University of Chicago)

2. From the point of view of economic incentives we would need to know to what extent farmers respond to price changes as distinct from income changes in making their decisions and insofar as it is price changes we need to know to what extent they react to the current or some other concept of normal or permanent prices. (Mellor — Cornell)

3. A study of the benefit-cost ratios needed to get farmers to adopt new techniques in developing countries. (Adams — AID, Washington)

4. The relative foreign-exchange costs of agricultural and industrial programs and influences that can be drawn from studies of individual crop response. (Adams — AID, Washington)

5. What is the extent to which export taxes (that is, on tea, cotton, karakul, jute, etc.) distort incentives to produce and export? And if governments were fully aware of the effects would they have the incentive to abolish such taxes? (Mohmand, Saunders, Kittrell — Afghanistan)

6. Studies of output response to the mix of inputs. (Raj Krishna — India)

7. Comparative analyses of the effectiveness of various input subsidy and price support programs. (Raj Krishna — India)

8. Studies of the effects of particular programs and the individual and family level. (Raj Krishna — India)

9. The relative efficiency of the free market and government marketing boards. (Forker — Cornell)

10. Study of the problem of default on small loans and procedures to maximize collections. (Rhodes — AID, Turkey)

11. Evidence is that middlemen (grain traders, millers, etc.) do not make exorbitant profits from their services, but the wide gap between remuneration to the grower and cost to the consumer suggests the need for study and innovative improvements in marketing, processing, and distribution to seek unit cost savings. (Rees — AID, Washington, as suggested by reading of Mellor, Forker, and others)

12. Others (Please and Mellor) show that existing credit institutions favor owners of larger farms, so the challenge is to find mechanisms which will direct credit to the segment of farmers that the nation will wish to support. (Rees — AID, Washington)

13. Many participants referred to the question of effective demand or consumption consideration, suggesting the need for re-

search in income or price elasticities of demand for different agricultural products and in particular the need for studies of cross-elasticities. (Rees, as suggested by Ranis, Krishna, Mellor comments)

14. Can taxes be used to get farmers from subsistence farming to cash farming? (Morss — Harvard University)

15. The ways and the extent to which land reform will affect development are seldom spelled out in scientifically testable relations between empirically identifiable factors. (Anthony Koo — Michigan State)

16. In view of the significance of jute industries to Pakistan and India and the decline in world market returns, what is the future of world markets for this product? (A. K. M. Ghulam Rabbani — E. Pakistan)

17. What are the underlying causes of the enormous differences in efficiency of the Pakistan jute mills? (Rabbani — E. Pakistan)

18. To what extent should agricultural mechanization be encouraged in a surplus labor economy? (Should an undervalued exchange rate be allowed to prevail as a price inducement to this input?) (Bose, Clark — Pakistan and Williams College)

19. How should the price of mechanization be adjusted to accommodate the divergence between social and private benefits and costs? That is, if mechanization produces unemployment, how will its consequence be dealt with? (Bose, Clark — Pakistan and Williams College)

20. Research is needed into the means for making credit available on economic terms to small farmers who en masse constitute the most numerous segment in the agricultural sector. (Tilikaratne — Ceylon)

21. As farmers prosper and surpluses seem imminent, to what extent should tax or other fiscal inducements be afforded agro-input industries in order to increase the use of inputs by farmers by enhancing the benefit-cost? (Ward, as reflected in Billings, AID/India paper)

22. Turkey has an extensive system of input and output incentives covering subsidized fertilizer, seed production and credit for a variety of inputs, including irrigation and land improvement projects, price supports on a variety of commodities, and numerous government-supported services. It is not clear, however, to what extent these incentives compensate for high-cost, protected domestic output of inputs (fertilizer), or consider the longer-run objectives of an optimum agriculture in Turkey. A coordinated study is needed of the basic economic effects and incidence of these incentives on food self-sufficiency objectives, diversification prospects, and export potentials. (Ward, as derived from Karachahisarli Turkey study)

23. How might selective subsidies to fertilizer (by commodity) create incentives for crop diversification as countries reach food-grain self-sufficiency? (Ward, generated from F. Kahnert, OECD, Paris)

24. Fertilizer price policies are widespread, but there is a clear difference between Latin America, where they are least common, Africa, which is in an intermediate position; and Asia, which pays most attention to fertilizer price policies. The scope of such policies varies widely. Some are general, like price review, control, or fixing policies, either by nutrient, by product, by crop, or by farmer category. Some discrimination is conscious and sometimes inspired by motives alien to agricultural development; some discrimination between products arises inadvertently from methods of applying a subsidy. In general, information on the schemes is fragmentary and not precise enough to come to well-founded conclusions (F. Kahnert — OECD, Paris)

Research on Incentives in Taxing Land, Income, and Wealth

1. What are the real incentive (and incidence) effects of agricultural taxation, especially the land tax, on development (that is, revenue gains versus private motivation and public investment?) (Holland — MIT)

2. Agricultural tax measures are inevitably concerned with aggregate agricultural output. However, there is an inadequacy of empirical research "relating to the responsiveness of supply and of marketed supply of agricultural output to changes in effective producer prices." (S. Please — World Bank)

3. What are the relative virtues or disadvantages, direct and indirect effects of the land tax as compared to an income tax or a tax on output of agriculture? (Bulutoglu — Turkey)

4. There are differences of view reflected in conference papers (Holland, Yucelik, Rawat, for example) as to the real effectiveness and purposes of a land tax. Research is needed to test hypotheses and assumptions about the land tax as an incentive either to optimize land use or resource allocation within agriculture as between crops or other uses or as between agriculture and other sectors. (Ward — formerly AID)

5. Although the effect of an income tax on product prices has been studied for many years in developed countries through economic analyses which seek to appraise the extent to which forward shifting of the (agricultural) income tax may be expected, the final word has not been said. (Mülayim — Turkey) Professor Mülayim deals with the Turkey case in his paper, not only in the effect on

product prices, but on size of farm holdings, on savings, investment, and efficiency. Musgrave and others have also indicated the need for further research in this area.

6. How can a country match an effective cadastral survey process which generates substantial revenues with equally effective development-oriented government fiscal policies? (Mohammed Jalallar, Kittrell — Afghanistan)

7. Given the experience in Nepal, what does it profit the agricultural sector to garner the unexpectedly ample savings of the peasants only to find that effective outlets for investment of the savings collected is thwarted by supply and infrastructural constraints? Or what is worse, why collect savings if governments spend them foolishly? (Ward, as reflected in Dhital — Nepal)

8. Numerous proposals are being made to increase mobilization of rural resources (Rawat — India; Dhital — Nepal, others.) This leads to a lateral think proposal for research: "Mobilize? For what?" Assuming a successful drive to accumulate savings in appropriate institutions, who will make the decisions as to how such funds should be invested?

9. How do you balance the flow of capital out of agriculture with effective growth in all sectors? Or, which sector is to carry the major burden of development over what period of time? (Kivanc — Turkey)

10. If it is true that land revenue, the major tax on Indian agriculture, is regressive or at best proportional and that most of the agricultural subsidies benefited the big farmers more than the small ones, then one cannot escape the hypothesis that tax-subsidy policy of the Indian government might have led to an increase in the inequalities of incomes and wealth in the agricultural sector. However, this hypothesis needs to be tested by further research. (V. Gandhi — India)

11. Just as new genetic varieties of seeds need adaptive research to determine their value in differing national and regional circumstances, so also is there need for "adaptive" research on the whole spectrum of farmer response, institutional acceptability, and political feasibility. Questions of tax policy, tax administration, marketing, urban-rural terms of trade, regional differentiation within nations, are not questions which can be decided for any nation based solely on experience elsewhere. They should be decided on the basis of principle, reinforced by the findings of research by indigenous researchers. (Rees — AID, Washington)

It is clear that fiscal strategies cannot be confined only to agriculture. The agricultural upsurge has produced a new generation of problems, some of which seem to have taken us by surprise. From ominous droughts to near self-sufficiency in potentially mass famine areas of the world has led us to wonder what to expect next. Certainly droughts have not been consigned only to history yet; there will be more. Nevertheless, it is generally accepted that there has been an upward kink in the production trend line and with it have come problems relating to surpluses, shifts from cereal production to other foods of higher nutritive value, and to nonfood agricultural items valuable for export. It has also brought rising problems relating to transportation, storage, marketing, the development of agrobusinesses of every conceivable kind, and all the other problems related to abundance in the face of fairly slowly changing demand elasticities. There are a number of other problems incidental to this revolution, pertaining to distortions in income distribution as between regions, between small farms and large farms, and between families and individuals within regions. This, in turn, has raised tensions between town and country, between landowners and tenants, and between village leaders and peasant workers.[10]

The underdeveloped countries themselves are not adequately equipped to deal with these problems in research that could suggest solutions to them. They will have to be assisted with imported scientific competence. As Moseman has illustrated in a dramatic way, the shortage of scientific skills in agricultural fields is critical in the underdeveloped countries. He reports that "the Minnesota Agricultural Experiment Station has as many Ph.D.-trained personnel at its Northwest Experiment Station at Crookston and at the Southern Branch Experiment Station at Weseca as does the entire research branch of the Ministry of Agriculture and cooperatives of the Government of Malaysia. And the latter organization is responsible for its nation-wide program of research on all crops, soil, water management, disease and pest control and related problems for all aspects of agriculture except rubber."[11] This is a serious problem, even if this overstates the case (Minnesota's income is high and its population not that much less), and it suggests that not too many innovative fiscal measures are likely to emanate from these overburdened facilities and men in countries such as India or Pakistan. There is a real need, therefore, to provide the incentives which will contribute to increasing the availability of trained agriculturalists, trained not only in the physical aspects of agriculture but in its broader economic impact. Scholarships or other forms of subsidy may be implied, but the real problem may be at the other end — the relative financial and psychic compensation for such services. What new shaft of wisdom can we cast on this problem?

A broader fiscal outlook is also essential in the current atmosphere in view of the major impact that agriculture is now seen to have on the rest of the less-developed economies. India's economy has been struggling to mount a full-scale revival, spurred on by the upsurge in agricultural incomes. However, this in turn has put pressure on the demand for imports in the nonagricultural sector which cannot be met unless India's exports, together with foreign assistance, help meet the demand. Given the foreign-aid climate of recent years, what innovative fiscal policy can be applied to agricultural products to put them in a better competitive position in world markets? Fiscal policies seem to have been conducive to promoting agricultural productivity through price supports and input subsidies; how can it now be used to improve the efficiency of handling the output, processing the food or the nonfood commodities, devising better strains of the higher-yielding nonfood crops, moving the commodities through the maze of trade imperfections and on through equally imperfect port storage facilities and, not least, overvalued exchange rates to world markets?

We may have focused too narrowly in some of our papers and discussions on particular aspects of price policy with respect to fertilizer or other given inputs or outputs or in terms of particular kinds of agricultural taxes and not enough on the kind of fiscal measures which will guide the agricultural sector into its proper role and formation toward the optimum growth path desired for underdeveloped countries. We need to view the total scene and to approach the management of a country's agricultural sector in a total, optimal sense vis-à-vis the other sectors of the economy. For example, it is sometimes said that Indian industrialization has expanded rapidly and raised output from this sector sufficiently to place India well up in ranking of industrial countries. In fact, India is below Sweden, the Netherlands, or Brazil in this respect, and its value added in industry is less than one-third of Italy and less than one-fourth of Japan. In 1966 the value of industrial output in India was only $8.5 billion, Brazil $9 billion, Italy over $25 billion, Japan over $34 billion. The per capita industrial output puts such countries as India and Pakistan in an even far worse comparative light. Unless industrialization is vastly increased in such densely populated areas, the development task would become insurmountable in time. The current agricultural revolution should not be permitted to becloud this fact. Ultimately, therefore, a broad fiscal outlook which addresses the total development task is the only wise beginning of a sound development program.

Notes

1. Clifton Wharton, Jr., "The Green Revolution: Cornucopia or Pandora's Box?", *Foreign Affairs,* April 1969.

2. The problem of price relationships has not, of course, just recently been discovered. Cf. OECD, *Interrelationship Between Income and Supply Problems in Agriculture* (Paris, 1965).

3. Gordon Conway, "Pests Follow the Chemicals in the Cocoa of Malaysia," Natural History Supplement to the Conference on the Ecological Aspects of International Development Programs, December 1968 (The Conservation Foundation, Washington, D.C.).

4. The whole range of ecological and environmental problems associated with raising agricultural productivity is covered in FAO, *The State of Food and Agriculture, 1968* (Rome, 1968), especially Section III, "Role of Science and Technology." Problems in adopting the new varieties led to a high-level Spring Review Seminar, sponsored by AID in Washington, 13–15 May 1969. Numerous papers prepared for that seminar contained many researchable problems.

For example, R. Newberg, "Emerging Problems"; John Mellor, The Role of Government and the New Agricultural Technologies"; Joseph Willett, "The Impact of New Varieties of Rice and Wheat in Asia"; Alex Daspit, "The Role of Research". These and other papers presented in that conference are available from AID, Washington, D.C.

5. I witnessed from personal experience the gains derived from large irrigation improvements (R. Ward, "Focus in Jordan Agriculture," *Land Economics,* May 1966).

6. Wharton, ibid., p. 465.

7. Cf. Forrest Hill and Arthur Mosher, "Organizing for Agricultural Development," in R. J. Ward, ed., *The Challenge of Development* (Chicago: Aldine, 1967), p. 207 ff.

8. The argument is heard commonly today that the industrial sectors of the underdeveloped world cannot absorb their rapidly growing labor forces and that therefore the agricultural, or at least rural, sector must. It is a common occurrence that the green revolution, through double cropping, far larger harvest, and hence greater marketing of crops has called for greatly increased use of labor. Even mechanization, which often makes double cropping and rapid harvesting possible, results in increased employment. By transferring Japan's labor absorption experience to India and other less-developed countries, I have argued that employment in agriculture can increase greatly. Cf. R. Ward, "Absorbing More Labor in LDC Agriculture," *Economic Development and Cultural Change,* January 1969. Bruce Johnston and John Cownie have made similar argument almost simultaneously in an as yet unpublished piece, "The Seed-Fertilizer Revolution and the Labor-Force Absorption Problem," Food Research Institute, Stanford University, 20 January 1969. The bibliography on this theme is growing. The OECD is in the process of producing numerous studies on the unemployment problem.

9. In nearly all cases I have identified the author of the paper from which the research ideas were culled. In a few instances where the idea was mine or that of Herbert Rees, director of the Division of South Asia for AID, but was engendered out of reading of a paper, I have so indicated. Some of the papers of the Istanbul Conference will be published in a forthcoming book (R. Hinrichs, E. Morss, R. Ward, eds., publisher undetermined.)

10. Research on the income inequality issue badly needs updating and more intensive survey. I have covered some of the ground and issues, but do not profess to having broken new ground in my review (cf. R. Ward, "Aspects of Income Inequality in Less Developed Countries," *Economia Internazionale*). The regional inequality issue is perhaps most acute in the East-West Pakistan case. Research into the appropriate fiscal approach to this problem is needed (although insights have been provided by John Beyer, "Regional Inequalities and Economic Growth in Malaysia," *Yorkshire Bulletin of Economic and Social Research,* May 1929).

11. Quoted in AID document, *The Role of Research* (Spring Review of the New Cereal Varieties, 13–15 May 1969), p. 4.

Index